Democracy
at Risk

Stephen Macedo
Yvette Alex-Assensoh
Jeffrey M. Berry
Michael Brintnall
David E. Campbell
Luis Ricardo Fraga
Archon Fung
William A. Galston
Christopher F. Karpowitz
Margaret Levi
Meira Levinson
Keena Lipsitz
Richard G. Niemi
Robert D. Putnam
Wendy M. Rahn
Rob Reich
Robert R. Rodgers
Todd Swanstrom
Katherine Cramer Walsh

Democracy at Risk

How Political Choices Undermine Citizen Participation and What We Can Do About It

BROOKINGS INSTITUTION PRESS
Washington, D.C.

ABOUT BROOKINGS

The Brookings Institution is a private nonprofit organization devoted to research, education, and publication on important issues of domestic and foreign policy. Its principal purpose is to bring the highest quality independent research and analysis to bear on current and emerging policy problems. Interpretations or conclusions in Brookings publications should be understood to be solely those of the authors.

Copyright © 2005
THE BROOKINGS INSTITUTION
1775 Massachusetts Avenue, N.W., Washington, D.C. 20036
www.brookings.edu

Library of Congress Cataloging-in-Publication data
Macedo, Stephen, 1957–
  Democracy at risk : how political choices undermine citizen participation and what we can do about it / Stephen Macedo ; with Yvette Alex-Assensoh . . . [et al.].
       p.   cm.
Summary: "Documents how recent trends in civic engagement have been shaped by political institutions and public policies and recommends ways to increase the amount, quality, and distribution of civic engagement, focusing on elections, the metropolis, and the nonprofit sector and philanthropy"—Provided by publisher.
  Includes bibliographical references and index.
  ISBN-13: 978-0-8157-5404-6 (isbn-13, cloth : alk. paper)
  ISBN-10: 0-8157-5404-3 (isbn-10, cloth : alk. paper)
  ISBN-13: 978-0-8157-5405-3 (isbn-13, paper : alk. paper)
  ISBN-10: 0-8157-5405-1 (isbn-10, paper : alk. paper)
  1. Political participation—United States. 2. Citizenship—United States. I. Alex-Assensoh, Yvette M. II. Title.
  JK1764.M33 2005
  323'.042'0973—dc22   2005012395

9 8 7 6 5 4 3 2

The paper used in this publication meets minimum requirements of the American National Standard for Information Sciences—Permanence of Paper for Printed Library Materials: ANSI Z39.48-1992.

Typeset in Minion

Composition by Circle Graphics
Columbia, Maryland

Printed by R. R. Donnelley
Harrisonburg, Virginia

CONTENTS

PREFACE   vii

1 Toward a Political Science of Citizenship   1
What Is Civic Engagement?   6
What Dimensions of Civic Engagement
     Should We Care About?   8
Can Civic Engagement Be Bad?   10
Our Report and the American Political
     Science Association   16
Roadmap to What Follows   18
Conclusion   19

2 National Electoral Processes   21
Basic Trends   22
Diagnosing Our Civic Malaise   30
Personal Factors   32
Structural Factors   41
Cultural Factors   49
What Is to Be Done?   52
Conclusion   64

3 The American Metropolis   67
The Promise and Perils of Local Politics   68
Changing Patterns of Metropolitan Life   73
Place, Context, and Civic Activity   82
Engagement with Electoral Politics   83
Political Engagement between Elections   90

Community Engagement through Nongovernmental
Institutions and Groups 97
What Is to Be Done? 104
Conclusion 114

**4 Associational Life and the Nonprofit
and Philanthropic Sector 117**
Associations and Civic Engagement 119
Two Positive Trends: Volunteering and Growth
of the Nonprofit Sector 122
How Policy Creates and Regulates Nonprofits 128
Reshaping the Civic Context for Associations 131
What Is to Be Done? 148
Conclusion 152

**5 Conclusion: Assessing Our Political Science 155
of Citizenship**
America's Democratic Deficit 156
Our Agenda for Reform 159
Pitfalls of Our Political Science of Citizenship 170
Conclusion 177

NOTES 179

THE AUTHORS 219

INDEX 221

PREFACE

T HE GENESIS OF THIS REPORT WAS THE FORMATION, IN THE SUMMER of 2002, of the American Political Science Association's first Standing Committee on Civic Education and Engagement. Our idea from the start was to operate for two years as a task force and to produce a report that would bring the insights of political science to bear on the problem of civic engagement. This book is the fruit of our labor. It tests the proposition that modern social science has useful insights into the state of democratic life and what might be done to improve it. This is no small task, and we have tried to be scrupulous about what we know and the limits of what we know. We speak to the public—to everyone who is interested in democracy in America—but we also address our fellow researchers by pointing out the many important questions on which more work remains to be done.

We, as authors, speak only for ourselves and not for the American Political Science Association (APSA) and its members. This collective effort is, however, part of a renewed commitment on the part of the American Political Science Association to take civic education and civic engagement seriously and to encourage political scientists to work together to address important public issues.

We seek to cast light on the ways in which choices about public policies and the design of institutions shape patterns of civic life: how and when citizens act, with whom, and for what ends and how citizens' identities, dispositions, and interests are formed. Our central concern is the educative or formative impact of political design. We focus on institutions other than schools and policies other than educational policies because political choice offers so many other formative possibilities. This is one of the oldest themes in political science: Plato and Aristotle sought to analyze how the laws as a whole form the character of citizens, and many modern political thinkers have also pursued this project.

We do not disparage the role of schools in forming citizens; indeed, a number of us have worked, and will continue to work, on schools and education, and we are all educators. It seems to us a mistake, however, to ignore the formative dimension of the laws as a whole, including collective choices about institutions and policies of many sorts. Even in a liberal democracy that avoids objectionable forms of paternalism, public policy is pervasively educative. A clearer recognition of this should help to support rather than demean the important work of schools.

We split our large theme into three more manageable topics and then divided into working groups. Several of our original committee members—all of whom made important contributions and offered valuable support—were not able to participate in our discussions and writing. Several coauthors were added for their expertise and commitment to the project.

The principal coauthors of chapter two, on the electoral process, were David E. Campbell, William A. Galston, Richard G. Niemi, and Wendy M. Rahn. The principal coauthors of chapter three, on American metropolitan areas, were Yvette Alex-Assensoh, Luis Ricardo Fraga, Stephen Macedo, and Katherine Cramer Walsh. Robert D. Putnam also worked with this group throughout. The principal coauthors of chapter four were Jeffrey M. Berry and Rob Reich, with substantial contributions from the beginning by Michael Brintnall, Margaret Levi, and Meira Levinson, all of whom also contributed to other parts of the document. These were all original members of the first American Political Science Association Standing Committee on Civic Education and Engagement (Putnam and Brintnall, ex officio), and they participated fully over two years.

The original group was joined in mid-course by Archon Fung and Todd Swanstrom, who worked closely with the metropolitan areas group and by Keena Lipsitz, who worked closely with the electoral processes group. Christopher F. Karpowitz and Rob Rodgers worked closely with Stephen Macedo for many months as roving editors and contributors; they worked especially intensely on chapters one and three and, with Macedo, brought the whole text together.

The foregoing paragraphs do not do justice to the degree of collaboration that went into every aspect of this report, from its initial conception to its final stages. Suffice it to say that every coauthor made important contributions, and every one contributed in many ways and at many different stages.

In addition, we had substantial help and contributions from many others. E. J. Dionne, Pamela Johnston Conover, and Keith Reeves made important early contributions as members of the original committee. We received extensive written comments from Chris Achen, Jane Junn, Leslie Lenkowsky, and Jessica Trounstine. Henry Brady, Jean Elshtain, and Margaret Weir provided very helpful and constructive comments at and after a panel held at the 2004 Annual Meeting of the American Political Science Association.

We received significant comments and suggestions from many colleagues; these improved our text substantially. At the Princeton workshop, we heard from Richard Alba, Larry Bartels, Kayla Dragosz, Walter Feinberg, Miriam Galston, Donald Green, Fredrick C. Harris, Michael Jones-Correa, Michael Lipsky, Nolan McCarty, Tali Mendelberg, and Iris Marion Young. At a daylong workshop at the Kennedy School of Government, we were joined by David Barron, Xavier de Souza Briggs, Gerald Frug, and Edward Glaeser. Barron and Frug supplied detailed comments over several months. At other meetings or via e-mail, we received comments and suggestions from Alan Abramson, Elizabeth Boris, Jeffrey Brudney, Juliet Gainsborough, Martin Gilens, James Jennings, Michael Jones-Correa, Greg Markus, Eric Oliver, Markus Prior, Douglas Rae, Lester Salamon, Bruce Sievers, Theda Skocpol, Steven Rathgeb Smith, Clarence Stone, and Sidney Verba.

We also gratefully acknowledge the generous support of Princeton's University Center for Human Values and its Center for the Study of Democratic Politics (and its director, Larry Bartels) for cosponsoring a two-day meeting at Princeton University in February 2004. The Midwest Political Science Association also allotted us panels at its annual meeting for three years running. We thank the program officers and annual meeting staff, especially Director William D. Morgan, for giving us these opportunities.

Finally, we are grateful to the officers and members of the American Political Science Association for giving us the opportunity and the support to undertake this effort. Thanks to Executive Director Michael Brintnall and staff assistants Kelly Baden and Corinne Ferrara for their logistical support. Thanks especially to APSA past president Robert D. Putnam and successive teams of officers for their leadership role in establishing this committee and for naming us to it.

1

Toward a Political Science of Citizenship

AMERICAN DEMOCRACY IS AT RISK. THE RISK COMES NOT FROM some external threat but from disturbing internal trends: an erosion of the activities and capacities of citizenship. Americans have turned away from politics and the public sphere in large numbers, leaving our civic life impoverished. Citizens participate in public affairs less frequently, with less knowledge and enthusiasm, in fewer venues, and less equally than is healthy for a vibrant democratic polity. Americans can and should take pride in the historical accomplishments of their constitutional democracy—in many ways, America remains a shining example to much of the world. But our democracy is not all that it could be. Although some aspects of civic life remain robust and some citizens still participate frequently, Americans should be concerned about the current state of affairs. The risk is not to our national survival but to the health and legitimacy of our shared political order.

Consider some straightforward indicators of political participation. American voter turnout ranks near the bottom among democratic nations.[1] Other political activities, such as writing letters to the editor, participating in rallies and demonstrations, and volunteering in campaigns, fell by about half between the mid-1970s and the mid-1990s.[2] Citizens need public information, but the number of civics courses taken in public schools has declined by two-thirds since 1960, and, at least by some measures, college graduates nowadays know as much about politics as the average high school senior did fifty years ago.[3]

The political activity we do observe is distributed unevenly across the population. Disadvantaged Americans, who may have the most reason to get involved, participate far less than the well-off.[4] Participation has plummeted precipitously among the young. For instance, from the mid-1970s to the present, the number of adolescents who say they can see themselves working on a political campaign has dropped by about half.[5] As our national politics has become more polarized, participation has declined especially steeply among independent and moderate voters, who should play an important centripetal role in keeping the two parties from drifting toward the extremes.[6] Meanwhile, in national politics and across metropolitan areas, long-standing inequalities in patterns of participation across racial and ethnic groups persist.

The 2004 presidential election witnessed a rebound in voter turnout, including among young voters. The campaign was widely regarded as the most intense and closely contested race in a generation, and yet, by the standards of a not-too-distant era, the turnout was not especially high: at approximately 60 percent, it was about the same as in 1956, when an incumbent president handily and predictably defeated the same challenger he had faced four years earlier. It remains to be seen whether 2004 marks a new trend or is a mere blip in a long-standing decline.

In addition to the decline in political participation, Americans have also withdrawn from a wide range of civic engagements. Published in 2000, Robert Putnam's *Bowling Alone* initiated a vigorous debate about the scope and dimensions of civic participation, but almost all agree that the fabric of our civic life has frayed significantly and that the youngest generations of Americans participate the least in civic life, a worrisome indicator for future trends.

These declining levels of civic engagement and participation are in many ways surprising. Income and education have long been viewed as the best predictors of civic engagement, and Americans are now far wealthier and enjoy more years of formal schooling than their parents and grandparents did. So why are Americans turning away from politics and civic life? More important, what, if anything, can we do about it? Do we know enough to diagnose the cause and cast light on possible remedies?

Our aim here is not simply to join the chorus of those who chronicle civic decline. Nor is it to cast blame on Americans for being poor citizens. Rather our aim is constructive. We believe America can do better by improving the design of institutions and policies that govern our civic and political life. Our central argument is that the levels and distribution of civic activity are themselves political artifacts. Whether consciously intended or not, the design of our current political institutions and practices turns citizens off.

If Americans find the presidential primary process long and boring, it is because that process is indeed longer than it should be, and its lengthy and episodic nature discourages sustained attention and continued political learning.

If Americans find congressional elections dull, it may be because they are rarely competitive. Our systems of redrawing district boundaries and financing campaigns, as well as our increasingly candidate-centered politics, all work to the advantage of incumbents—an advantage that has grown in recent years. For example, in 2004, 98 percent of the incumbents running in House races won. When elections are not competitive, citizens have little incentive to pay attention, become informed, take part in the campaign, and vote in the election.

If Americans find partisan politics excessively ideological, nasty, and insufficiently focused on practical problem solving, there is reason to think they are right: American citizens tend toward the political middle, but safe congressional seats may empower the ideological bases of the two parties at the expense of moderates, intensifying party conflict in Washington and hindering efforts to work across party lines.

If poorer Americans believe that local political institutions are incapable of addressing their problems, if racial minorities find American politics to be exclusive rather than inclusive, and if better-off Americans seem disconnected from the problems and experiences of their poorer fellow citizens, this is partly because our metropolitan political institutions encourage privileged Americans to move to suburban enclaves, defying the promise of common public institutions and a sense of shared fate.

In short, if the American public square is far less vibrant than it should be, if the quality of participation is disappointing, if the tone of national politics is nasty, and if the distribution of political activity and influence favors the socially and economically advantaged, the responsibility in substantial measure is our own. But we cannot solve the problems as individuals. Instead, we must act collectively to improve our institutions and thereby to foster a richer civic life for all citizens.

The authors of this book are political scientists, and in what follows, we do our best to present in clear prose what is known about the ebb and flow of civic and political activity in America: who participates, how much, with whom, and why. We know that the capacity and willingness of citizens to get involved in politics depend on a variety of personal factors. We draw on a rich set of research traditions that highlights the relationship between political participation and such individual characteristics as psychological dispositions, learned habits or skills, and socioeconomic standing.

Our motivating idea, however, is that the political arrangements under which we live—the policies and institutions we make together as a political society—

shape the incentives, interests, identities, and capacities of citizens to participate effectively in civic life. In writing this report, we seek to bring the expertise of political science to bear on the task of improving our political arrangements and, thereby, the quantity, quality, and equality of civic engagement.

Why do we believe that improving our institutions to promote robust citizen engagement is essential to American democracy? First, civic engagement enhances the quality of democratic governance. Democratic decisionmaking requires knowledge of the interests of the people. Citizens make their preferences known through various forms of civic engagement: casting a ballot, attending a rally, writing a public official, volunteering time, or showing up at a meeting. While there surely is a role for expertise in politics and public administration, citizen input has the potential to improve the quality of public decisions by marshaling the knowledge and registering the preferences of the entire community. As Gregory B. Markus puts it, "When citizens do more than merely provide 'input' to professional decisions, when they instead possess sufficient information, resources, time, and space for deliberation, and power to transform input into action, then the planning, the implementation, and the results can be more insightful, more legitimate, and more effective than anything that officials and planners could have devised on their own."[7]

Second, the promise of democratic life is not simply that government by the people yields the most excellent governance. It is also—and perhaps mainly— that government is legitimate only when the people as a whole participate in their own self-rule. Insofar as important classes of citizens are considerably less active and influential than others—especially when participatory inequalities are a consequence of the design of the political system—then the reality of collective self-rule is doubtful, and the legitimacy of the political order is compromised. Democracy is supposed to represent the interests of the people as a whole, but ample evidence supports the notion that political institutions are most responsive to those who mobilize.[8] Government "by the people, for the people" founders when only narrow and particularistic interests are mobilized or when important sectors of the political community are left out. "The rights and interests of every or any person are only secure from being disregarded," John Stuart Mill declared, "when the person interested is himself able, and habitually disposed, to stand up for them."[9]

Third, participation can enhance the quality of citizens' lives. We believe that civic engagement is valuable in itself, that popular self-rule involves the exercise of distinctive human capacities and is an intrinsically noble enterprise. We follow Alexis de Tocqueville, John Stuart Mill, and many others in holding that participation has the potential to educate and invigorate citizens to expand their understanding and capacities. Mill praised "the ennobling influence of free government—the nerve and spring which it gives to all the faculties, the larger and higher objects it presents to the intellect and feelings, the more unselfish public spirit, and calmer and broader views of duty, that it engenders."[10] We recognize, however, that the benefits of political and civic activity often compete with other good things in life. There can be trade-offs between time spent at a political meeting and the joys of private life, including time spent with family and friends. While acknowledging the existence of important trade-offs and allowing that people frequently lead good and fulfilling lives without engaging in political activity, we maintain that civic engagement is part of the good life and that, under favorable conditions, civic activity complements rather than detracts from other valuable activities.

Indeed, civic engagement can enrich citizens' lives in more diffuse ways. Beyond formal institutions of government, voluntary and nonprofit organizations, supported in part by the contributions and participation of individuals, provide a wide variety of goods and services that neither the state nor the market can replace. Some evidence even suggests that higher levels of civic engagement, especially active membership in groups and involvement in social networks, are associated with greater individual satisfaction with the quality of community life and, indeed, one's own life.[11] Quite simply, when citizens are involved and engaged with others, their lives and our communities are better.

In sum, we share the widespread—if not unanimous—concern with the state of American citizenship, and we agree with President George W. Bush when, in his first inaugural address, he told the American people,

> What you do is as important as anything government does. I ask you to seek a common good beyond your comfort, to defend needed reforms against easy attacks, to serve your nation, beginning with your neighbor. I ask you to become citizens. Citizens, not spectators. Citizens, not subjects. Responsible citizens, building communities of service and a nation of character. . . . When this spirit of citizenship is missing, no government program can replace it. When this spirit is present, no wrong can stand against it.[12]

To help Americans better understand the plight and the promise of civic engagement, we undertake three tasks. First, we describe and document recent trends in civic engagement. Second, we explore the influence that the design of public policies and political institutions has had on these civic trends. Finally, and perhaps most important, we recommend policies and institutional reforms to increase the quantity, quality, and equality of civic engagement in the United States.

We have set out to test the proposition that political science casts light on the problem of civic engagement and on reforms that could improve the practice of citizenship. We focus largely—though not exclusively—on the educative impact of institutions other than schools and practices besides the directly and specifically educative. We fully realize that schools have played and will continue to play an essential role in promoting civic education and engagement in the United States. Nevertheless, we choose not to focus on schools for several reasons. Many others have explored the topic of civic education in schools, and excellent summaries of this literature are already available. Indeed, ever-increasing numbers of organizations and groups focus attention on school-based civic education.[13] Much less attention has been given to the many ways in which institutions and policies other than those concerned directly with schools and education shape civic life and educate citizens in critical ways. The first political scientists, Plato and Aristotle foremost among them, recognized the importance of viewing all political institutions as broadly educative. We believe that modern political scientists and those engaged in crafting public policy too often neglect the formative dimension of politics as a whole.

In this sense, schools are part of the larger political order: they respond to imperatives set forth by the polity and work hand-in-hand with other community institutions, from parents and families to the federal government. Hence school-based efforts to foster civic engagement should be placed within a broader political framework. Schools did not create our current civic engagement crisis single-handedly, and they cannot solve it on their own.

What Is Civic Engagement?

Citizens enter into public affairs in many ways and for many reasons. They may seek information about candidates or policies or express support for, or opposition to, particular candidates or programs. They may act to extend their own or others' rights, to protect their own interests, or to promote what they view as the public good. They may be moved by a sense of civic duty: the belief that citizens have an obligation to volunteer, to vote, to serve. Or they may desire to build a community or network in support of some cause or to address some common problem. Of course, people also get involved partly because they enjoy the social interaction that accompanies many forms of civic activity.

Just as we take a broad view of the reasons and motives for political action, so too do we favor a capacious understanding of the means of civic engagement. For us, *civic engagement includes any activity, individual or collective, devoted to influencing the collective life of the polity.* This includes the acquisition of relevant knowledge and skills as well as a wide range of acts. We do not draw a sharp distinction between "civic" and "political" engagement because we recognize that politics and civil society are interdependent: a vibrant politics depends on a vibrant civil society.[14] Political voice can, for example, mean participation in formal government institutions, but it may also involve becoming part of a group or organization, protesting or boycotting, or even simply talking to a neighbor across the backyard fence.

Civic engagement most obviously includes voting. As John Dewey reminded us, however, the moment when a vote is cast is the culmination of a much richer process that includes a host of prior conversations, judgments, and actions. Scott Keeter and his colleagues identify various "electoral indicators" of civic engagement that lead up to voting; these include working for an organization on behalf of a candidate or campaign; attending a political rally, speech, or dinner; contributing money to a campaign or cause; displaying a campaign button or bumper sticker; and persuading friends, neighbors, or strangers why they should vote for or against a party or candidate.[15] We should never forget that the electoral process includes far more than the act of voting and the quality of voters' choices depends on this wider set of activities.[16]

Important as they are, elections and the activities that precede them are but one aspect of political activity. Protesting and marching, attending a public meeting, lobbying a government official, writing to a newspaper about a public issue, signing an e-mail or written petition, boycotting, canvassing a neighborhood, or engaging in political mobilization and debate are all forms of civic engagement. Beyond these well-established methods of advocacy, nonelectoral political involvement can also include new avenues of engagement, such as the growing number of deliberative forums where private individuals can meet face-to-face to talk about public problems.[17]

If politics includes far more than elections, it is also true that "civic" activity includes more than electoral and pressure politics. Citizens frequently gather either formally or informally to address collective problems themselves, sometimes, but not always, with the support of public institutions. Civic activity includes public service and collective actions to improve our society: serving one's country in civilian or military capacity when needed, volunteering for programs such as Volunteers in Service to America (VISTA), AmeriCorps, or the Peace Corps, or participating in a neighborhood watch. Numerous Americans volunteer their time or give money and support to groups and organizations that are concerned with serving the disadvantaged, protesting injustices or promoting other moral values, protecting the environment, or improving our cultural institutions, schools, and communities. Voluntary and community groups of all sorts, including nonprofits, labor unions, and churches, help citizens to mobilize on behalf of matters of common concern.[18]

Civic activity also includes learning about our political system and the issues of the day. Civic education takes place in schools, unions, voluntary associations, and places of worship, among other venues. Campaigns and elections are educative exercises in important respects. Citizens acquire knowledge about political affairs by reading the newspaper, watching the news and other television programs, listening to the radio, surfing Internet sites, studying voter pamphlets, talking to friends, volunteering their time, and participating in a host of other ways.

What Dimensions of Civic Engagement Should We Care About?

Given that such a wide range of activities qualify as civic engagement, we need to pick out those aspects of civic engagement that matter most for the health of American democracy. Throughout this book, we concentrate on three critical dimensions of civic engagement: quantity, quality, and equality.

QUANTITY

We care about the overall amount of civic engagement. Democracy is better, we assert, if participation is widespread. Generally, though not always, the problem is to get citizens interested, to encourage them to turn out in an election, or to get them involved with an organization or group. This, in any event, is the challenge in the contemporary United States. Many ordinary citizens express a lack of interest in politics at all levels and an extreme hesitancy to play a role in democratic decisionmaking.[19] We are especially worried about declining involvement among the young—a tendency that may portend an even greater impoverishment of democratic life in the years ahead. Whether or not one believes that there is a crisis of civic engagement, a concern with encouraging an interest in, and capacity for, active citizenship runs through many reflections on modern mass society, including those of Adam Smith, Benjamin Constant, and Alexis de Tocqueville.[20] We agree that the number of participants (or nonparticipants) is important, and we believe that institutional and policy choices can increase these numbers by influencing the environment within which individuals develop and act on their civic interests and identities.

QUALITY

Of course, numbers alone are not enough to ensure the legitimacy, stability, and health of a democratic government. The quality of participation matters too. In a large, diverse, extended republic, citizens need to learn to cooperate across lines of racial, religious, political, social, and economic differences. Political engagement is not confined to the first Tuesday after the first Monday in

November; it extends beyond the ballot box to myriad other opportunities for expressing one's voice. At its best, it involves learning about public issues and understanding the political system. It means being heard as well as being able to explain and justify one's opinions to others in civil dialogue. It encompasses the capacity to affect the agenda and do more than just respond to given choices. The most valuable forms of civic engagement address important issues on which people of goodwill disagree, finding points of common agreement, while seeking ways to deal productively with enduring conflicts. Quality civic engagement maintains bonds of political community even after the votes have been counted and the majority has spoken.

Individual acts of participation have qualitative dimensions, but so too do institutions such as elections. At their best, elections hold incumbents accountable for their past performance and offer citizens clear choices between candidates with well-articulated programs and positions. Poor elections generally feature entrenched incumbents who, for numerous reasons (including their fundraising advantage, name recognition, or the way their district lines have been drawn), easily trounce their opponents. Quality civic environments prompt deliberation and debate about a range of political issues, including those important to disadvantaged segments of the population. We recognize, of course, that although healthy competition is good, excessive polarization is bad. We discuss this distinction in chapter two. While acknowledging that qualitative judgments about civic and political activity are often controversial, we argue that political activity is increasingly uninformed, fragmented, and polarized.

EQUALITY

Implicit in the idea of governance by and on behalf of the people as a whole is a concern with who participates and who does not. We realize that distributive concerns are often controversial and partisan, and we recognize that inevitably some people will choose not to be involved. Nevertheless, we worry about the uneven distribution of civic participation. We are especially concerned about institutional obstacles that undermine civic engagement among the disadvantaged. Certainly, the young, the poor, the less educated, and many racial and ethnic minorities participate far less than the population as a whole; these persistent or even increasing inequalities impoverish our civic life and call into question the democratic credentials of our politics. In some respects, racial and socioeconomic inequalities are rooted in discriminatory policies of the past, and the effects persist most visibly in educational inequalities and residential housing patterns. Significant progress has been made in eradicating discriminatory laws, and the variation in participation across racial and ethnic groups seems attributable largely to differences in income, education, and citizenship status. Nonetheless, many political scientists have worried that the political chorus "sings with a strong upper-class accent."[21] We share this worry and add to it the concern that the chorus is older and whiter—not to mention more male—than American society as a whole.

Ultimately, we believe that improving the quantity, quality, and equality of civic engagement will improve the quality and legitimacy of self-governance, and it should increase our collective capacity to pursue common ends and address common problems. There is, of course, a great deal of disagreement about what our most pressing problems are and how we should address them; improved civic engagement will not end disputes about what our common ends should be. But we will be better off as a nation and as individuals if more Americans participate in an informed and capable manner. If, however, we choose to do nothing and unfavorable trends continue, the decisions of an increasingly unaccountable political elite will reflect the interests of a smaller and increasingly unrepresentative pool of highly mobilized citizens. Our democratic ideals will ring increasingly hollow.

Can Civic Engagement Be Bad?

Not all observers—not even all political scientists—agree with our basic premise that citizen engagement is fundamental to healthy democratic politics. Some are untroubled, even comforted, by low levels of citizen participation.[22] There are, indeed, numerous arguments against our effort to bolster citizen activity, and we want to take their measure briefly before moving on.

Citizens may have good reasons not to get involved or stay informed. Public engagement can be demanding, and many citizens may decide not to participate in the political life of their communities because they prefer to delegate political activity to others, such as other voters, their elected representatives, or other political elites.[23] As John Hibbing and Elizabeth Theiss-Morse put it, "The last thing people want is to be more involved in political decisionmaking; they do not want to provide much input to those who are assigned to make these decisions; and they would rather not know all the details of the decisionmaking process. Most people have strong feelings on few if any of the issues the government needs to address and would much prefer to spend their time in nonpolitical pursuits."[24] Lack of political involvement may signal widespread satisfaction with the status quo rather than a crisis of democracy. When circumstances change or problems arise, citizens will become more involved. Mancur Olson expresses a related idea by casting citizens as rational maximizers of self-interest. In this view, the costs associated with participation will, for many if not most, outweigh any benefits that might accrue to them.[25] In addition, people may act privately rather than publicly to attain the sorts of public goods they want. For example, people may move their place of residence within a metropolitan area to live in the community that matches their personal preferences with respect to public services and to live with others who share those same preferences; they may "vote with their feet" rather than cast ballots.[26]

Participation in political affairs can cause people to feel injured. Citizens may emerge from attempts to participate in even normal and relatively tame political settings feeling frustrated at the inefficacy of their efforts or dismayed by the disharmony commonly found in a diverse democracy. We take seriously the cautionary observations of Hibbing and Theiss-Morse, who argue that many citizens recoil from the disagreements and differences that naturally emerge in any open democratic forum concerned with important issues. Political participation can spark feelings of powerlessness and frustration.[27]

Other arguments against our concern with participation focus on the consequences for public governance rather than for individuals. Low participation may not be troubling if the preferences of voters are, for the most part, representative of the entire society, so that nonvoters would not alter election results by going to the polls.[28] Elitists, however, worry that more widespread popular engagement would undermine good governance. Critics of democracy, beginning with Socrates, have bristled at the people's capacity for capricious decisions.[29] Although few now advocate nondemocratic forms of government, many scholars still worry that extensive citizen participation encourages unwise decisions. According to these critics, elites are more competent than ordinary citizens, who tend to have less knowledge and less information and to be less consistent in their opinions.[30] As Joseph Schumpeter rather derisively puts it, "The typical citizen drops down to a lower level of mental performance as soon as he enters the political field."[31] Intense citizen engagement may hamper the ability of politicians and other elites to broker policy compromises. Samuel Huntington claims that "some of the problems of governance in the United States today stem from an excess of democracy."[32] He argues that heightened participation leads to political polarization, which makes it more difficult for political elites to satisfy the demands of citizens. As a result, citizens lurch between overly passionate involvement and cynical withdrawal in a kind of "democratic distemper."[33]

Still worse, highly engaged majorities may repress minorities and produce other injustices. Democracy allows citizens to organize on behalf of particular interests averse to "justice and the public good"; as James Madison warned,

"Freedom is to faction as air is to fire."[34] Participation may be aimed at righting constitutional wrongs, but citizens sometimes mobilize to defend an unfair privilege or to deny other citizens their basic rights. If the civil rights movement was an exercise in political engagement, so were many aspects of the massive resistance to it. Voluntary associations, praised for their contribution to civic life by political scientists such as Robert Putnam and Theda Skocpol, sometimes foster racism rather than tolerance, insularity rather than bridges across particular identities, or sectarianism rather than a commitment to a larger public good.[35]

Our commitment to increased popular engagement faces, it is now clear, a powerful litany of criticisms. How can we answer these arguments? And what can we do about the potential pathologies of popular involvement in political and civic life?

Let us begin with the view that popular civic engagement can undermine the capacity of wise and virtuous elites to govern. The obvious problem with this view is that there is not now, and never will be, a class of empathetic, non-self-interested elites who can be trusted to advance the common good.[36] Unless they are held to account by a vigilant public of engaged citizens, elites tend to advance their own interests and the interests of that small portion of the electorate that actively supports them. Expertise, leadership, and excellence play important roles in politics, but elites must be held accountable by the people as a whole. As Thomas Jefferson put it, "I know no safe depositary of the ultimate powers of the society but the people themselves; and if we think them not enlightened enough to exercise their control with a wholesome discretion, the remedy is not to take it from them, but to inform their discretion by education."[37] For these reasons, we worry about the decline of civic engagement and popular attention to politics—and so the weakening of the popular capacity to hold leaders accountable.

But what of Schumpeter's dictum regarding the political foolishness of citizens? We would turn his charge on its head: there are many issues on which political and bureaucratic elites are likely to be ignorant and on which citizens are especially expert. Citizens as subjects feel first and most deeply the effects of many kinds of policy decisions in areas such as education, the environment, and social policy. Contestatory democratic institutions help to bring out the relevant information needed to make intelligent decisions. For this reason, civic engagement often enhances the quality of governance.

In addition, the activity of ordinary citizens is often vital because many public goods are the joint product of the activities of public officials and ordinary individuals: education, public safety, a clean environment, and public health are among the goods that can be achieved only when citizens and public officials collaborate. We would also note that "voting with your feet" by moving to another jurisdiction to find improved public services, such as schools, is often a very poor substitute for political action on behalf of better services for all. We explore both of these themes further in chapter three.

Finally, leaving aside the quality of governance, it remains the case that the basic legitimacy of our system of government rests on the democratic ideal: government by and for the people as a whole. Whatever the wisdom of many laws and policies, many people accept them because they can be plausibly connected to popular assent. This connection becomes less plausible as levels of civic and political engagement diminish and as the active electorate ceases to represent the people as a whole. Ample political science research confirms that the poor, for example, participate considerably less than the better-off. It is not plausible that greater satisfaction is the reason; nor is there any evidence that the disadvantaged have consciously delegated custodianship over their political interests to the better-off. There are a variety of respects in which the unengaged differ from the engaged, and evidence suggests that those who are active do a poor job of representing the interests of the inactive.[38] The theory of "virtual representation" was abandoned long ago, for good reason. When the half of the electorate that votes in national elections and the far smaller percentage that votes in state and local races are unrepresentative of the people as a whole, government legitimacy ebbs. Without a strong sense of legitimacy, citizens can become reluctant or even unwilling to obey the laws, let alone cooperate in the joint production with government of a host of public goods.[39]

In the end, then, we stick to our guns: accountable, effective, and legitimate government requires substantial civic and political engagement by "the people themselves."

This does not mean, however, that political action and civic engagement are costless. We acknowledge the costs, which include deflection from valuable private pursuits, potentially tedious meetings, the discomfort of open conflict, and the frustration that comes from being on the losing side of decisions. We contend, however, that many of these costs and pathologies of engagement stem from weaknesses in particular forms of civic engagement rather than participation per se. Through institutional design, it may be possible to reconcile, or at least lessen the tensions between, just and good government, on the one hand, and enhanced participation, on the other.

And, of course, there is an important role for "elites": we advocate popular engagement within the frame of constitutional self-government. Representative government, federalism, and a complex system of shared powers among separate institutions providing "checks and balances" should help to refine and elevate the popular opinion.[40] Constitutional limitations on political majorities are a significant part of this system, and courts should help to sustain stable support for democratic fairness and basic constitutional principles such as freedom of speech and minority rights.

We may not altogether agree with Al Smith that "all the ills of democracy can be cured by more democracy," but we believe the evidence shows that some of them can be. Institutions and policy choices shape the quality (as well as the quantity and equality) of engagement, and this may have an impact on citizens' satisfaction with political activity. For example, problems in citizen participation may arise because citizens are shut out of the process or because elites do not trust ordinary citizens: this may encourage citizens to take a distinctly adversarial approach to participation. Public hearings may become contentious and uncivil. Participation may improve, however, if citizens are invited to take part earlier in the process of policy formation. Democracy depends on citizens being willing to make an effort, no doubt, but the nature and consequences of much popular political activity are deeply influenced by the context in which citizens must act. That context may inhibit, frustrate, and deter valuable political activity. In well-designed contexts, civic participation may lead from a vicious circle of alienation and exclusion to a virtuous circle of trust and inclusion.

The lesson we draw is that if politics can, from the perspective of the citizen, seem "a remote, alien, and unrewarding activity,"[41] that is partly the consequence of poor design. We can construct institutions that encourage the better forms of civic activity and that promote a healthy exchange of ideas without deteriorating into cantankerous and destructive polarization.

Finally, we believe that citizens can learn to participate in civic life in healthy and productive ways. Civic education occurs in a variety of places—at school, at home, at work, in religious organizations, in the great variety of voluntary associations that Tocqueville saw Americans creating and joining with astonishing frequency, and through ongoing activity within well-designed democratic institutions. As we seek ways to increase public participation and decrease unnecessary polarization, we believe citizens will come to better appreciate the inevitability and legitimacy of disagreement in a diverse democracy: "People need to understand that disagreements can occur among people of good heart and that some debating and compromising will be necessary to resolve these disagreements and come to a collective solution."[42] Citizens who are averse to political conflict often misunderstand the nature of democratic politics. Many wrongly assume a greater level of consensus about the common good than may, in fact, exist.[43] Indeed, civic educators and public actors need to make it clear that disagreement and public debate are often the best way of discerning the truth.[44] When democratic institutions are designed properly, citizens who participate can learn that disagreement, contention, and the giving and demanding of reasons are not necessarily signs of political dysfunction, but salutary parts of democratic life. Then, too, they should come to better understand the opinions of others, and they may come to accept decisions that they disagree with (or might have disagreed with initially). Their interests and their self-conceptions may be modified; they may truly become citizens. Hannah Pitkin expresses eloquently the hope that civic engagement can promote genuine deliberation:

> Drawn into public life by personal need, fear, ambition, or interest, we are there forced to acknowledge the power of others and appeal to their standards, even as we try to get them to acknowledge our power and standards. We are forced to find or create a common language of purposes and aspirations, not merely to clothe our private outlook in public disguise, but to become aware ourselves of its public meaning. We are forced, as Joseph Tussman has put it, to transform "I want" into "I am entitled to," a claim that becomes negotiable by public standards. In the process, we learn to think about the standards themselves, about our stake in the existence of standards, of justice, of our community, even of our opponents and enemies in the community; so that afterward we are changed.[45]

We hold that, as things stand, increased civic engagement would improve our democracy and the lives of our citizens. Conflicts are rarely resolved by being swept under the rug, and problems are unlikely to be addressed in ways that are widely acceptable if only a few participate. While we know that some disagree, we believe that the predominant danger is not excessive widespread political zeal but widespread apathy that allows the zeal of a relative few too much sway over Americans' lives.

One last point. Our argument is *not* that we should *maximize* participatory demands on citizens. In that respect, we share a concern that too many demands (too many elections, for example, held at too many different times) can cause exhaustion and a decline in participation as well as skewed participation. When few take part in public decisions, those few who do turn out are likely either to have a special interest in the outcome or to be motivated by principled purity and zeal that are not shared by mainstream, moderate voters. It is worrisome when few participate, and it is also worrisome when those who do are not representative of the people as a whole. One way to get more citizens to vote is to ask them to vote less frequently. The point can be generalized: one way to increase participation is to be reasonable in our expectations about the number and extent of the occasions on which we expect citizens to participate. Increasing participation is important not only for its own sake but because higher turnouts are liable to produce electorates that are less dominated by the ideological extremes and more reflective of the broad interests of the public as a whole.[46]

To conclude, we argue that civic and political participation in the United States today is too low. We do not argue that extremely high rates of participation are necessary, that high participation has no negative consequences, or that democracies "always" need more participation. When and where participation falls to a point where perceived legitimacy is low, individual cynicism about government decisionmaking is high, and indifference to government and collective life is excessive, then *increased* engagement is called for. The current situation in the United States features these characteristics—questionable legitimacy, high cynicism, and great indifference—and, in response, we call for increased participation, more equal participation, and a higher quality of participation.

Our Report and the American Political Science Association

The collective endeavor that has produced this book is part of a recent effort by the American Political Science Association (APSA) to enhance the contributions of political scientists to our nation's conversation about democracy. This may seem anything but novel—political scientists talking about politics—but in truth, while individual political scientists routinely comment in the press or in popular writings about the wisdom of this policy or that reform, as a profession we have been silent.

We have not spoken collectively in large part because the members of our profession—like the rest of the public—disagree on many issues of the day. In spite of our expertise, or because of it, political scientists disagree not only about the way the world ought to be but also about how it is and why it is that way. Given our disagreements, it seemed inappropriate (and perhaps unwise) for a committee of the American Political Science Association to speak on matters of policy or institutional practice. Until the initiation of our project, the APSA had not encouraged the formulation of a set of public policy or reform recommendations since 1950. In that year, the APSA Committee on Political Parties issued a report advocating a more "responsible" party system.[47] That study proved highly controversial.

Recently, however, the officers and council of the APSA reexamined this matter and decided that the inhibition against collective contributions by political scientists to national discussion of issues on which we have some expertise has been overly broad. When we work together, collaborating across subdisciplinary boundaries, we should be well positioned to present the state of knowledge in an informed and nonpartisan manner. Whether we succeed is for readers to judge. Nonetheless, we emphasize that we do not speak for the APSA as an organization or for its membership as a whole. As authors of this book, we speak only for ourselves: we have, under the auspices of the APSA, tried to discern what political science has to say about citizenship—the sources of its current malaise and the means of its possible renewal—but the judgments that follow are ours alone.

Wherever possible, we rely on evidence backed by a strong consensus among our peers. However, here as elsewhere in life, evidence is often conflicting, uncertain, and subject to competing interpretations. Significant forms of civic and political engagement are influenced by a host of factors, and understanding causal connections can be extremely difficult. Further complicating the task is the fact that reliable measures are often hard to come by and some important aspects of public life have received little attention from scholars. Frequently our judgments are, by necessity, based on the preponderance of the available evidence, and it is rare that we can claim to have proof "beyond a reasonable doubt" (a strict standard appropriate for criminal law but inappropriately demanding for many other spheres of life). An additional complexity is that there are many positive political values, and these sometimes conflict (for example, the goals of securing more, versus more equal, participation). Our assertions often rest on contestable value judgments, but we try to avoid narrowly sectarian claims. When evidence pulls up short, we marshal our best hypotheses, believing that offering an educated guess is better than remaining silent, so long as we are clear about the speculative nature of our recommendations. We sometimes address ourselves to our fellow researchers, pointing out important questions on which not enough is known. Even then, however, we believe that ordinary citizens and policymakers will benefit from understanding more about the limits of our shared knowledge.

In short, we do the best we can with what we have. Scholars agree, for example, that many forms of civic engagement have declined, and there is a substantial body of excellent research that we can draw on to describe the problem. There is less agreement on the causes of the decline and on what can or should be done about it. We ourselves do not always agree. We try, in what follows, to be scrupulous in emphasizing the limits of what we know and the limits of what we agree on. We hope to clear a path along which a great deal more work remains to be done.

Most important, we agree that Americans are less involved in civic life than they should be and that inequalities of involvement reflect persistent hierarchies of wealth and privilege to a disturbing degree. Not all of our news is bad. Many Americans remain active in civic affairs. Some forms of participation—notably volunteering—remain robust. But the overall health of our democracy has been compromised by a decline in participation across a broad range of activities. From neighborhood life, to city politics, to state affairs, and to matters involving the whole nation, we believe that expanded and improved participation will strengthen our democratic way of life.

Roadmap to What Follows

The concerns at the center of this report are large, but in the chapters that follow we try to deal with manageable aspects of the problem of American citizenship.

Chapter two discusses engagement with electoral politics at the national level. We consider some debates about the degree to which voting has declined but emphasize that, given increasing education and wealth, voting and other forms of political activity are far lower than they should be. Political participation among the young, moreover, has not held steady but has decreased; this bodes ill for the future of American democracy. We also canvass persistent inequalities of participation across various groups within the population and emphasize that civic inequalities among Hispanic and non-Hispanic white Americans, for example, are important in their own right, even if they are explained largely by differences in income, education, citizenship status, and language proficiency. We find that important features of the political process itself depress turnout: these features include noncompetitive elections and the interminable nature of presidential campaigns. We agree with those who observe that our national politics is excessively polarized, and we identify a variety of likely causes. Most important, we argue that practical reforms could improve the prospects for more widespread, representative, civil, and well-informed campaigns and elections. The most important of the practical reforms we advocate in chapter two is nonpartisan redistricting of congressional districts.

Chapter three takes up a very different set of institutions and policies that shape political and civic engagement: those that structure American metropolitan areas. Here we confront the fact that political scientists lately have given far less attention to local and regional politics than they have to national politics. In this domain we have less evidence than we would like, and both our critical analysis and our recommendations are tentative. We argue, nevertheless, that local and regional political structures often have profound effects on the composition and form of political communities, and this, in turn, has significant implications for political interests and identities, the ways in which citizens act in their communities, and the winners and losers in metropolitan political life. Because of the relative dearth of research, and because especially difficult and complex trade-offs seem to confront metropolitan civic reformers, many of our practical recommendations in chapter three call for more research. Nevertheless, the most important practical recommendation that emerges out of chapter three is that we must find ways to overcome the tremendous and growing inequalities associated with places of residence, inequalities that defy democratic ideals of equality and inclusion.

Chapter four examines policies and institutions that influence the health of a domain that has recently been at the center of discussions of citizenship: associational life and the nonprofit sector. Here we report both encouraging and discouraging trends. As is well known, participation in many civic groups and social organizations has declined considerably over the past forty years. Yet volunteering has increased, especially among the young, and important voluntary associations remain vibrant—notably religious institutions. In addition, the sheer numbers and resources of nonprofit organizations in the United States are nothing short of astonishing. No nation rivals the United States with respect to the extent of the resources and responsibilities we assign to nonprofit organizations. A great deal of responsibility for the delivery of social services has devolved to the nonprofit sector. These organizations interact extensively with disadvantaged segments of the population, and they should be capable of playing a role in enhancing the political voices of the disadvantaged. However, as we discuss, various rules unnecessarily inhibit the political activity of nonprofit organizations. Our most important recommendation in chapter four may be our call for more adequate public funding of a variety of programs of national service.

Conclusion

Our central argument is that the amount, quality, and distribution of political and civic engagement are themselves largely the product of our political choices. For this reason, the future of American democracy is, in important measure, up to us. Although there are significant limitations to political scientists' understanding of why some people are actively engaged in civic life while others are not, sometimes we know enough not only to describe and diagnose but also to prescribe.

In the chapters that follow, we clarify the nature and limits of what we know about our collective civic and political lives: we offer a portrait of important aspects of American citizenship, a diagnosis of our ills, and some prescriptions for improvement. We hope to clarify the vision of democratic reformers and to refocus the energies of political scientists. We fully recognize that politics is not an exact science. We offer no blueprint for a democratic utopia, but we have labored to produce a rough sketch of where we succeed and where we fall short as a democratic community. We offer this not as the best that can be done but as the best we could do, in the hope of helping our colleagues and our polity to do better.

- *Between 1974 and 1994, engagement in twelve key political activities, such as writing letters to the editor, participating in rallies and demonstrations, and volunteering in campaigns, fell significantly.[1]*

- *In 2002, only fifteen of 435 congressional races were decided by four percentage points or less. Of the fifty congressional incumbents who ran in California, not one lost, and all got at least 58 percent of the vote.*

- *In the 2004 presidential election, despite a massive voter-drive ground war in which interest groups alone spent more than $350 million to get out the vote, voter turnout, at 59 percent, was only five percentage points higher than in 2000.*

- *Also in 2004, just 2 percent of House incumbents and a single Senate incumbent—the aggressively targeted Senate minority leader—lost.*

- *From the mid-1970s to the present, the number of adolescents who say they can see themselves working on a political campaign has dropped by about half.[2]*

2

National Electoral Processes

THIS CHAPTER FOCUSES ON ELECTIONS AND THE WAYS IN which people get involved in the electoral process. We devote considerable attention to voting, of course, but also discuss the wide range of other activities that lead up to elections. We draw on a voluminous and venerable literature within political science, and our discussion by necessity reflects the strengths and weaknesses of generations of work on electoral participation. For example, we focus mainly (though not exclusively) on presidential and congressional elections because they have been subject to the most scrutiny by political scientists. Along the way, we draw attention to topics that deserve greater attention from researchers.

We do not pretend to be morally neutral about civic engagement. In contemporary America, we believe that virtually all indicators of involvement are lower than ideal and that many are declining. We start from the premise stated in chapter one that, under current circumstances, democratic politics would be healthier if the *quantity*, *quality*, and *equality* of political participation were improved. We also recognize, however, that the pursuit of these three goals may involve trade-offs. Electoral reforms that make voting easier, for example, thereby boosting by a few percentage points the "quantity" of participation, may worsen underlying inequalities in the composition of the electorate, as political scientist Adam Berinsky argues.[3] We do our best to describe these trade-offs when we encounter them and to suggest ways of managing them productively.

We begin this chapter by describing the levels of electoral participation in the United States and trends in participation over time. Next we seek to diagnose some of the causes of low, uneven, and declining levels of electoral involvement. Here, as elsewhere in this book, we emphasize that the institutional context in which citizens act may inhibit, frustrate, and deter valuable forms of popular political activity. In the end, we offer recommendations on ways to improve the overall amount, distribution, and quality of voting and other forms of electoral engagement. Our prescriptions, therefore, address both the *levels* and distribution of political participation in America and the *declines* in those levels during the previous generation. Prescription, however, can only follow explanation.

Basic Trends

We begin with voter turnout, the bellwether of electoral engagement. Consider the contrast between the elections of 1960 and 2000, two presidential contests that have much in common. Both races featured a vice president who had served for two terms and who faced a relatively young and unknown opponent. More important, both elections featured a photo finish, as voters were split evenly between the two candidates. In 1960, 63 percent of eligible Americans went to the polls. In 2000, that percentage had dropped to barely half of eligible Americans: 51 percent.

The 2004 presidential election is also instructive. Again the nation experienced a presidential contest that, heading into election day, was "too close to call." Democrats and Republicans and their allied groups implemented massive efforts to mobilize voters, and pundits predicted a record turnout. And turnout did rise, to roughly 59 percent,[4] which put it at the same level as in 1956, an election in which a popular incumbent won handily. In other words, only an extremely close and passionately contested race along with unprecedented efforts at voter mobilization seem able to boost turnout to the level of an unsuspenseful election in an earlier era.

There is a consensus among political scientists that contemporary voter turnout rates are lower than they were in 1960. More contentious is the question of whether turnout has been stable since 1972. The conventional wisdom is that turnout has declined more or less steadily, with occasional blips upward, as in 1992 and 2004.[5] More recently, however, Michael McDonald and Samuel Popkin argue that the decline since 1972 has been more apparent than real because increasing numbers of residents are ineligible to vote.[6] We know that since the 1970s the number of noncitizens in the adult population has risen due to higher rates of immigration, and we know that a larger fraction of the population has been incarcerated. Since noncitizens, felons in prison (in virtually all states), and felons who have completed their terms (in some states) cannot vote, their increasing numbers within the overall population result in lower estimates of voter turnout in recent years, unless we recalibrate for the number of eligible voters in the adult population base (the denominator). When McDonald and Popkin make these and a few other small adjustments (like accounting for U.S. citizens living abroad), it appears that turnout in presidential election years has been relatively flat since 1972 (although the readjusted figures still show modest increases in 1992 and 2004) and that turnout in midterm congressional elections has fallen from an average of 44 percent in the 1950s and 48 percent in the 1960s to just over 40 percent in the 1990s (see figures 2-1 and 2-2).[7]

It is fair to ask why we should be concerned about voter turnout in presidential elections if—and this is a contentious "if"—it has remained flat for roughly thirty years. One answer is that, trends aside, American voter turnout ranks near the bottom among democratic nations. Only the Swiss have lower turnout. Even the rate of voter participation in the 1960s—high by American standards—is low when compared to the average turnout in other democratic nations. Some might say it is unrealistic to expect Americans to participate at the same level as citizens in nations with different electoral systems and constitutional frameworks. This may be so, but there is still a great deal we can do short of fundamental constitutional change. While some features of our constitutional and electoral framework are "hard-wired" in a way that makes them nearly immune to change (the fact that we have a federal system of states, for example), other important and relevant aspects of our electoral system are not beyond reform (creating more competitive congressional districts, for example).

A second reason to be concerned with the level of voting since 1960 is that there is every reason to expect turnout to have risen sharply over that period. Americans' levels of education rose dramatically during these decades, and education has long been recognized as having a huge impact on whether people turn out at the polls and participate in myriad other political activities. In addition, African Americans began to register and vote in large numbers during the 1960s. As a result of the civil rights movement, registration rates that were below 25 percent in several southern states in 1960 had increased to above 50 percent by 1968.[8] More generally, voter registration, long considered a major impediment to higher turnout, has been made markedly easier over the past forty years. The effort required to cast a ballot has been reduced, thanks to reforms such as the "motor-voter" law, unrestricted absentee voting, vote-by-mail, and same-day registration.[9] Indeed, even if voter turnout had remained steady, the fact that voter participation did not increase in the wake of these

FIGURE 2-1 Voter Turnout in Presidential Elections, 1952–2004

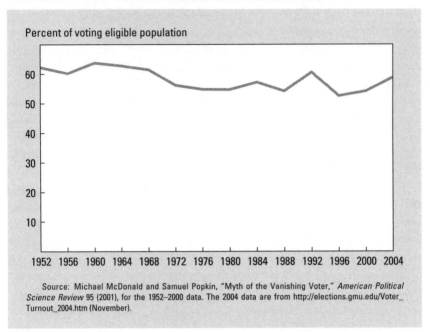

Source: Michael McDonald and Samuel Popkin, "Myth of the Vanishing Voter," *American Political Science Review* 95 (2001), for the 1952–2000 data. The 2004 data are from http://elections.gmu.edu/Voter_Turnout_2004.htm (November).

FIGURE 2-2 Voter Turnout in Midterm Congressional Elections, 1950–98

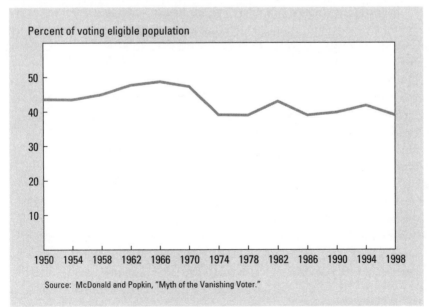

Source: McDonald and Popkin, "Myth of the Vanishing Voter."

massive changes within the American electoral environment is cause for con-cern. In this case, even a flat line represents a net loss of civic effort. This is not to disparage the value of these and other reforms: participation might have declined more steeply in their absence.

Yet another reason that we are troubled by trends in voter participation is that modest changes for the population as a whole mask sharper trends within impor-tant parts of the electorate. Voting by young people, for example, has declined substantially.[10] The percentage of eighteen- to twenty-four-year-olds voting in presidential elections dropped from 55 percent in 1972 to 42 percent in 2000 (adjusting for noncitizens), while turnout among those twenty-five and over held steady at around 70 percent. Registration among eighteen- to twenty-four-year-olds also dropped by 14 percentage points during this time.[11] Voting in midterm congressional elections in nonpresidential years has undergone a similar decline (see figure 2-3). At this writing, figures for the 2004 presidential election year are still preliminary, but the best available evidence indicates that voter turnout among young people increased by almost 13 percentage points from 2000, to 54 percent.[12] With higher turnout across the board, evidence on young people's *share* of the voting public in 2004 is mixed. Some analyses indicate it was the same as in 2000, while others note an increase. For all the talk of extraordinary efforts to mobilize young voters in 2004, early indications are that these voters only voted at a rate that was slightly higher than in 1992 (when their turnout was 51 percent) and about the same as in 1972 (figure 2-4).[13] It remains to be seen whether 2004 will prove to be something more than a temporary "blip." Even with an increase in 2004, however, younger citizens' levels of turnout over the past thirty years have been nothing to celebrate. Since eighteen- to twenty-four-year-olds have the lowest level of turnout, they have the most room to grow.

That young people today are less likely to turn out than people their age in previous generations is an especially portentous development given that life-long electoral engagement is rooted largely in habits developed in one's youth.[14] In fact, current turnout levels would be much lower if Americans born between roughly 1910 and 1940, who vote at high rates as a group, did not constitute such a large portion of the electorate. But they will not live forever. As more civically engaged generations diminish as a share of the population, voter turnout will decline.

Generational differences in political activity are worthy of attention, we believe, because they are key to understanding why overall participation rates have stagnated in the United States. We are also concerned about the persistence of other inequalities: between whites and nonwhites, the wealthy and the poor, and men and women. Such inequalities are pernicious because they lead to "participatory distortions" in which the voices that are heard and heeded in

FIGURE 2-3 Voter Turnout in Midterm Congressional Elections, Eighteen-to Twenty-Four-Year-Olds, 1974–98

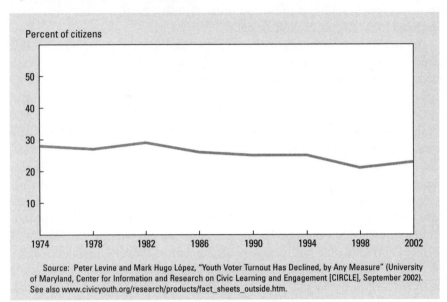

Source: Peter Levine and Mark Hugo López, "Youth Voter Turnout Has Declined, by Any Measure" (University of Maryland, Center for Information and Research on Civic Learning and Engagement [CIRCLE], September 2002). See also www.civicyouth.org/research/products/fact_sheets_outside.htm.

FIGURE 2-4 Voter Turnout in Presidential Elections, Eighteen- to Twenty-Four-Year-Olds, 1972–2004

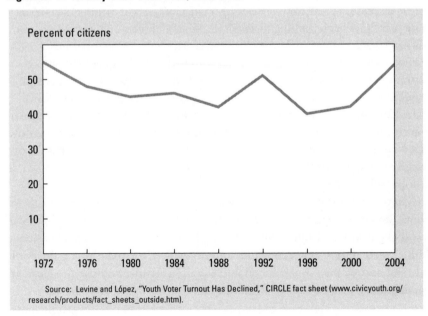

Source: Levine and López, "Youth Voter Turnout Has Declined," CIRCLE fact sheet (www.civicyouth.org/research/products/fact_sheets_outside.htm).

politics are not representative of the public as a whole.[15] Some of these inequalities have lessened since the 1960s. The participation gap between African Americans and non-Hispanic whites is far less than it was. Indeed, although African Americans still vote at somewhat lower levels and contact public officials less frequently than whites, they engage in some other forms of participation at higher rates than whites. There is a greater gap between whites and both Latinos and Asian Americans, two groups whose numbers are growing. These differences can be explained largely by differences in education, income, English proficiency, and recent immigration status, but they are important nonetheless. Even though women now vote at the same rate as men, they engage in other forms of political activity at significantly lower rates and consistently demonstrate lower levels of political knowledge; moreover, this gender gap cannot be explained by differences in education, income, and political interest.

Perhaps most striking, there are sharp differences in the rates of political participation of richer and poorer Americans.[16] One study has found that the richest 10 percent of Americans engage in various forms of participation at rates that are three and a half times that of Americans in the bottom 10 percent in terms of income.[17] Such stark discrepancies testify to the importance of asking not only how much people are participating, but *who* is participating. Although the participation gap between the socioeconomically advantaged and disadvantaged has not worsened in the past thirty years, it has not improved either.[18]

Voting is only the most visible indicator of political participation. In fact, declines in other forms of engagement are even more precipitous than the drop-off in voting. From 1974 to 1994, the Roper Center conducted roughly ten surveys a year in which people were asked whether they had engaged in twelve key political activities, such as writing letters to the editor, participating in rallies and demonstrations, and volunteering in campaigns. Engagement in every single one of these activities fell over this twenty-year period, most by about half.[19] The steepest declines were observed for those activities that are done in tandem with other people, like belonging to groups and attending meetings. Not only are Americans pulling out of the political process, they also are pulling away from one another. As with voting, the most dramatic declines of all were found among the young.

Of particular relevance to a discussion of engagement in the electoral process is the dramatic decline in the percentage of Americans who get involved in political campaigning. Even the simple act of wearing a campaign button or displaying a sign has become less and less common. In the 1950s and 1960s, 15 to 20 percent of Americans would display their political allegiance during a presidential campaign. Today, that has dropped to roughly 10 percent (see figure 2-5).[20] The young seem especially disconnected from political campaigns, as evidenced by the percentage of high school seniors who report that they envision themselves volunteering to work on a political campaign. In the mid-1970s, roughly one in five seniors said that they could see themselves working on a campaign, but in the last few years that has dropped to only one in ten (see figure 2-6).[21]

Consistent with this story of declining participation are trends in attentiveness to and knowledge of public affairs. The events of September 11 and their aftermath only temporarily interrupted a long-term decline in the percentage of Americans who regard politics as important and follow it closely. Even during the presidential election campaign, when we would expect attention to politics to be greatest, few Americans reported paying much heed to this most important political contest. Whereas 37 percent of Americans said that they were "very much interested in following the political campaigns" of 1952, by the 2000 election, its historic closeness notwithstanding, the corresponding figure was only 26 percent (though 2004 may represent a departure from this trend). Again, this decline was particularly acute among the young. In the mid-1970s, more high school seniors said that they had "a lot" or "very great" interest in current events than had "none" or "very little" interest. When we plot trends in political interest among seniors from 1976 to 2001, we see a startling change (figure 2-7). By the mid-1990s, more young people expressed a lack of interest in current events than said that they follow public affairs.[22]

No group is more aware of Americans' declining interest in current events than the nation's newspaper publishers. Newspapers have traditionally served as a principal source of civic information, but newspaper subscribership has declined from about 35 percent of the population in the early 1950s to under 20 percent in the early 2000s.[23] Even during presidential election campaigns, fewer and fewer Americans are turning to newspapers for information about the race. In 1952, 79 percent of Americans reported that they read a newspaper during the presidential campaign, compared with only 57 percent in 2000.

Once again, the decline is steepest among the young. Thirty years ago, newspaper reading among young adults was roughly where it is for their elders now: 44 percent of young people regularly read a paper. At present, according to a recent Pew Research Center report, only 23 percent of those under thirty said they read a newspaper "yesterday."[24] Nor does it seem to be the case that either television or "nontraditional" sources such as the Internet have served to enhance the political knowledge of young Americans.[25] Despite a huge increase in median levels of formal education over the past fifty years, which we would expect to have boosted their knowledge about public affairs, today's young adults know no more about politics than did their parents and grandparents.[26]

FIGURE 2-5 Share of the Population Wearing a Campaign Button or Displaying a Campaign Bumper Sticker during a Presidential Election, 1956–2000

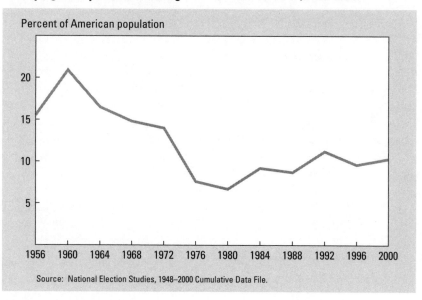

Percent of American population

Source: National Election Studies, 1948–2000 Cumulative Data File.

FIGURE 2-6 Share of High School Seniors Saying They Can See Themselves Working on a Political Campaign, 1976–2001

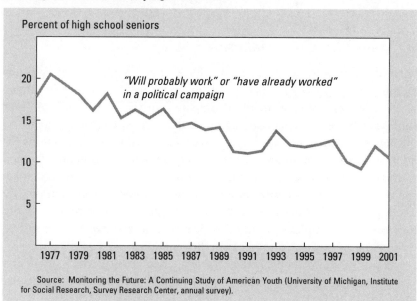

Percent of high school seniors

"Will probably work" or "have already worked" in a political campaign

Source: Monitoring the Future: A Continuing Study of American Youth (University of Michigan, Institute for Social Research, Survey Research Center, annual survey).

FIGURE 2-7 Share of High School Seniors Expressing an Interest in Current Events, 1976–2001

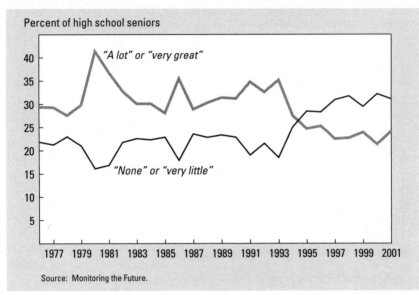

Source: Monitoring the Future.

As with voter turnout, the fact that political knowledge has held steady in the wake of a massive increase in education is really a "net loss."

Diagnosing Our Civic Malaise

Current levels of political engagement in the United States are the result of numerous factors, some of which are more amenable to change than others. Americans' low rate of voter turnout compared with that of citizens of other nations is partly the result of long-standing features of our electoral system. The simple fact that Americans are asked to vote a lot—in staggered elections for multiple offices at different levels of government, not to mention on referenda and initiatives in many states—reduces the number of voters who participate in any given election. Turnout is also dampened by the fact that even though registering to vote has become easier in the United States, it remains more burdensome and complex than in other countries: here the onus for registration is still on the individual rather than the state.[27]

Our diagnosis draws on the best available political science, which frequently diverges from claims that are advanced by pundits on television and in the nation's op-ed pages. For example, recent years have seen much speculation that the way political campaigns are financed has a deleterious effect on voters' engagement with the electoral process. Researchers have yet to establish a direct link between campaign finance and levels of electoral involvement, so we do not discuss, let alone attempt to settle, the knotty problem of campaign finance.[28] Similarly, term limits for elected officials have been a recurring theme among American reformers, but again, there is as yet no good evidence on the possible effects of term limits on electoral involvement, so we leave this topic aside.

Likewise, when we discuss changes in political engagement over time, a number of ready explanations do not withstand empirical scrutiny. It is easy to speculate about the long-term impact of events such as Vietnam and Watergate on political participation but hard to be precise about their effect. Nonetheless, social scientific research has helped to narrow the range of indeterminacy and identify the more plausible causes. Such explanations must meet two criteria. First, they must be factors that can be shown to be related to electoral engagement independent of other influences on the vote. Second, they must be factors that have undergone change over the past generation.

By narrowing our attention to factors that meet both criteria, we have been able to eliminate some that might, at first blush, appear to be relevant. Thus we do not devote much attention to voters' sense of political efficacy: voters' level of confidence that their participation matters. While people who are politically involved have higher levels of political efficacy than those who are not, past research suggests that efficacy itself is largely the product of other factors known to influence engagement and thus has little independent impact on whether people get involved in political activity.[29] Similarly, Americans' trust in their government has declined dramatically over the past thirty years, suggesting that it might be a large part of the explanation for the decline in engagement over the same period. On its own, however, trust in government has little direct impact on whether people get involved in political activity.[30] There is no simple, straightforward connection between increased distrust of government and declining electoral participation, although distrust may have other consequences. We are also unable to offer any firm conclusions about another oft-mentioned damper on electoral engagement: negative campaign advertising. Laboratory experiments suggest that exposure to negative campaign advertising drives turnout down, while studies outside of the lab provide contradictory results. In the absence of any scholarly consensus, we simply note that the sheer volume of political advertising compels further research on the subject.[31]

There are three categories of causal factors that we think compose the most plausible explanations for the trends in electoral involvement:

▌ *Personal:* those that reflect the characteristics of individual voters.
▌ *Structural:* those that reflect the characteristics of America's political system and institutions.
▌ *Cultural:* those that reflect the characteristics of American society and culture.

We acknowledge that there are not necessarily bright lines between these categories, as some of the factors we discuss straddle more than one. Nonetheless, this tripartite division helps us to impose some structure on what could otherwise become a deluge of facts and figures. These factors interact with one another to influence patterns of civic engagement, and all can be influenced to some degree by the design of policies and institutions.

Personal Factors

As we have argued, improving our democratic processes requires enhancing not only the quantity and quality of engagement but its equality as well. We must pay close attention to *who* engages in political activity and, in particular, which personal characteristics make people more likely to participate in civic life.

POLITICAL KNOWLEDGE

Citizens' acquisition of political knowledge is important in its own right, and it is also linked to both the quantity and the quality of other participatory activities. As James Madison put it, "A well-instructed people alone can be a permanently free people."[32] People who know more about politics are more actively engaged in it: those with a higher level of political knowledge are more likely to engage in every type of political activity. The quality of that participation is also enhanced because knowledge increases the consistency of views across issues and time, facilitates the acquisition and comprehension of new information, and enhances the ability of individuals to see the connections between public policy and their own interests.[33] Better-informed voters are more likely to rely on sophisticated criteria, such as a candidate's positions on issues, and less likely to rely on simple cues, such as partisan identification, when making voting decisions.[34] Relatedly, politically knowledgeable voters are also less likely than their less informed counterparts to cast their ballots for incumbents, suggesting that they rely on more than mere name recognition or comfort with the status quo in making their voting decisions.[35]

The amount of schooling enjoyed by Americans has risen dramatically in the decades since World War II, and yet Americans' political knowledge has not kept pace. Comparisons are difficult, but it appears that the average college graduate today knows only as much as the average high school senior did fifty years ago.[36] If Americans are much better schooled, why do they not know more about politics? It could be because reading newspapers, watching the nightly news, and staying informed in other traditional ways have declined dramatically over the past generation. Consider also that during this same period, public high schools have retreated from their historic mission of civic education: they have reduced by fully *two-thirds* the median number of civics and government courses taken in the high school years. Since the 1970s, they have introduced social science courses that incorporate numerous disciplines such as history, economics, geography, and sociology, often to the detriment of civics and government; furthermore, to the extent that they do include civics topics, they often teach *about* citizenship and government without teaching students the skills that are necessary to become active citizens themselves. There is evidence, for example, that many students learn about the history of voting in the United States but do not connect that knowledge with the disposition or skills to become voters themselves.[37] In effect, the older texts were "how-to" manuals for citizens, conveying a sense of the importance of citizenship and describing how citizens can get involved and affect politics. The newer texts are less empowering.[38]

While we recognize that reasonable people disagree about how to teach about citizenship and government systems—and we see great value in social scientific analysis of political institutions and behavior—the sad fact is that, in an era of increased schooling and general well-being, political and civic knowledge has stagnated. It appears that just as individuals are making less of an effort to acquire knowledge, so too political communities are doing less than they once did to impart crucial civic knowledge via schools, our primary collective agency for direct civic education. In this regard, particular groups within the population may be poorly served by a "one-size-fits-all" approach to civics and social studies. As James Gimpel and his coauthors argue, teaching civics and social studies "with the aim of stimulating participation is a very different enterprise in African American inner-city classrooms than it is in white suburban classrooms."[39]

Some argue that the rise in levels of education has not led to a rise in political knowledge because education serves primarily as a mechanism to sort people relative to others. In this view, one's level of education relative to others is what determines social status and thus one's level of political engagement (including one's political knowledge, which is one of the best indicators of engagement with the political process).[40] By this reasoning, an overall increase in education is not expected to lead to an overall rise in political participation or knowledge. While research continues on the usefulness of this "sorting model," it seems clear that simply increasing overall amounts of education is not likely by itself to "fix" current trends in political attentiveness and knowledge.[41]

Here, as elsewhere, it is important to ask not just about the *quantity* and *quality* of Americans' civic capacities and political engagement but about the distribution or *equality* as well. Political knowledge is spread extremely unequally across the population, with poor, nonwhite, and immigrant people, on average, possessing far less political knowledge than their middle-class, white, and native-born counterparts. As early as fourth grade, for example, African American, Hispanic, and poor students perform worse on the civics test of the Nation's Report Card (the National Assessment of Educational Progress, or NAEP) than white, Asian, and middle-class students.[42] These gaps are also evident among ninth-grade students in the United States on an international test of civics knowledge and skills.[43]

It is not surprising that racial and income-related disparities in political knowledge among children mirror similar disparities among adults. In a comprehensive study of adults' civic and political knowledge, political scientists Michael Delli Carpini and Scott Keeter conclusively demonstrate that "men are more informed than women; whites are more informed than blacks; those with higher incomes are more informed than those with lower incomes; and older citizens are more informed than younger ones." These disparities are not small: out of the sixty-eight questions posed, "in no case was the percentage correct for blacks as high as [that] for whites or [the percentage correct] for low-income citizens as high as that for upper-income ones."[44] Because political knowledge is correlated with civic and political participation, these knowledge gaps presage worrisome inequalities in political participation as measured by age, class, race, ethnicity, and immigration status.

POLITICAL INTEREST

A survey researcher asked a respondent why the American people are so ignorant and apathetic about politics. The citizen replied, "I don't know, and I don't care." We repeat this standard joke among survey researchers to call attention to the fact that, beyond political knowledge, political interest in campaigns is itself an important indicator of electoral engagement and, moreover, an indicator that has dropped precipitously. Campaigns are supposed to make noise, and the more noise the better, for political interest is the single most important factor influencing political participation, even when accounting for other demographic factors. For example, consider the comprehensive model that

Sidney Verba, Kay Schlozman, and Henry Brady have developed to describe the factors that lead people to become engaged in political activity. Among the many factors they examine, political interest heads the list, topping even political knowledge and education.[45] In an exhaustive model of turnout and campaign participation in the 2000 election, Joanne Miller and Wendy Rahn similarly give a preeminent place to political interest in accounting for political participation, political knowledge, party mobilization, and organizational involvement.[46] Interest in the campaign is a powerful antecedent of turnout, second only to habit (that is, previous turnout). For expressive political acts, such as attending a campaign rally or wearing a campaign button, it is the most powerful precursor.

Given that political interest, or "the degree to which politics arouse[s] a citizen's curiosity,"[47] is tremendously important as an explanation of political participation, it is perplexing that political scientists have not shown more recent interest, as it were, in political interest. Instead, they have preferred to concentrate on political knowledge or political mobilization.[48] Political interest typically is seen as such a "close" or "obvious" precursor to political participation that analysts have not wasted time conceptualizing or explaining it in its own right, other than to note that resources, such as education and income, play their usual roles as determinants.[49] However, "taking an interest in something" and "doing something" are clearly distinct, and we want to pay careful attention to the importance of political interest.[50]

We do know that some component of adult political interest is a legacy of pre-adult experiences, including the stimulation provided by frequent political discussion at home and participation in high school activities.[51] But the role of parental transmission of political interest is modest in comparison with parents' influence over other political orientations, such as partisanship.[52] Furthermore, these pre-adult experiences do not change rapidly enough to account for the difference between the 1992 presidential election, where 39 percent of Americans reported being very interested in the fall campaigns, and the subsequent election of 1996, where only one-quarter felt similarly engaged. To a large degree, then, levels of political interest hinge on the stimulation provided (or not) by the political environment, and the political environment is something that we can collectively exercise some control over.

PARTISANSHIP

Parties are one of the most important features of the political environment—among other things, they provide information and provoke interest. The people most likely to turn out to vote and participate in other forms of campaign activity are partisans—people who identify with a political party. Beginning in the 1970s, scholars spoke of declining partisanship in the United States. Rather than an electoral *realignment* (a periodic reshuffling of the coalitions supporting America's major parties), some described the partisan environment in the United States as being in a period of *dealignment* (widespread disaffection from the parties altogether).[53] More recently, however, partisanship has taken on renewed importance in American elections. Larry Bartels has shown that party identification is now a more reliable predictor of someone's presidential vote than at any time over the past fifty years.[54] In other words, people who identify themselves as Republicans are more likely to cast a ballot for a Republican today than in the 1950s, while Democratic identifiers are more likely to vote for a Democratic candidate. As the parties have become more ideologically cohesive over the last generation, voters have responded by pulling the lever more consistently for candidates of one party over another. Polls heading into the 2004 election also showed that support for the major party candidates very strongly reflected voters' party affiliation.

The fact that party identification has become a more reliable predictor of how someone votes is not a troubling development in and of itself. Elections are inherently partisan contests, and modern politics is organized around the idea that reasonable differences should be argued out by organized parties linking groups of public officials and voters who advance contrasting visions of the public good and differing policy strategies. While the term "partisan" may have a negative connotation to a general audience, we join other political scientists in affirming that effective elections are properly regarded as "good fights" among candidates and parties with real differences. Indeed, many scholars of American politics have long lamented the ideological incoherence of the U.S. party system. When the parties do not have clearly differentiated policy positions, it is difficult for voters to hold elected leaders accountable for their policies, hindering responsible government.[55] Ideological cohesion, or clear differences between the major parties, is helpful to voters: it means that party labels stand for real differences and real choices.

This rise in partisanship, however, has a troublesome dimension: ideological polarization among elites occurs when the system produces candidates who are more ideologically extreme and far more sharply divided than the electorate. While much of the rhetoric from political pundits about the divide between the "red and blue states" is overblown (there is little evidence that the public is polarized), it is nonetheless the case that ours is an era of sharp partisan differences among political elites, and this seems to be accompanied by increasing political rancor.[56] One worrisome consequence of this polarization of politics is that independent voters—those who do not identify themselves as either Democrats or Republicans—are less and less likely to vote and otherwise engage in the electoral process.[57] Independent voters serve as a centripetal force, holding the parties from drifting toward the extremes. As independents exit the electoral process, we fear that the parties will not simply offer clearly delineated political choices, but instead will diverge so far from one another as to become increasingly unrepresentative of mainstream voters' preferences, driving overall levels of electoral engagement down even further.

The bottom line is that partisan conflict is an essential part of modern politics: the voters need organized parties to present clear alternatives that lay out competing visions of political ends and policy means. Healthy partisanship may become excessive polarization, however, when institutions discount the views of centrists and amplify the voices of the ideological extremes. We understand that it will sometimes be difficult to discern which of these conditions hold, but we believe that it is important not to confuse genuine disagreement with divisive conflict, whenever possible.

SOCIOECONOMIC STATUS

One of the enduring findings of political science research over the past fifty years is that poor people participate less than the wealthy across the entire spectrum of political activities. To take just one example from myriad studies, the American Political Science Association (APSA) Task Force on Inequality and American Democracy reports that nearly 90 percent of people with family incomes above $75,000 claim to have voted in presidential elections, compared with only half of individuals with family incomes under $15,000.[58] Voting, however, is just one form of participation and arguably the most egalitarian. Data from the Roper Center's surveys reveal enormous disparities across income levels in all forms of participation. If one compares participation rates between those in the top tenth of the income distribution with those in the lowest tenth, one finds that the wealthy are three and a half times more likely to attend a meeting on town or school affairs than the poor, three and a half times more likely to contact their congressional representative or senator, and four times more likely to work for a party. We know less about giving contributions to causes, campaigns, and candidates, as apparently the data have not been gathered to allow us to assess trends over time. The data we do have show, not surprisingly, that people with more money give more money. In 2000, 95 percent of people who gave $1,000 or more to a presidential candidate had a yearly household income of $100,000, while people with this level of income only constitute 12 percent of the population.[59]

Two recent studies suggest that these participatory inequalities may indeed be affecting policy outcomes. One study of U.S. senators' roll call votes finds senators to be consistently more responsive to the opinions of high-income constituents on issues such as civil rights, government spending, abortion, and the minimum wage.[60] A more recent study by political scientist Martin Gilens finds that, when the wealthy disagree on issues with the middle and working classes, the former are much more likely to see their policy preferences enacted. Gilens goes so far as to argue that "influence over actual policy outcomes appears to be reserved almost exclusively for those at the top of the income distribution."[61]

Constructively addressing these participatory inequalities is not easy. In chapter three, we discuss ways to get citizens from lower socioeconomic circumstances more involved at the local level through neighborhood councils, the creation of deliberative forums for citizen input, and involvement in actual policy implementation, especially in areas such as schooling and public safety (such as block watches and citizen patrols). Reforms such as these may increase citizens' sense of personal political efficacy and eventually lead to increased political participation, although this connection has not been established empirically. In terms of the electoral process itself, it seems clear that political parties are more likely to try to mobilize lower-income and less educated citizens if they have incentives to do so—that is, if they are likely to succeed in getting poorer citizens to actually vote.[62] As a result, changes to electoral law, such as making election day a national holiday and mailing out sample ballots and polling place information, may be the best method for increasing turnout among citizens with low socioeconomic status.[63] Recent studies also suggest that citizens in lower socioeconomic circumstances are especially responsive to personal and face-to-face efforts at political mobilization.[64]

It is suggestive that the recent decades of declining political interest and participation have coincided roughly with a period of rising economic inequality. The links between inequality and participation are a nascent, but burgeoning, field of research, and much has yet to be learned. At this point, about all we can conclude is that the relationships between inequality and various forms of political participation are complex. Economist Richard Freeman, for example, thinks that rising income inequality is partially responsible for the decline in turnout over the previous generation.[65] In contrast, Henry Brady argues convincingly that rising income inequality over time does not appear to be responsible for the drop in other forms of political participation. In fact, his evidence suggests that "participatory inequality *de*creased for at least some forms of political participation as income inequality *in*creased" (emphasis in original).[66]

Brady does find evidence, though, that income inequality across states is a factor explaining why some states have higher levels of participation than others. Although there is no agreement that rising economic inequality during this period has affected overall equality of participation, it is difficult to be satisfied with a political system in which participation tracks inequalities of income and education as closely as ours does.[67]

GROUP-BASED INEQUALITIES IN PARTICIPATION

The United States has long been characterized by unevenness in participation across different demographic groups.[68] Members of some groups participate more, on average, than others. However, these differences are not immutable. In the not-so-distant past, the electoral engagement of African Americans lagged far behind that of whites, which is understandable given the racially discriminatory barriers to black enfranchisement in the Jim Crow South. The Voting Rights Act of 1965 worked swiftly to close the electoral participation gap between African Americans and whites: the political participation of African Americans is now fairly similar to that of whites. African Americans report voting at moderately lower levels and are less likely to contact a public official or to be affiliated with a political organization, but they are more likely than whites to report doing campaign work and participating in protest.[69]

Similarly, women were largely excluded from participating in the electoral process until the Nineteenth Amendment. Today, men and women vote at approximately the same rate, although other participatory inequalities persist: women are less likely than men to discuss politics, make campaign contributions, contact public officials, and affiliate with a political organization.[70] These differences are explained in part by lower education levels among women, but they are also driven by the fact that women are less interested in and knowledgeable about politics and are less likely to think that they can influence government decisions.[71] The fact that holding office and running for office continue to be predominantly male preserves in America may help to explain the differences between men's and women's interest in and sense of efficacy with respect to politics: several studies find that women are more likely to know female politicians than male ones and may be more likely to try to persuade others how to vote when there is a woman on the ballot.[72]

Despite some lingering participatory inequalities, the examples of women and African Americans demonstrate that constitutional and policy changes can promote more equal participation by groups that were once largely or entirely excluded from the public sphere. Attending to the ways in which policy choices can affect rates of participation across demographic groups is especially important now, at a time when America is experiencing a boom in immigration, particularly from Asia and Latin America. As we explain in chapter three, these sweeping changes have made many communities far more diverse than they once were. In California, non-Latino whites now constitute less than half of the state's population. Changes in America's ethnic-racial composition have implications for political engagement, as people who are Latino, Asian American, or foreign born participate in politics at much lower levels than whites born on American soil.[73] Yet it is not ethnicity per se that pulls these groups out of politics. For example, research has found that the relatively low rates of engagement for Latinos can be explained largely by their language proficiency, citizenship status, education, and income.[74] Not being a citizen is obviously a barrier to voting, but it also affects other variables that are themselves causes of participation, such as mobilization. Compared with citizens, for example, noncitizens are less likely to be asked to contact a public official.[75]

English proficiency is another strong predictor of Latino participation, not only for voting, but for nonelectoral political activities and for school-based civic engagement as well.[76] While there is comparatively little research on Asian Americans, several studies have found that a constellation of factors, including English proficiency, foreign-born status, and political socialization account for much of the low participation of Asian Americans.[77]

As these immigrant groups become fully incorporated into American society—particularly as English proficiency and naturalization rates rise—we can expect their levels of political engagement to increase also. To that end, our public policy choices may be able to influence these attributes in important ways. Research suggests, for example, that the sponsorship of adult education classes by state and local governments increases English language proficiency and, in turn, political knowledge and engagement in the Asian community. Also, targeted mobilization efforts, particularly among low-resource Asian groups, may boost turnout.[78] It seems reasonable to assume that non–English speakers are more likely to vote when voting materials are provided in their own language. Under the Voting Rights Act, political jurisdictions are required to provide written and oral assistance to voters who belong to a language group that accounts for at least 5 percent of the voting population in a single jurisdiction and whose English literacy rate is below the national average. This provision expires in 2007, and Congress will consider its reauthorization. In the absence of any empirical research on the effects of non-English ballots, we tentatively recommend that Congress reauthorize the voting materials provision, while at the same time exhorting our colleagues to give this subject more attention.

Structural Factors

We have tried to spell out what we know about which personal characteristics matter and why. This is part of what we need to know about why some citizens are active and others are not and what we might do as a political community to enhance political activity and to address some of the imbalances in activity across different groups of citizens. But if personal characteristics certainly matter for political activity, it is likewise also the case that people live within institutional and policy structures that influence their capacity and willingness to act in politics. We now turn to these less personal, more contextual conditions that influence political and civic activity. As is likely already clear, it is difficult to separate out these two sets of considerations, and the political choices we make can influence both personal and structural factors.

MEDIA ENVIRONMENT

Given the extent and complexity of the public sphere in modern America, the media—though not a formal political institution or branch of government—provide an essential component of meaningful civic engagement; quite simply, the media play a critical role in the electoral process. Our discussion of the news media here relates to what we have said about political knowledge and interest, as there is a symbiotic relationship between individuals' knowledge of and interest in politics and the media's coverage of it, particularly political campaigns. And just as many individual-level factors have changed over the past forty years, so too have the media. The communication environment surrounding American political campaigns has been altered irrevocably by such technological advances as cable and satellite television and the Internet. Here, as elsewhere, technological changes interact with and can be influenced by policy choices. We want to resist the tendency to view changes such as the rise of the Internet as the technological and economic equivalents of acts of nature, whose consequences the political community must grapple with but whose fundamental shape and effects must simply be accepted. As Paul Starr argues, in the past "American law and policy have . . . actively used government to promote communications."[79] We have at least some capacity to shape the media and their consequences for political life.

One consequence for political participation that stems from the greater number of choices afforded by the proliferation of media options is that the audience for network news, once captive to the three major broadcast networks, has shrunk considerably, declining from nearly 40 percent of the potential viewing audience in 1980 to slightly more than one-quarter in the 2000–01 television season. Such declines prompted one former network news executive to declare that "network news is basically a corpse that hasn't been pronounced [dead] yet."[80] One response of the networks to this increased competition for viewers has been to scale back their coverage of elections and other political events, such as presidential news conferences and political party conventions.[81] For example, in 2000, the "big three" networks spent an average of only 268 minutes on the fall campaigns, down from a record high of nearly 500 minutes in 1992.[82] Larry Bartels and Wendy Rahn suggest that the extent of network coverage, all else equal, is strongly related to the average level of interest in the campaign reported by citizens: they argue that more coverage results in more engagement in the campaign, which in turn spurs turnout and other forms of engagement in the electoral process.[83] Of course, it could be that the networks spend less time covering political campaigns because interest among the public is low, but even so, the declining level of network coverage is a telling indicator of Americans' disengagement from the nation's politics.

The network news, like the daily newspaper, serves as a "general interest intermediary." General interest intermediaries, according to Cass Sunstein, perform important integrative functions in large, modern, and increasingly heterogeneous democracies by providing a shared focus of attention for millions of viewers and readers.[84] We have already pointed to the decline in newspaper reading; the magnitude of this decline is simply stunning. In 1960, the ratio of newspaper subscriptions to the number of American households was just over 1, indicating that the average American household received slightly more than one newspaper. By 2000, the ratio was down to 0.54.[85] There is no sign that this long-term decline in newspaper reading is leveling off; indeed, it may be accelerating. Data on newspaper readership collected by the Pew Research Center for the People and the Press show that in 1995 over half of those surveyed indicated that they had had "a chance to look at a newspaper yesterday." The percentage fell more than 10 points, to 39 percent, by 2002.

Even in the absence of political news coverage on the major networks, abundant political information is available to Americans with cable or Internet access: roughly 80 and 50 percent, respectively. Yet as more channels make accidental exposure to political information less likely, only those motivated to seek out political content stay informed. Markus Prior shows that greater choice between different media content has widened the knowledge gap between people who like news and people who prefer entertainment.[86] Those motivated enough to follow the news despite greater availability of other media content are also more partisan. The audience that remains for the news is, therefore, more ideologically polarized than in the past.

The impact of the tragic events of September 11, 2001, on the levels of political engagement provides a compelling example of how the mass media can unite Americans. The networks covered the tragedies for four days without breaks for commercials, and even entertainment-oriented cable television networks, such as MTV, interrupted their usual programming to carry news feeds.[87] However, despite the extraordinary round-the-clock coverage, the events of 9-11 are not the largest attention-grabbing story in recent memory. Instead, that distinction belongs to the Space Shuttle Challenger disaster, where a record 80 percent of the public reported following the story "very closely," according to the Pew Research Center's News Interest Index (74 percent of the American public followed the story of the terrorist attacks very closely). But 1986 was a different world, before the Internet and the proliferation of channels on cable served to fragment the news audience.

With new communication technologies allowing individuals to create their own personalized versions of the news or avoid news altogether, the individualism that is already so dominant in America now has an even greater capacity to overwhelm the common public culture. Exposure to political news and public information is now more than ever not simply an inevitable result of living among our fellow citizens; rather, it is one among many options requiring a choice. The "interested citizen" becomes just another market segment to be pursued, a niche left to specialty cable outlets or political websites.

Efforts at reengaging Americans with the electoral process should grapple with the challenges inherent in a fractured media market. And yet there are no obvious policy solutions to these changes in the media environment. One thing that would help is for those engaging in congressional redistricting to keep media markets in mind—along with other relevant factors—when drawing congressional district boundaries. Recent research by Marty Cohen, Hans Noel, and John Zaller indicates that voters in districts in which there is a high degree of overlap with a major media market may receive better coverage of political campaigns than voters in districts that cut across media markets.[88] They argue, moreover, that the higher degree of political coverage makes it harder for parties to select candidates whose views are more ideologically extreme than those of voters. The greater flow of information to voters in high-media districts could, therefore, check the tendency toward elite polarization. This is just a small piece of a very complicated media puzzle, and, as always, more research is needed.

We join with others in calling on the media to enrich and expand their coverage of campaigns, political conventions, and public affairs more generally.

Other policy levers might help to increase Americans' exposure to political information as well.

POLITICAL CAMPAIGNS

Ironically, one reason that Americans express less and less interest in political campaigns is that campaigning has become pervasive. In the past, political contests were conducted in a limited period of time, in which voters' attention could be focused on the campaign. That is no longer the case, as campaigns have lengthened dramatically. Rather than a concentrated period of campaigning, which serves to heighten voters' interest, the long campaigns that characterize the American electoral environment produce what Thomas Patterson aptly calls the "politics of tedium."[89]

Because of their two-year terms, members of the House of Representatives have always had to return to the campaign trail frequently. Now, however, they never really leave it: they are essentially engaged in a permanent campaign.[90] At the presidential level, the process of winning a major party's nomination has become a true marathon, and the nomination fight is just the precursor to the general election. Presidential candidates begin their public campaigns at least two years before the general election in order to build support for the early caucuses and primaries that they must navigate to win their party's nomination. Just as the media market's fragmentation has diminished the public's shared focus on political campaigns, so too the sheer length of the presidential campaign means that only political "junkies" pay close attention from the start. Even news organizations genuinely committed to thoroughly covering political campaigns have a difficult time sustaining the public's interest over such a prolonged stretch of time.

Another obstacle to keeping the general public interested in the presidential nominating process is the fact that the primary season has become heavily front-loaded: it is not surprising that residents in states holding early primaries turn out in much greater numbers than those in states holding primaries after the nomination has been all but decided. After Super Tuesday—the massing of a number of primaries on the same day in early March—the race may be effectively over, but with the conventions still months away, the voters experience what Patterson calls a "Silent Spring" in which interest declines and Americans forget much of what they had learned about the candidates and their positions on issues.[91]

Campaigns should be educational exercises—helping citizens to learn about candidates, their positions, and the relevant issues—but they are now structured so as to dampen interest and discourage citizen involvement and learning. It may be difficult to muster the political will to create a more rational process for selecting presidents—our federal structure devolves considerable power to individual states—but it is time to try.

POLITICAL COMPETITION

Presidential elections are often competitive, but they go on for way too long. Congressional elections also go on for a very long time, and they are rarely competitive. In both cases, the problems are partly the result of poor institutional design.

One of the least disputed facts about recent American politics is that both major political parties have used increasingly sophisticated information technology to protect incumbents during the decennial redistricting process. The result has been a surge over the past two decades in the number of safe seats dominated by one party or the other. By 2002, the number of congressional races decided by four points or less had declined to only 15 out of 435—less than 4 percent of total seats—and outright defeats of incumbents had all but disappeared. California offers a perfect example of this process at work. After 2000, a major-party duopoly cooperated to eliminate "marginal" seats. In 2002, fifty incumbents (out of fifty-three congressional districts) ran for reelection. All fifty succeeded. Forty-eight received more than 60 percent of the vote in their districts; the lowest incumbent total was 58 percent. The same is true of state legislatures, where the percentage of uncontested seats has tended upward since the 1960s and 1970s, and the percentage of marginal seats has declined.[92]

Studies of congressional races have found that the closeness of an electoral contest has far-reaching effects, altering the behavior of candidates, journalists, and voters alike. Candidates not only mobilize voters more aggressively in competitive races but also are compelled to be more specific about their issue positions in campaign communications.[93] In addition, editors use preelection polls to determine how many resources to devote to campaign coverage, and press reports are more likely to discuss issues in "intense" races.[94] Finally, voters in competitive congressional elections do a better job of recalling and recognizing candidates' names and can articulate more likes and dislikes about the candidates than their counterparts in safe districts and states.[95]

The decline in contested (as opposed to safe) districts may not only depress turnout but also the quality of political life by, for instance, increasing ideological polarization and divisiveness among elected representatives. Safe seats empower the bases of the two major parties, increasing the chances that successful candidates will be either very liberal Democrats or very conservative Republicans. The result may intensify partisan conflict and diminish the capacity for legislators to work effectively across party lines. For example, researchers have shown that fewer members of Congress are ideologically "cross-pressured" today and that this has caused a significant decline in bipartisan cooperation. This dynamic is especially evident in the U.S. House of Representatives.[96] With the exception of intense partisans, most citizens react negatively to what they experience as incomprehensible and counterproductive bickering, and many respond by withdrawing from what they see as a system that does not represent their desire to "get things done."[97] Citizens who identify themselves as "moderates" and "independents" are less likely to participate than strong ideological partisans, a trend that is especially evident among young adults.[98]

We observe a similar process in presidential elections. While redistricting per se does not apply to presidential candidates, states that are deemed uncompetitive receive little or no attention from the presidential campaigns. For example, in the 2000 presidential election neither Al Gore nor George W. Bush purchased any advertising in seven states: Alaska, Arizona, Connecticut, Hawaii, Rhode Island, Utah, and Wyoming. At the same time, in Arkansas, Delaware, Michigan, Missouri, Pennsylvania, Washington, and Wisconsin, these candidates purchased enough advertising so that *every voter* would see an average of 350 ads![99] The attention that a presidential candidate gives to a state has a profound effect on the information environment of its voters. For instance, in 2000, residents of battleground states knew more about the candidates' issue positions, were more likely to discuss their vote choice with family, friends, and co-workers, and were less likely to believe that they have "no say" in who is elected president.[100] Unfortunately, the number of states that are closely contested in presidential campaigns has declined since 1960, and the average state margin of victory for one presidential candidate or another has increased from around 8 percent in 1960 to 14 percent in 2004.[101]

The absence of political competition in so many jurisdictions is paradoxical, given that at the macro level the nation as a whole is evenly divided politically (witness the 2000 and 2004 presidential elections). Lack of a fighting chance in "safe" districts may discourage those in the minority and make the election seem a fait accompli for those in the majority. At the national level, the sharpness of the political divide likely contributes to political brinksmanship among elected officials, intensifying partisanship among political elites. Such intense partisanship has additional negative consequences, one of which is to drive away voters who themselves are not strongly partisan. The process of excessive polarization feeds on itself.

Localized political competition spurs political engagement. Parties and candidates respond to the electoral landscape, focusing their mobilization efforts in places where they are competitive, whether these are states in a presidential election or districts in a congressional election. And when it comes to engaging people in the political process, mobilization efforts are hugely important. Admittedly, a call for greater competitiveness may seem inconsistent with our concern for polarization among political elites. We contend, however, that one plausible way to curb polarization among members of Congress is to ensure that, to the greatest extent possible, they represent districts with healthy political competition. In other words, maintaining competition at the local level is fully compatible with seeking ways to check destructive polarization in Washington.

As we have already said, it is no simple matter to distinguish, as we have, between "healthy partisan competition" and "destructive polarization." These phrases involve a number of complex judgments. Nevertheless, this distinction is important, no matter what one's ideological preference may be: one of our principal aims is to recommend ways of crafting a political system that encourages real debates among competing parties over important policy issues and that forces competition throughout the system, including congressional races.

POLITICAL MOBILIZATION

Political scientists have accumulated considerable evidence demonstrating the great impact that mobilization has on engaging people in the political process, whether turning out at the polls or undertaking more intensive activities such as attending political meetings or volunteering for a campaign.[102] As Sidney Verba and his colleagues put it, one reason people do not get involved in politics is simply that nobody asks them to. In light of what we know about the significance of political mobilization, a likely culprit for the low and declining levels of electoral engagement is the well-established deterioration of what might be called mobilizing institutions. Three instances are of particular importance. First, the kinds of multitiered national voluntary organizations that dominated American civic life until the 1960s (such as parent-teacher associations, fraternal groups, and professional organizations) have lost members, status, and élan.[103] Second, membership in labor unions as a share of the workforce has declined by almost two-thirds from its peak in the 1950s, a topic we return to in chapter four.[104] Finally, the post-1968 transformation of political parties has empowered pollsters, consultants, and the media (as well as those who have the money to pay for them) at the expense of grassroots activities and face-to-face politics. Thus, while the volume of party mobilization efforts has not necessarily been declining (and by some accounts has actually increased in recent years), the nature of that contact has changed.[105] The parties generally engage in mobilization of the faithful rather than persuasion of the agnostic, which means they target their own supporters for get-out-the-vote drives. And among those supporters, they seek out those who are already the most likely to vote.

Among the groups in the population least likely to be contacted, therefore, are (a) young people, who are often politically or geographically unsettled and have had fewer opportunities to establish themselves as regular voters; (b) poor people, who have historically voted at low rates and have few tools for interest-based mobilization; and (c) immigrants, who may not be eligible to vote because of their citizenship status. The decline in mobilizing institutions is especially consequential for these groups of individuals, who are less well endowed with basic political skills and resources and may therefore encounter more obstacles (material and psychological) on the road to political participation.[106] During the past three decades, for instance, younger voters and those with lower socioeconomic status have been especially likely to drop out of official politics or not to enter in the first place. Not entering is significant, in turn, because of mounting evidence that political participation is a "habitual" activity: early acts spill over into subsequent acts, forming enduring patterns of behavior.[107] Hence, the quantity and equality of political participation are harmed over the long term, as these groups of potential voters are neither mobilized at particular points in time nor habituated to participate over the course of their lives.

OBSTACLES TO ENFRANCHISEMENT

One explanation that *can* be invoked to explain the level of voter turnout in the United States compared with other industrial democracies, but that *cannot* be invoked to explain the decline in electoral engagement over the past forty years, is the difficulty of registering to vote. Although registration remains more difficult in the United States than in virtually all other nations, it has become increasingly simple. After the passage of the motor-voter law, individuals can register to vote while renewing a driver's license or applying for state assistance in all but a few states, where registration is arguably even easier because it can be done on the same day as the election.[108] Numerous states have also simplified the process of absentee voting, while Oregon conducts its elections entirely by mail.

Two groups of individuals, however, continue to face hurdles to voter registration. First are those who have been convicted of a felony—a group whose numbers are growing. Some states permanently bar ex-felons from the polls, even once they have paid their debt to society.[109] Because ex-felons still constitute a relatively small share of the overall population (approximately 1.7 million as of 2000), their disenfranchisement cannot explain much of the aggregate decline in electoral engagement.[110] Nonetheless, high incarceration rates among some subgroups of the population, most notably young African American males, have created communities in the United States with heavy concentrations of disenfranchised voters, exacerbating race-related inequalities that stem from income and education. By one estimate, for example, approximately 7.5 percent of voting-age African American males no longer enjoy the right to vote because of felony convictions.[111]

Second, college students sometimes bear an added burden because they cannot easily register in their college town and may have to register in a location far removed from where they spend most of their time. (They also must deal with the additional difficulties of voting by absentee ballot.) In some instances, local registrars create significant hurdles for students who claim residency in their college community. Genuine questions remain as to what identification is required for registration or first-time voting (for example, whether an out-of-state driver's license is adequate) and about the implications of registering to vote in one's college town (that is, whether this changes one's legal residence for other purposes, including, for example, automobile registration and taxes).[112] These questions of enfranchisement raise obvious questions of justice. Although we realize that some of our colleagues may disagree, permanent disenfranchisement of ex-felons seems to us indefensible.

Cultural Factors

The personal factors that shape civic engagement include, as we have seen, one's socioeconomic status and the tendency to identify with a political party. By structural factors we mean those institutional and policy structures that provide part of the context within which citizens live and make decisions. Various cultural factors also help to compose a citizens' environment. Cultural factors are a bit more diffuse than the structures we have been describing, but they can also be influenced by policy choices.

SOCIAL CAPITAL

Among the many factors known to have an influence on civic engagement is the nation's level of social capital, an analog to both physical and human capital. In the words of Robert Putnam, "Social capital refers to connections among individuals—social networks and the norms of reciprocity and trustworthiness that arise from them."[113] While the social capital literature is vast, among political scientists research on social capital has focused on two key indicators: trust and participation in the voluntary sector.

Over the past four decades, standard measures of both interpersonal and political trust have registered sharp declines, although the relationship between each and political participation is a matter of ongoing research. As noted previously, it is well established that there is no uniform connection between *trust in government* and political participation, although they may be related to one another under some conditions. For example, a distrust of government in combination with political efficacy appears to boost voter turnout.[114] Regarding the relationship between *interpersonal trust*—that is, how much an individual trusts his or her neighbors and fellow citizens—and participation, the political science community has not yet reached a consensus. Some scholars have found evidence that various forms of social trust are related to participation, particularly local participation, but other researchers question the relationship between the two.[115] It is interesting that voter turnout appears to be driven less by an individual's own level of trust and more by whether one is surrounded by others who have a high degree of interpersonal trust.[116]

Trends in associational life are no less contested, but we may conclude (tentatively) that overall levels have declined somewhat and (less tentatively) that the mix and characteristic structures of associational life have changed significantly. The work of both Robert Putnam and Theda Skocpol suggests that the shift away from associational structures integrating grassroots activity with state and national agendas and toward Washington-focused organizations staffed by lobbyists and experts may well diminish opportunities to acquire key political skills and to participate in public life.[117] We discuss the voluntary sector, especially the professionalization of nonprofit associations and their impact on civic engagement, in chapter four.

Religious organizations, in particular, can play a considerable role in facilitating civic and political engagement. Indeed, of all the factors that influence voting and other forms of political participation, religious practice appears to be a motivator nearly as powerful as any.[118] Political scientists, in general, do not pay sufficient attention to this connection, so we do not understand it adequately. Is this effect the result simply of the fact that churches are communities that establish connections among people? Or is it significant that religious communities typically articulate socially conscious values in public settings? Or is it that they engage in actual grassroots mobilization? We do not really know.

This is not to say, however, that most places of worship in America are heavily involved in political mobilization. While some clergy explicitly mobilize their parishioners into political action (constrained by the legal limits on such activity by tax-exempt organizations), most do not engage in direct mobilization. Instead, faith-based institutions generally operate in other ways to enhance an individual's likelihood of engaging in political activity. For one, they are important venues for the acquisition of politically relevant skills. Also, people who attend religious services are usually embedded in social networks of like-minded parishioners; such networks facilitate political mobilization by other parishioners.[119]

Research on the civic life of young people adds a layer of complexity to the analysis of social capital. Many observers have noted that the recent rise in voluntarism among young people has been accompanied by a decline in their political activity, suggesting that voluntary sector activities serve not as a bridge but rather as an alternative to political engagement. It is true that even more than older Americans, young adults tend to regard public institutions as remote and unresponsive and as unreliable mechanisms for transforming individual efforts into desired social outcomes. However, it turns out that people who volunteer, including youth, are also more likely to engage in political activity and that volunteers are less, not more, likely to be alienated from public institutions.[120] Far from being alternatives to one another, voluntarism and political participation appear to be complements. We have more to say about voluntarism in chapter four.

PUBLIC CULTURE

Judged against other societies, the United States has an unusually individualistic public culture. Through most of our history, however, that individualism has been counterbalanced by forces such as strong neighborhood and local ties and by moral and religious doctrines that emphasize duties and obligations to others. During the past generation, though, these forces have weakened, and a form of individualism centered on unfettered choice has become a dominant cultural norm. Not surprising, therefore, young adults are more likely than their parents (and especially their grandparents) to see civic life as a matter of choice rather than responsibility. According to data collected by Scott Keeter and his colleagues, young people from fifteen to twenty-five years of age are the least likely to see citizenship as accompanied by obligations to the wider community.[121]

Although largely neglected in political science research, a sense of civic obligation, or duty, is one of the primary reasons that people participate in politics. It is, indeed, difficult to make sense of the fact that large numbers of people do vote and get involved in other ways without relying on the notion that they feel a sense of duty. The infinitesimal chance that any individual voter could cast a deciding vote would seem to mean that a cost-benefit analysis of voting would always point toward greater costs than likely benefits—and thus no one should ever bother to vote. The same logic applies to other forms of political activity. Yet people do vote and participate in other ways, and many say they do so because they feel it is their duty. In their massive study of why people become involved in civic life, Sidney Verba, Kay Schlozman, and Henry Brady find that a sense of obligation is the most commonly cited reason that political participants give for their engagement.[122] All other things being equal, as the percentage of Americans who regard voting and other public acts as a civic obligation declines, so does participation.

What Is to Be Done?

In the foregoing discussion, we have provided an account—grounded in evidence as solid as we could find—of the personal, structural, and cultural factors that influence the overall levels and unequal distribution of participation in elections and activities related to campaigns. Political participation and civic engagement can be seen, we have argued, as the consequence of a complex interaction of personal, structural, and cultural factors. There are reasons to expect more participation than we see. Both registration and the act of casting a ballot have been made easier through reforms like the motor-voter law. Similarly, Americans have more of what are normally considered prime resources for participation—education and wealth—than in times past. Nonetheless, voting and many forms of civic engagement have declined or stagnated.

Inequalities of participation have not really worsened, so far as we can tell, and some have improved markedly: African Americans and white Americans are far more equal in their rates of participation than was the case fifty years ago. Nevertheless, many inequalities of participation across different groups in the polity are substantial and, we believe, troubling. For example, we are not convinced that the much lower levels of participation among poorer Americans can be explained by the premise that they are happiest with the political system.

We acknowledge that certain basic structures of politics in the United States tilt against high rates of political participation. For example, our complex federal system both multiplies the number of elections in which citizens are asked to participate and increases the diversity and complexity of voting rules among jurisdictions.[123] A plausible case can be made that these features of our system tend to depress turnout. Similarly, it is likely that two-party systems with "first-past-the-post" winners (in which the candidate with the most votes wins) are less likely to mobilize marginalized citizens than are multiparty systems with some form of proportional representation.[124] Our recommendations would not fundamentally alter our constitutional structure. It is, however, both possible and desirable to *reform* many aspects of existing institutions to encourage more, more equal, and higher-quality participation.

There is, of course, disagreement about many of these matters within the scholarly community. Some of our colleagues and some ordinary Americans will deny that civic engagement is a problem, as we discussed in chapter one. We do not wish to short-circuit this or other legitimate debates or to settle complex issues by fiat. We have tried to focus on claims for which there is substantial evidence, but we also recognize that much of what we have said involves contestable value judgments. This is even more true of the recommendations that follow. Nevertheless, we are far from alone in worrying about America's civic health: observers have regarded low levels of civic engagement as a problem in mass democracies for centuries, and we believe they are right to do so. There is every reason, moreover, to believe that inequalities in the rates of participation between rich and poor Americans and across other social divisions will result in inequalities of political influence. Insofar as the political system produces these inequalities by design, it is unfair. Democratic politics in the United States would be healthier if the *quantity*, *quality*, and *equality* of political participation were improved.

We believe that citizens should expect more of themselves and of their political system. There is much that can be done if we have the will. So what should be the plan of action to increase participation and make it more equal and deliberative? We conclude this chapter by outlining the primary recommendations that gain support from recent work in political science. Our prescriptions follow the same pattern as our diagnoses and are thus divided into personal, structural, and cultural factors affecting involvement in the electoral process. To be sure, diagnoses outrun prescription, and so we do not feel that we can offer empirically grounded proposals to address every factor that depresses civic engagement. Not surprising, most of our recommendations consist of changes to the structural elements of the electoral process, as these are perhaps the easiest to reform.

PERSONAL FACTORS

More should be done to provide information so that potential voters, especially those coming to the polls for the first time, are familiar with the electoral process. The provision of information to prospective voters can significantly boost turnout. For example, mailing polling place information to registered voters prior to election day increases overall turnout by roughly three percentage points, while mailing sample ballots yields an increase of two points. The impact is greatest for the least-educated voters with the fewest alternative sources of information. Among registered voters with less than a high school education, advance polling place information yields a seven-point gain; the corresponding figure for sample ballots is about six points. Even more promising findings obtain for young registered voters ages eighteen to twenty-four. Mailing sample ballots to this group produces a very large gain in voting: almost fourteen percentage points.[125]

While we have focused mainly on institutions other than schools, formal education does play a significant role. Education policymakers should renew their commitment to the teaching of civics in a way that will inform younger Americans and empower these future voters. We believe that it would also be sensible for schools to increase newspaper reading and exposure to other in-depth news sources among high school students. Governments at all levels should support programs to increase English language proficiency among immigrants via adult education classes and other means.

It is also important to note recent research on high schools as sources of civic information.[126] A study now in progress highlights the potential of school-based sources of information. A survey conducted in 1999 by the National Association of Secretaries of State found that many young people were staying away from the polls out of embarrassment or fear that they would not know what to do if they showed up.[127] In response, a random assignment experiment has tested the effects of providing high school seniors with school-based instruction in the mechanics of voting. Preliminary evidence suggests noteworthy results, with gains of more than twenty points in voting.[128] Other research suggests that student governments can trigger political engagement among young people. Students in schools where they report having a meaningful voice in at least some aspects of school governance also have higher levels of both political knowledge and engagement.[129]

Given the need for more effective civic education and increased political information about the electoral process, we recommend the following policies:

- Mail polling place information and sample ballots to registered voters prior to election day.
- Place greater emphasis in schools on civic education that empowers citizens.
- Offer English language proficiency classes for immigrants.
- Provide high school students with school-based instruction in the mechanics of voting.

STRUCTURAL FACTORS

Over the past two decades, states have put in place numerous reforms to lower the costs of voting with measurable, albeit modest, results. A simple reform that has been shown to boost turnout, if only a little, is extending the voting day earlier and later than normal working hours: the total number of hours available for voting is linked directly to turnout. Younger voters, in particular, respond strongly to longer voting hours. An even more significant change would be to declare election day a holiday or move elections to the weekend. In the words of Clyde Wilcox, "Estimates vary of the likely impact of holding elections on a holiday or weekend, but all agree that the impact would be great."[130] Puerto Rico designates election day as a holiday and has very high rates of voter turnout.[131]

Other institutional changes to decrease the costs of participation also have a significant impact on younger individuals. A recent analysis shows that election-day registration boosts youth voting by an estimated fourteen percentage points in presidential elections and by an estimated four percentage points in midterm congressional elections, while mail-in balloting also substantially increases youth turnout during presidential elections.[132] Other options—unrestricted absentee voting, in-person early voting, and motor vehicle registration, among others—have either ambiguous or no effects whatsoever. It is, likewise, not clear at this point whether turnout increased as a consequence of the extended voting periods adopted by Florida and several other states in the 2004 presidential elections. (In Florida, voters had the option of voting during an eleven-day period preceding election day.)

Congress should make voting easier in immigrant communities by reauthorizing those provisions of the Voting Rights Act that require localities to provide written and oral assistance, including bilingual voting materials, to communities with below-average rates of English literacy.

Concerning college students, we recommend that colleges, universities, and other organizations continue and expand the extensive efforts made in 2004 to encourage and assist students to register. Minimally, all schools should fully implement the 1998 Higher Education Act, which requires colleges and universities receiving federal funds to make good-faith efforts to distribute voter registration forms to every student.

To review, then, we recommend the following strategies for reducing the costs of voting:

- Declare election day a holiday or move elections to the weekend.
- Employ election-day registration wherever possible.
- Reauthorize the voting materials provision of the Voting Rights Act.

▮ Continue efforts to register college students and fully implement the 1998 Higher Education Act.

Those who commit felonies are denied the right to vote in nearly every state, and there is considerable agreement that imprisoned felons should not be allowed to vote. Opinions vary on whether the right to vote should be restored when felons are on parole or probation, although a majority feels that they should be given back the franchise under both of these intermediate circumstances. Once these periods are over, the public strongly supports the restoration of voting rights, and most states in fact restore them.[133] Unfortunately, some states refuse to permit ex-felons to vote.[134] Restoration of this basic right once all of one's time has been served is an important signal to the individual that he or she will once again be allowed, indeed expected, to participate in the most important tasks of citizenship.[135]

We readily admit that this change carries with it partisan implications. Given that nearly half of convicted felons are African Americans and that most are not well off economically, one would suppose that they will tend toward the Democratic Party, and evidence supports this supposition.[136] Obviously this is not a good reason to deny restoration of the right to vote. Other groups also have decidedly partisan tilts. Cuban Americans lean heavily toward the Republicans; African Americans tend toward the Democrats; in recent years, women have been more supportive of Democrats, men of Republicans (although this tendency was less pronounced in the 2004 presidential election). Indeed, the 2004 election seems to show that, contrary to popular myth, increases in turnout can favor Republicans and that Republican efforts to mobilize voters at the grassroots level can be extremely effective. It is perfectly acceptable for a political party to urge its own supporters to vote, while not seeking to mobilize groups likely to oppose it. But this is very different from using institutional barriers to prevent participation by certain categories of adults. Presumably, no one presently thinks it acceptable to deny the right to vote to Cuban Americans or women, and it is unconstitutional to bar individuals from voting based on race or color or by imposing a financial requirement in the form of a poll tax. No state should find it acceptable to bar voting by felons who have served their complete sentence.

Our policy proposal here is straightforward:

▮ Restore the right to vote of felons who have served their complete sentence.
▮ Consider restoring the right to vote to felons on parole or probation.

No aspect of our political system evokes more partisan energy than does defining electoral districts, and the idea of "taking politics out of redistricting" faces formidable obstacles. Nonetheless, it is possible to shift the locus of redistricting power to reduce the partisan control that has made a mockery of the ideal of competitive elections. For example, Arizona established a citizen redistricting commission in 2000 that must be composed of people with limited ties to government and political parties. Moreover, the statewide proposition that created the commission stipulated that, in addition to respecting the Voting Rights Act and striving to achieve traditional redistricting goals such as equal population, the commission must create competitive districts when doing so "would create no significant detriment to the other goals."[137] Thus, mechanisms do exist for minimizing political influence in the redistricting process. Promoting competitive districts is likely to improve participation by increasing the importance of small numbers of votes, creating incentives for parties to expand the electorate, and promoting the sense of excitement that often accompanies elections with uncertain outcomes. It may also dampen the extreme partisanship that many Americans find distasteful. What should *not* happen, from the point of view of increasing competition, is redistricting multiple times in a single decade in back-and-forth gerrymanders, as was attempted in Colorado (but ruled by the state supreme court to violate the state constitution) and was done in Texas (and upheld by a three-judge federal panel, whose ruling the U.S. Supreme Court refused to review).[138] We are not sure that ten years is the ideal period to wait before redistricting, but we worry that redrawing district lines too frequently fosters cynicism among voters.

Greater competition might ensue if the U.S. Supreme Court made it easier to identify political gerrymandering. In *Davis* v. *Bandemer* (1986), the court ruled that political gerrymandering was "justiciable" (that is, subject to a ruling by the court), but the standards enunciated in that case have made it virtually impossible for individuals or parties to successfully challenge a districting plan on the basis of partisan fairness.[139] The court recently revisited political gerrymandering in *Vieth* v. *Jubelirer* but upheld the Pennsylvania redistricting plan in question because the five-justice majority concluded that "no judicially manageable standards for adjudicating political gerrymandering claims [had] emerged."[140] Five of the justices indicated that they believe such standards might exist, but it seems clear that the court will not hear another case of this nature until it believes that such standards have been found.[141] Until then, the search for an adequate definition of excessive political gerrymandering must continue among scholars and the engaged public.

We applaud the widespread concern with the partisan and racial impact of gerrymandering. However, the public and especially judges should also recognize that the current practice of giving the power to redraw district lines to incumbent partisan politicians, armed with ever more powerful computers and more accurate voting maps, allows them to craft noncompetitive congressional districts ever more effectively. This, in turn, undermines political interest and, along with it, voting and a host of other vital participatory activities. It may also promotes polarization among candidates and elected representatives, making our politics nastier and less capable of dealing with serious problems.

Reforming the districting process is, we believe, the single most important thing that could be done to increase competitiveness and spur political participation. And the single most important reform is the creation of nonpartisan commissions to draw district lines. Currently, twenty states use commissions at some point in their redistricting process, but only a handful of these commissions are designed to be nonpartisan—most are designed in a manner that encourages parties to create "bipartisan gerrymanders," which protect incumbents of both parties.[142] Such bipartisan compromises are largely responsible for the decline of competitive congressional districts that occurred following the last two rounds of redistricting.[143] Scholars have found that two types of commissions especially encourage bipartisan gerrymandering: (1) commissions with an equal number of political appointees who must adopt a map by a supermajority vote and (2) commissions with an equal number of political appointees who must themselves select a tie-breaking member. In contrast, Arizona's unique commission, which is composed of citizen members who must apply politically neutral criteria when drawing district lines, appears to offer the best model for a commission that will produce competitive districts.[144] Finally, it should also be noted that California Governor Arnold Schwarzenegger recently proposed another commission design that may be effective in producing more competitive districts in his home state: a three-member panel of retired judges.[145] This judicial model may be worth considering.

Our specific recommendations in this regard are the following:

▌ Do not allow states to engage in redistricting multiple times in a single decade.
▌ Use nonpartisan commissions for establishing new political boundaries for congressional and state legislative districts.

Starting in the early 1970s, political parties shifted away from grassroots activities and toward a top-down politics dominated by pollsters and the media. Lately parties have taken some tentative steps to begin redressing the balance. Recent research suggests that a more systematic shift toward face-to-face contacts will increase participation, particularly for groups otherwise less likely to get involved. More specifically, Donald Green and Alan Gerber have spearheaded an ambitious research enterprise involving scores of randomized experiments—the most precise method of determining causal relationships— in order to determine which mobilization methods have the greatest effect on voter turnout.[146] They have found that by far the most effective form of mobilization is old-fashioned shoe-leather politicking, namely, doorstep conversations. Close behind are personalized phone calls (*not* automated calls that simply play a recording). Leaflets and direct mail also have measurable effects, but they pale in comparison to more personalized methods of communication; e-mail appeals have no effect whatsoever.[147]

Evidence also suggests that mobilization, competition, and cost reduction can interact to increase turnout. Candidates and parties in states with same-day registration are more likely to reach out to younger voters, who are (as we have seen) especially influenced by this opportunity. And the competitiveness of individual races influences investments in mobilization by parties and candidates. For example, during the 2004 presidential race, John Kerry campaigned heavily for the Native American vote in western battleground states—a group that typically votes Democratic but that often has low turnout rates, partly because candidates rarely bother to campaign on reservations.[148]

In short, then, parties and other organizations should undertake the following:

▌ Encourage face-to-face contacts urging voter turnout.

Cross-national research suggests that multiparty systems employing some form of proportional representation tend to have higher rates of participation than do two-party, first-past-the-post (or winner-take-all) systems, like that of the United States.[149] We neither anticipate nor recommend shifting U.S. electoral rules in this direction. Nonetheless, it is worth considering whether it would be possible to incorporate some of the pro-participatory features of a system of proportional representation into the basic structure of U.S. politics. For example, demographic groups that find themselves in permanent minority status in single-member districts may gain new electoral opportunities (and thus incentives to participate) in multimember districts. Indeed, evidence from a number of sources suggests strongly that incumbents are less advantaged in multimember state legislative districts.[150] This incentive would very likely be enhanced if a cumulative voting system were used, in which voters in multimember districts were allowed to cast their multiple ballots for a single candidate instead of casting only one vote per candidate. Similarly, cumulative voting at the municipal level, which is essentially a form of partial proportional representation, appears to boost turnout by about five percentage points.[151]

One change that would encourage more geographically dispersed national campaigning for the presidency is for states to give two electoral college votes to the statewide winner and one vote to the winner of each congressional district (as is presently the case in Maine and Nebraska).[152] Under such a system, candidates would be less likely to ignore select states on the grounds that the statewide popular vote is highly predictable from polling information and, therefore, that the disposition of its entire bloc of votes in the electoral college is known. Such a system would also be likely to yield closer votes in the electoral college. By carrying the campaign to more places and increasing the overall level of competition, this reform would probably stimulate greater turnout across the country, although we admit that this conclusion is based more on inference than on empirical analysis.[153] This reform is more appealing than eliminating the electoral college altogether because adopting it would not require amending the Constitution.[154] A drawback of the district plan, however, is that it would considerably raise the stakes of congressional redistricting. Thus states that adopt this way of allocating electoral votes should also reform their redistricting process to insulate it as much as possible from partisan politics.

In sum, we call for an adjustment in the way states allocate electoral college votes:

▎ Give two electoral college votes to the statewide winner and one vote to the winner of each congressional district.

Thus far, we have considered structural factors that affect mainly the *quantity* and *equality* of participation. We have paid less attention, however, to how these factors—or any other factor for that matter—affect the quality of civic engagement. In chapter one, we argued that the *quality* of participation has many features. Participants should have information that allows them to form judgments, they should interact with citizens from various backgrounds, and they should have the power to shape—not simply respond to—the political agenda. We believe that the quality of citizens' political engagement increases to the extent to which such engagement is deliberative. In deliberations about politics and public problems, individuals can acquire information, encounter diverse perspectives, improve their reasons for supporting or opposing policies or politicians, and ultimately alter their preferences and views though discussion or discourse with others. Political deliberation occurs in countless venues, including not only public hearings and meetings but also discussions around kitchen tables, at barbershops or bars, and on top of soapboxes. Some of the factors discussed above, such as the media environment and the character of mobilization by political organizations, affect the quality of political deliberation.

Over the past decade, dozens of civic innovators have created models for intentionally gathering citizens to discuss local, and sometimes national, issues with one another and with their representatives. Unlike traditional public hearings, most of these efforts employ a range of methods to bring together diverse participants who not only express their own views but seriously consider differing ones. Some of these gatherings, such as the Minnesota E-Democracy project, occur in the electronic space of the Internet, but most are face-to-face.[155] In terms of binding influence, one of the most striking examples comes from outside the United States: British Columbia's Citizen Assembly on Electoral Reform. The 160-member group of randomly selected B.C. citizens met regularly between January and December 2004 to determine how the province's electoral system should be reformed. Their recommendations framed a referendum question that citizens voted on in May 2005. With regard to scale, the most ambitious of these ideas for integrating a more deliberative element into American politics is Bruce Ackerman and James Fishkin's "Deliberation Day," which involves paying citizens $150 to participate in face-to-face community discussions across the country just prior to general elections.[156]

By selecting participants at random or by engaging in targeted outreach, some of these initiatives have the potential to generate more equal patterns of participation, where wealthier and highly educated citizens are not overrepresented. Furthermore, there is evidence that participants gain substantive knowledge and, in the case of deliberative polls, alter their positions as a result of deliberation.[157]

With the exception of Deliberation Day, which is itself a proposal rather than an institutionalized practice, reforms of this kind have less potential to affect citizen deliberation on a large scale. Moreover, without random selection or special outreach efforts, individuals who are politically interested, knowledgeable, and efficacious—precisely the people who need deliberation less—are more likely to participate in these forums. Almost all of these efforts issue public reports and attempt to garner media coverage that will affect the broader public debate. James Fishkin, inventor of the deliberative poll, has gone further by organizing television broadcasts. Despite considerable media interest, no work has assessed whether the polls are having widespread effects either by triggering substantial informal public deliberation or by providing political cues—cognitive shortcuts—to other citizens.

We applaud all of these efforts for their creativity and believe they have the potential to create a more informed and engaged electorate. We encourage scholars to devote more attention to what takes place in these forums, especially how deliberative agendas are set, who participates, what they discuss, and how they discuss it. Moreover, scholars proposing reforms that create deliberative shortcuts need to assess whether they can possibly affect the engagement of the larger public.

Therefore,

▮ Provide more opportunities for deliberative engagement within the political system.

▮ Pay more attention within the field of political science to the conditions under which deliberative opportunities contribute to a more enlightened citizenry and better-informed political participation.

CULTURAL FACTORS

While decreasing the costs of voting has lifted turnout a little, the fact that previous reforms in this regard (like the motor-voter law of 1993) have had a muted impact suggests that costs are not all that stand in the way of more people voting. Another likely reason is a diminished sense of civic duty, which, as noted earlier, has a major impact on political participation. Compared with the costs of voting, however, there has been far less research into what fosters civic duty. We do know that, as a personal moral norm, civic duty is hard to shape through specific institutional devices, at least in the short term. Nonetheless, it is worth thinking about ways to enhance the norm of civic duty.

Civic duty can also be understood as justifying a legal obligation, which presents one possibility: making voting mandatory. Making jury duty a legal requirement induces many citizens who would not volunteer for it to show up on the appointed day, and there is no evidence that jury "draftees" are on average less competent to perform their duties than are volunteers. It would be perfectly possible for individual states to experiment with mandatory voting systems. There is precedent for this in countries with political cultures reasonably close to our own. For example, Australian states that instituted compulsory voting in the 1990s saw an overall 23 percent increase in voting.[158]

However, it remains to be seen whether these gains have been purchased at an acceptable cost, measured along other relevant civic dimensions. While it is true that mandatory voting would increase turnout, the psychological literature on "insufficient justification" suggests that giving people an external reason for their behavior (that is, "I voted because I have to") decreases their intrinsic motivation for the task. Similarly, cross-national research suggests that higher rates of voter turnout are negatively correlated with other forms of civic activity and that, in nations where the costs of civic membership are low (for example, Scandinavia), people are less likely to spend time actively participating.[159] In sum, there is evidence that there are civic costs to making participation mandatory or even easier. Any steps taken in this direction, therefore, should be accompanied by a careful consideration of the potential consequences coupled with rigorous research regarding its effects.

Short of making voting mandatory, there are other avenues by which a sense of civic duty can be thickened. Schools are one; the mass media are another. One useful model would seem to be campaigns to discourage smoking and drinking, which have successfully fostered social norms discouraging such activities.[160] Perhaps similar efforts could be made to encourage political participation, especially among young people. One place to begin would be to encourage the recognition of a young person's "first vote" as a significant rite of passage, much like getting a driver's license. Schools can play a part in such an effort, as can parents. As mentioned, a growing body of evidence demonstrates that, because voting is habitual, the earlier people start voting, the more likely they are to continue voting throughout their lives. Moreover, schools should reexamine civics curricula and seek improved ways both to impart relevant information about the various tasks of citizenship and to instill a sense of the responsibilities of citizenship. These efforts should take account of the differing experiences of various groups within the population.

To foster a heightened sense of civic duty, especially among young people, we recommend the following:

▌ Encourage recognition of a young person's "first vote" as a significant rite of passage.
▌ Focus on the responsibilities of citizenship in a reinvigorated civics curriculum that addresses the specific circumstances of different groups.

While our proposals for reform are targeted mostly toward the public institutions most amenable to changes in public policy, the family is also an absolutely critical component in promoting civic and political participation among young people. Growing up in a home where other family members discuss politics has an impact on political participation long after one has left home.[161] Similarly, young people are more likely to vote and otherwise get involved in politics if they have seen their parents do so. Any public campaign designed to promote the political engagement of young people must not neglect the home as an institution in which youth learn to be engaged.

Conclusion

We began by setting ourselves the challenge of understanding the mechanisms that shape civic life in order to recommend ways to improve the *quantity*, *quality*, and the *equality* of civic engagement in our electoral system. We wish we knew more about a number of important points. However, a great deal is known, and we believe that there is much that can be reliably recommended. We conclude by considering how the reforms we propose would affect each of these three criteria.

We acknowledge that most of the recommendations in this chapter focus on the quantity of engagement. They are designed largely to increase the number of people who vote and otherwise participate in the electoral process. Reforms that make voter registration easier, for example, are intended to enhance overall participation at the polls. Likewise, efforts targeted at young people will swell the numbers of those involved in the electoral process. Furthermore, we have sought levers to enhance electoral competitiveness at the district level because competitive elections beget engagement. The fact that our main focus has been on ways to increase the quantity of engagement, specifically voter turnout, is largely a reflection of the current state of research. We simply know more about turnout than other types of engagement. Nevertheless, while we do not have evidence to prove their effectiveness, we believe that experiments with new deliberative opportunities are well worth exploring, studying, and encouraging.

In addition, quality and equality would be enhanced by some of the other reforms we propose. Ensuring the re-enfranchisement of people who have committed a felony but paid their debt to society, for example, equalizes their opportunities for electoral engagement. In general, measures targeted at young people will address the inequality of engagement across younger and older voters. Promoting newspaper reading among high school students would serve to keep them informed of public affairs, boosting the quality of their engagement because informed voters are better able to connect their own preferences to candidates' policies. More systemically, efforts to restore competition to congressional elections would, we argue, enhance the overall quality of the electoral process. No longer would the parties' congressional delegations be dominated by representatives elected from districts in which their party is effectively an oligopoly and, barring a scandal, their reelection rarely in doubt.

As acknowledged at the outset, our three criteria may sometimes be in tension. Political science can help us to understand how these dimensions are related, but it cannot tell us which one is most highly valued. Therefore, in closing, we argue that the nation would be well served if the three criteria for engagement that we have laid out were regularly invoked in discussions of the state of American politics so that these trade-offs might be explicitly weighed by would-be reformers and better understood by citizens.

We believe that our proposed reforms would have a salutary effect on electoral engagement. We also know that ours will not be the final word on this important subject.

Local politics makes important contributions to civic life:

- *More than 96 percent of all elected officials in the United States serve at the local level.*[1]

- *Since 1970, the number of African American elected officials has increased nearly fivefold. Of those holding public office in 2002, more than 70 percent of African Americans and Latinos served in local government or on school boards.*[2]

- *In 2003, 24 percent of respondents to a national survey said that they belong to or work with a community group or neighborhood association.*[3]

- *Most large American cities have systems of neighborhood councils, with most being officially recognized by city government.*[4]

- *An estimated 50 million people belong to more than 250,000 home-owners associations, with well over 1 million serving on boards and committees.*[5]

But the trends are discouraging:

- *In 1987 only 35 percent of U.S. adults reported always voting in local elections, down from 47 percent in 1967. In 1990 only 21 percent of eligible voters reported voting in all local elections.*[6]

- *The number of candidates running for local offices dropped 15 percent nationally between 1974 and 1994.*[7] *Seven California cities reportedly canceled elections in 2003 because of a lack of candidates.*[8]

- *Between 1973 and 1994, the percentage of people attending a public meeting on town or school affairs declined from 22 to 12 percent, and the proportion serving on a committee for a local organization declined from 10 percent to just over 5 percent.*[9]

- *In 1990, 38 percent of people with family incomes over $75,000 had participated in some informal community activity and 6 percent had served on a local government board, compared with just 13 and 1 percent, respectively, of people with family incomes under $15,000.*[10]

3

The American
Metropolis

Place matters for civic engagement. Of course, personal characteristics such as education and income also matter, but the local circumstances in which citizens live and work have significant independent effects on whether they will get involved, with whom (and against whom) they will engage, and how successful their efforts will be. To begin with, a majority of Americans identify with their city or town and report that their place of residence gives them a sense of community.[11] Such identification can be an essential building block of citizenship, providing reasons for people to be interested and involved in political affairs.[12]

Moreover, place determines the civic landscape. The extent and character of social networks are in large part place based, and these networks in turn affect patterns of political mobilization. In addition, the institutions chosen by a locality provide the mechanisms through which citizens can take part in the collective life of their community. Different communities face different needs and have widely divergent resources for meeting those needs. At least in part, place shapes the issues individuals face as well as their responses to those issues. The characteristics of place thus influence the amount, the quality, and the distribution of civic engagement by providing opportunities for, and erecting obstacles to, participation.

But the places Americans call home are changing, and these changes exert important effects on place-based patterns of civic engagement. In particular, metropolitan areas are growing, spreading, and fragmenting. As in chapter two, where we chronicle declines in participation at the national level, many traditional forms of local political participation are eroding as well. This chapter explores the place-related factors that enliven or dampen civic engagement in metropolitan areas, where the vast majority of Americans now reside, but where the most serious challenges to healthy democratic life are also found. Because the nature of the places where we live is determined in large part by political choices, one overarching question drives our investigation: *How can we reshape local institutions, policies, and practices to encourage residents of metropolitan areas to work together, especially across geographic, racial, ethnic, class, and jurisdictional boundaries?*

Despite their problems, cities and their surrounding localities provide a vast array of opportunities for civic engagement—so many that one of the main challenges of local engagement may be providing productive opportunities for participation without overburdening citizens. With some notable exceptions, however, contemporary political scientists have paid too little attention to local politics. This neglect is troublesome, because what Robert Dahl said of the city nearly forty years ago is even truer of metropolitan places today: "It confronts us with a task worthy of our best efforts because of its urgency, its importance, its challenge, the extent of our failure up to now, and its promise for the good life lived jointly with fellow citizens."[13]

The Promise and Perils of Local Politics

As the country has grown, local institutions have spurred civic engagement by keeping government close and accessible to ordinary people. The crazy quilt of political boundaries affords an almost endless array of occasions to get involved in local politics. In 2002 there were 87,525 units of local government in the United States, including 35,933 municipalities, towns, and townships and 13,506 school districts.[14] Nearly 500,000 elected officials—twenty-four out of every twenty-five elected officials in this country—serve at the local level. (Thomas P. "Tip" O'Neill's famous quip that "all politics is local" is hardly an exaggeration.) Because there are so many points of access, it is relatively easy to get involved in local politics. In addition, many local governments, especially in larger cities, have created innovative mechanisms for citizen participation.

Americans and observers of American politics have long believed that a healthy democratic life rests on local institutions. As Alexis de Tocqueville argued, "Local institutions are to liberty what primary schools are to science; they put it within the people's reach; they teach people to appreciate its peaceful enjoyment and accustom them to make use of it. Without local institutions a nation may give itself a free government, but it has not of the spirit of liberty."[15] By "liberty" Tocqueville meant the capacity of free citizens to govern themselves in private and public life. It is through interaction with local institutions that citizens can directly connect their own interests with those of their community.

Local participation is important, not just for its own sake, but because it enables citizens and leaders to participate in the broader arenas of state and national politics. And the political stepping-stones provided by local institutions are especially important for those whose voices tend to be fainter at the national level. Many African American, Latino, and, increasingly, Asian American public officials gain office locally, often in places where these groups have a numerical advantage, making local politics especially important for these geographically concentrated but traditionally underrepresented groups.

Citizens are drawn into participation at the local level because ease of access is coupled with direct potential benefits of involvement. The actions of local governments affect the value of residential property, the primary economic asset of the majority of Americans. In addition, local public services are "vital to the preservation of life (police, fire, sanitation, public health), liberty (police, courts, prosecutors), property (zoning, planning, taxing), and public enlightenment (schools, libraries)."[16] Local governments spend close to a trillion dollars on service provision, and in doing so they directly address the "day-to-day vital interests" of ordinary citizens.[17]

The unique value of *local* government flows from its closeness to the people—closeness in the sense that city hall is nearer than Capitol Hill, city boundaries are narrower than those of an extended republic, and one's fellow citizens are more likely to be familiar. Proximity to the people is in part a product of size; government can be close when the jurisdiction is small. Although localities vary greatly in size, they still preserve vital space for the democratic virtues of the small republic.

The claim that democracy flourishes in small communities is as old as systematic reflection on politics. When Aristotle argued that a democracy should be small enough for citizens to recognize one another, he expressed what would be the common view for centuries. Robert Dahl summarized the thought two millennia later: "The city-state must be small in area and in population. Its dimensions are to be human, not colossal, the dimensions not of an empire but of a town, so that when the youth becomes the man he knows his town, its inhabitants, its countryside."[18] Indeed, an "extended republic" of the sort championed by James Madison and the other founders was a radical innovation, considered by many to be an impossibility.

Recent research supports the claim that smaller units of government invite political participation and civic engagement. In his study of citizen participation in 800 towns and cities in the United States, for example, Eric Oliver finds that rates for three kinds of engagement—contacting officials, attending board meetings, and attending organizational meetings—decline significantly as the population of one's place of residence increases.[19] In a decades-long study of town meetings in Vermont, Frank Bryan reports that town size is the single best predictor of participation rates: far greater percentages of residents attend town meetings in small than in large towns.[20]

Although not all of the evidence points in the same direction, there are reasons to believe that smaller places can draw citizens toward participation.[21] Dahl, Bryan, and others observe that individuals participate more in smaller places because they are more likely to be able to influence outcomes.[22] In a small jurisdiction, each vote has relatively more weight. Greater influence may also come because citizens of smaller localities face less complicated and more responsive bureaucracies and may find it correspondingly easier to make their voices heard. They may even know their elected officials personally.[23] It may also be that alienation is lower and political interest greater in smaller places, in part because smaller places tend to be more homogeneous and because residents of smaller places are more likely to be contacted by someone seeking to get them politically involved.

Robert Putnam, Wendy Rahn, and others muster a great deal of evidence showing that residents of smaller places are more likely to trust other people as a general matter and that those who exhibit greater trust are more likely to behave in a trustworthy manner.[24] These increases in interpersonal trust can have positive implications for civic engagement. Residents of smaller places are far more likely to be involved in their communities: they are more likely to volunteer, work on community projects, and give to charity.[25]

Local institutions help to form civic life, but the effects of place on political and civic activity are complex. Two central and related difficulties have drawn our attention: the dilemma of *scale* and the challenge of *diversity*.

First, there is the *dilemma of scale*: small size may increase the opportunities and inducements for engagement in the ways we have just described, but smaller political units also have their limitations. We care, of course, not only about the quantity of political participation but also about its distribution and the quality of governance. Relevant to the quality of governance is the fact that different levels of government in our federal system have specific advantages when it comes to promoting particular political values and interests. Larger governments have the capacity to address some public problems more effectively.[26]

Local governments, especially small ones, tend to be relatively homogeneous and exclusive. Many of the Anti-Federalists preferred the sorts of aims associated with smaller and more homogeneous communities; an Anti-Federalist writing as Agrippa warned that state control over immigration was necessary to allow citizens to keep "separate from the foreign mixtures" and preserve "their religion and morals."[27] Nearly two centuries later, Grant McConnell argued that larger and more diverse constituencies are more liable to promote encompassing public interests:

> It is not meaningless to speak of public values. They are public in the sense that they are shared by broad constituencies; usually, they must be achieved through mobilization of large constituencies. . . . A political order composed exclusively of small constituencies, whether drawn on lines of geography, function, or other dimensions, would exclude a variety of genuine values of real concern to the members of society. . . . Many of the values Americans hold in highest esteem can only be realized through large constituencies, some indeed only by a genuinely national constituency.[28]

Paul E. Peterson has given greater precision to McConnell's insight. While national governments have some control over entry, naturalization, and eligibility for public benefits, local governments do not. Because movement is easier across localities than across national boundaries, local political institutions are less likely than the federal government to promote certain sorts of policies, including redistribution and policies with broad and unconfined benefits. Small communities are relatively incapable of pursuing broad-based political goals. When local communities raise taxes in order to aid the disadvantaged, for example, they furnish incentives to the better-off to exit and the worse-off to enter.[29]

In addition to issues of size, there is also a *challenge of diversity or heterogeneity*. On the one hand, a large and diverse democracy needs settings in which citizens learn how to encounter, comprehend, and negotiate myriad differences of opinion, race, class, religion, ethnicity, and lifestyle. More diverse localities seem far more likely to realize democratic hopes of vitality, creativity, and innovation. Although cities have always contained neighborhood enclaves, the democratic promise of city life is that in their daily routines people encounter others who are different from themselves. As Iris Marion Young notes, "City dwellers frequently venture beyond . . . familiar enclaves . . . to the more open public of politics, commerce, and festival, where strangers meet and interact."[30] Douglas Rae similarly emphasizes that diverse and inclusive early-twentieth-century cities, where all classes and races lived and worked in relatively close proximity to one another, helped to realize core aspirations of democracy: "Central to the democratic experience is contact with difference—other races, other nationalities, other economic classes, other language groups."[31]

On the other hand, there is evidence that greater diversity, including racial and ethnic heterogeneity, decreases trust and undermines a shared sense of community. The greater diversity likely to be found in larger cities may bring citizens of different interests and backgrounds together to address important issues, but the greater levels of conflict that may accompany democratic politics among a diverse citizenry may prove off-putting and difficult to some, especially if local institutions do not encourage respectful interaction in a supportive context.[32]

None of this is really surprising. If our only aim were to maximize the opportunities for civic engagement, Americans would have done well to side with the Anti-Federalists and reject the Constitution's "extended republic." "Extend the sphere," as Madison argued in the tenth Federalist Paper, "and you take in a greater variety of parties and interests; you make it less probable that a majority of the whole will have a common motive to invade the rights of other citizens; or if such common motive exists, it will be more difficult for all who feel it to discover their own strength and act in unison with each other." Madison did not argue that politics on an extended scale would inhibit all forms of political cooperation equally. To the contrary, in a larger polity "unjust or dishonorable purposes" are inhibited more than others because "communication is always checked by distrust in proportion to the number whose concurrence is necessary."[33] Still, it is hard to escape the suggestion that greater size and diversity of interests inhibit political cooperation in general, even if these inhibitions apply most especially to dishonorable political purposes.

In sum, the structure of local political institutions provides both opportunities for and obstacles to civic engagement, and these institutions are built to favor some sorts of engagement over others. More encompassing institutions play a vital role with respect to the pursuit of our most inclusive aims, but they may not favor the greatest amount of civic activity. Active citizenship seems to flourish most naturally at the local level and in smaller communities. This does not mean that those who favor civic engagement should abandon wider and more inclusive goals or that those who favor diversity and inclusion should abandon local institutions. It does mean, however, that these two dilemmas— of scale and diversity—pose difficult political challenges.

In addressing these persistent dilemmas, we must, even more than in chapter two, grapple with both limited evidence and hard trade-offs. Vexing civic problems grow directly out of the local political structures that have long been celebrated in our political tradition, and it is difficult to say how these problems can be overcome. But we are not completely in the dark, and institutional and policy choices offer possibilities for managing trade-offs in better and worse ways.

Changing Patterns of Metropolitan Life

While localism has long been central to American politics, local community life in America has changed enormously over the past fifty years, and these changes have had a profound impact on civic engagement in metropolitan America. Our aim is to emphasize that the changes in metropolitan areas that are having a major impact on civic life—patterns of growth and decentralization and increased inequality and difference across places—are partly the result of particular political structures, laws, policies, and institutions that are subject to our collective control. Similarly, the choices we make now about policies and institutions will shape future patterns of civic life.

GROWTH AND DECENTRALIZATION

American metropolitan areas are growing rapidly in both population and territory, and this creates new challenges for civic engagement. The vast majority of Americans now live in metropolitan areas (80.3 percent, or 226 million people in 2000).[34] But the growth in metropolitan areas has not been in central cities. Over the past sixty years, the American metropolis has experienced a dramatic "decentering" due to suburbanization, with suburbs growing at twice the rate of central cities. This increase in size is evident not just in population but in land use as well. Metropolitan areas are adding urbanized or developed land at a much faster rate than they are adding population.[35] Increasingly, many Americans now reside on the fringe of metropolitan regions in unincorporated or "ex-urban" areas that lack any general-purpose local government at all. Across the metropolitan region, from the central city to the ex-urbs, growth strains the institutions of civic engagement.

DIVERSITY

In addition to becoming larger, American metropolitan regions are becoming much more diverse, although there is considerable variation in patterns of diversity among metropolitan areas and across regions of the country. Despite regional differences, it is clear that populations of African Americans, Latinos, and Asians in the nation's largest central cities are growing, while whites now constitute less than half the population in almost half of those cities. Census 2000 reveals that across the nation's 100 largest cities, "there was a consistent pattern of decreasing white population, rapidly growing Hispanic population, strong increases in Asian population, and modest increases in black population."[36] The unprecedented growth in the Latino and Asian populations constitutes one of the most dramatic demographic shifts in American political history, the implications of which have been most profound in metropolitan areas where Latinos and Asians are more likely to live.[37]

Diversity is not simply a characteristic of central cities: some suburbs are also diversifying. The proportion of minorities in the suburbs of the nation's 102 largest metropolitan areas grew from 19.3 percent in 1990 to 27.3 percent in 2000.[38] Across all metropolitan areas the rise in minority populations was even more substantial: the numbers of African Americans, Hispanics, and Asians residing in suburbs increased by 38, 72, and 84 percent, respectively, between 1990 and 2000.[39] Demographers have coined the term of "melting-pot metropolitan area" to describe places that were once predominantly white and are now populated by significant concentrations of two or more minority groups, whose shares of the population exceed those populations' national averages. Demographers also caution, though, that patterns of diversification are complicated and the dangers of oversimplification are great. As demographer William Frey puts it, "Only a handful of the nation's large and small metros can be considered true melting pots, based on recent census profiles. And it is not likely that any one of these multiple melting-pot areas will resemble any of the others."[40]

FRAGMENTATION

In some parts of the country, principally the South and the West, central cities have annexed territory and grown along with their suburbs. But in most metropolitan areas incorporation laws facilitate the formation of new suburban municipalities, constraining the ability of central cities to grow through annexation. From 1952 to 2002 the number of municipal governments grew by 15.6 percent, from 16,807 to 19,431.[41] More striking, the number of "special-district" governments—usually serving a single function such as fire protection or sewer maintenance—almost tripled in the half century after 1952, growing from 12,340 to 35,356. The average metropolitan area now has a complex and confusing array of more than 100 governments, including cities, towns, school districts, other special districts, and regional authorities.[42]

There are a number of reasons to be concerned about increasing fragmentation in the American metropolis. While the multiplicity of political institutions in metropolitan areas means smaller jurisdictions, greater choice of services, and more access points for civic engagement, it may also obscure power relationships, place onerous demands on citizens, and make local politics bewildering. As Samuel Popkin puts it, diffusion of political power "results in a system in which it is particularly hard to connect problems and votes, and a plethora of different campaigns and election dates."[43] Jurisdictional fragmentation can undermine engagement in other ways as well. Political boundaries may work to sever social relations as well as political relations, cutting off the free flow of communication, mutual understanding, and a sense of shared fate.[44] In addition, many issues that fall across jurisdictional lines, including transportation, balance between jobs and housing, and air and water pollution, appear on local agendas in an attenuated form, if at all. Thus many metropolitan areas are unable to confront a variety of important public issues.

For example, the St. Louis region, one of the most fragmented in the country, comprises *795 local governments*, including 300 cities and townships.[45] In such a setting, issues that affect the metropolitan area as a whole fall through the cracks. And the sheer extent of this fragmentation makes voluntary interjurisdictional cooperation extraordinarily difficult. Instead, municipalities often pursue their particular interests at the expense of any regional good. Heavy reliance on sales tax revenues encourages municipalities in the St. Louis area to engage in a beggar-thy-neighbor competition for big-box retail stores, dumping the traffic and the need for affordable housing on neighboring municipalities.[46] In the long run, these policies harm the entire region by encouraging a mismatch between jobs and housing that worsens traffic congestion and air pollution.

Fragmentation of metropolitan regions is especially problematic to the extent that political borders coincide with patterns of racial and economic segregation. True enough, it no longer makes sense to think simply in terms of the "city-suburb doughnut"; the stereotype of suburbs as lily-white middle-class enclaves is increasingly false. Although it is true that suburbs taken as a whole are more diverse, suburban diversity is mostly *between* suburbs, not within them. Across the patchwork of suburban jurisdictions, individual suburbs are likely to be characterized not by integration and diversity but by residential segregation and homogeneity. While there is some evidence that black-white racial segregation fell in American metropolitan areas after 1970, it remains stubbornly high.[47] According to one measure of racial segregation, on average about half of all blacks would have to move across census tracts to achieve an equal distribution of the population.[48] In addition to persistent racial segregation, economic segregation has become worse over the past thirty years. In 1970 the neighborhood of the average poor person was 13.6 percent poor; by 2000 that figure had risen to 24.6 percent. Similarly, the average affluent household lived in a 30.8 percent affluent neighborhood in 1970, but that figure rose to 33.8 percent in 2000.[49] Between 1970 and 1990, the number of people living in census tracts with poverty rates of 40 percent or more almost doubled.[50] In the 1990s the number living in such areas fell 24 percent, although much of this decline was due to the unusually tight labor markets that prevailed when the census took its snapshot in 2000.[51]

Despite these drawbacks, the fragmented structure of American metropolitan areas has its defenders. Charles Tiebout, for example, argued that metropolitan areas should be viewed as a kind of marketplace of jurisdictions in which "the consumer-voters may be viewed as picking that community which best satisfies his preference patterns for public goods."[52] Metropolitan consolidation should be avoided, therefore, on the grounds that a multiplicity of governments creates a system of choice compatible with market efficiency and American individualism.[53] A sophisticated "public choice" school of metropolitan analysis developed around this approach.[54]

The basic premise of the public choice approach to metropolitan governance is that citizens can "vote with their feet" on the particular bundle of local taxes and services that best meets their preferences. From this perspective, citizens' ability to exit a jurisdiction whose policies they disapprove of can be viewed as a substitute for other forms of political voice and citizen participation.[55] On the one hand, some scholars argue that the threat of exit can actually enhance citizen engagement because local leaders will be more attentive to citizen preferences. On the other hand, the public choice perspective also suggests that fragmentation will sort citizens according to their preferences for local public goods and reduce the need for traditional forms of participation; choice of residence will lead to communities in which citizens are essentially satisfied with the package of taxes and services provided by the local government. Absent fragmentation, many citizens would be forced to submit to taxing and spending decisions that strongly violate their preferences. The exit option thus means that citizens can satisfy their preferences via choice, making participation far less important.[56]

In our view, this model of "polycentric" metropolitan governance ignores the challenges faced by important segments of the population and offers an impoverished vision of civic life. Research has shown that preferences for local public goods do not vary a great deal.[57] People do care about how much they are taxed and the quality of local services; above all, they move in search of better public schools. Local governments compete not so much to satisfy different preferences as to attract residents and businesses that will contribute more in taxes than they cost in services. Perhaps most significant, households' capacities for exit and entry vary a great deal: for this reason, voting with one's feet does not serve as an effective mechanism for holding governments accountable to poor households. Indeed, exclusion of the poor can become a way that local communities compete against one another to enhance housing values and the quality of schools. Obviously, voting with one's feet can communicate information about personal preferences to local governments, but that does not make it a form of political or civic engagement. The choice to move often has more to do with fleeing the necessity of deliberating with others: it is the search for a private benefit rather than an engagement in public activity. Stephen L. Elkin puts it well: action is "public" when "others have to be convinced, justification is essential. I must, that is, move beyond assertions of what is beneficial to me."[58] Exit is often an alternative to political voice, and in today's metropolitan conditions, we believe it discourages civic engagement.

Of course, we cannot really blame people for seeking the best schools they can for their children or the best neighborhoods in which to raise their families. Homes are, moreover, the largest capital investment of most families. The problem is a system that promotes competition among communities to exclude poorer households, encouraging the population to sort itself along lines of class and race. The challenge, as we will see, is to repair an institutional context in which people are encouraged to pursue better public services, including schools, by seeking entry into local communities whose advantages include their capacity to exclude the less well off.

Systems of private choice often generate good collective outcomes: this is generally true of competitive economic markets (or at least most would argue). But within poorly designed frameworks private choice may lead to socially destructive consequences. Indeed, we worry that this fragmented metropolitan governance may shape the interests and judgments of citizens in perverse ways. As a well-known text in comparative urban politics puts it, highly fragmented systems of local government encourage "a narrow conception of public interests defined in terms of the individual jurisdiction, at the expense of wider metropolitan and regional common interests. So the problem of fragmented local government may not be that it produces a poor 'quality' of leadership but that it produces parochial leadership and defines the political agenda in narrow terms."[59] This constriction of the public agenda cannot help but diminish the quality of civic engagement.

STRATIFICATION AND POLARIZATION

As a result of residential segregation, suburbs vary tremendously in fiscal capacity, socioeconomic conditions, and demographic composition.[60] One study of fifty metropolitan areas finds that the percentage of suburban residents living in middle-class suburbs declined from 74.9 percent in 1980 to 60.8 percent in 2000.[61] In the twenty-five metropolitan areas studied by Myron Orfield, the fiscal disparity among suburbs increased 8 percent between 1993 and 1998.[62] Economic disparities across communities are promoted by competition among communities for well-off residents and businesses as local governments seek sales and property tax revenues. Once advantaged in this game, well-off communities frequently use exclusionary zoning measures to maintain their privilege and exclusivity.[63] Separation by race and class across suburban jurisdictions depresses the quality of civic engagement. As Rae explains,

> Too often, the end of urbanism has undermined [the democratic] experience by promoting social homogeneity within municipalities, leading to the evolution of regional hierarchies in which "purified communities" [Richard Sennett's term] . . . bring likes together, safe from contact with persons different from themselves. . . . The bottom rung more often than not lies in the formerly working-class neighborhoods of central cities, where opportunity is scarce, danger is commonplace, and democracy in any plausible sense seems out of reach.[64]

Instead of being microcosms of the larger society, our political jurisdictions are too frequently characterized by persistent racial segregation and worsening economic stratification.

Some scholars have argued that homogeneity within suburbs depresses not just the quality but also the quantity of civic engagement by decreasing the likelihood of controversies that would mobilize people to become more involved.[65] While that claim is debated, it is clear that the homogeneity within many suburban jurisdictions deprives local leaders of the opportunity or necessity to engage the full spectrum of issues that face a metropolitan region. "Boutique" suburbs—homogeneous upper-income enclaves— trivialize and dampen public engagement because important issues involving race and class never make it onto the agenda. As McConnell observed of narrow constituencies in general, "It often appears that the achievement and defense of particular status and privilege are the central goals of narrow and cohesive groups."[66] Acting more like private interest groups than truly public institutions, havens of privilege keep their agendas narrow by practicing the politics of exclusion. Indeed, some would argue that such exclusionary appeals to localism often mask underlying racism. It is hard to deny that the prospect of racial integration was among the factors that encouraged "white flight" to the suburbs. As Thomas Byrne Edsall and Mary Edsall argue, local political structures and the ideal of local control (or "home rule") allow for the defense of what amounts to class-based and (to some degree) racial exclusion without explicit appeal to either class or race.[67]

Stratification is especially harmful to those who live amid concentrated disadvantage.[68] Although many poorer neighborhoods exhibit impressive levels of civic activity, people's capacity to become involved in civic affairs is diminished greatly where inequalities are "cumulative rather than offsetting."[69] Impediments to civic engagement in disadvantaged areas include greater health problems, transportation difficulties, and safety concerns. Surrounded by neighbors who may not have developed critical civic skills, residents of disadvantaged communities have comparatively fewer effective models of civic engagement. Even if they overcome these obstacles, they are likely to encounter local public institutions that lack the resources to respond to their needs.

Recently, some have argued that, in addition to other forms of stratification, localities are also becoming more politically or ideologically polarized. In a series of articles in the *Austin American-Statesman*, Bill Bishop reports the results of a county-by-county analysis of voting in presidential elections. He finds that between 1948 and 1976 the proportion of American voters living in counties that were won by a landslide (defined as a margin of 60 percent or more in the division of the major two-party vote in presidential elections) declined to a low of 26.8 percent in 1976. Since then, counties have become increasingly lopsided in their voting so that, by 2000, 45.3 percent of Americans lived in a landslide county.[70] Bishop worries that as more ideologically like-minded people live nearby one another—as birds of an ideological feather flock together—minority political views will tend to be stamped out or driven underground, people will tend to become more ideologically extreme, and the electorate will become polarized. There is evidence to support these sorts of fears.[71] As James G. Gimpel and his coauthors argue, "The political segregation and partisan balkanization of neighborhoods promote a polarization of viewpoints that is intolerant of internal dissent among adherents of a particular party."[72] They also find that there is more political discussion and greater acquisition of political knowledge in more politically balanced settings, a conclusion that is consistent with our conception of the healthy democratic metropolis.

These noteworthy suggestions notwithstanding, others urge caution lest we draw overly pessimistic conclusions. Morris P. Fiorina argues that evidence of deep polarization among voters is lacking.[73] It is not clear that localities are becoming ideologically lopsided enough to have the consequences for citizens' views that Bishop fears. Insofar as concern is limited to the ways in which Americans as a whole array themselves along the political spectrum with respect to most issues, they are still clustered toward the middle. Nevertheless, even if Fiorina is right about public opinion as a whole, residential sorting and stratification by race and class across different localities furnish ample grounds for worry. Polarization is of concern insofar as it entails not only a shift in the distribution of public opinion as a whole but also in the geographic and institutional organization of that opinion. As we argue in chapter two, political parties are far more polarized than they were a generation ago, as conservatives have left the Democratic Party and liberals have left the Republican Party. Election results suggest that congressional districts are becoming politically far more homogeneous internally, which may empower activists within a district's dominant party. It is hard to believe that the geographic sorting we have described is unrelated to the ideological polarization among elites that hampers civil dialogue and constructive cooperation to solve important problems.

In sum, American metropolitan areas, taken in aggregate, have become among the most diverse urban areas in the world, but the fragmented jurisdictional fabric of many major metropolitan areas, including local control over property tax revenue and social services, has facilitated a sorting of populations by class and race that damages civic life by thwarting the effective pursuit of many inclusive political goals and short-circuiting the public encounters that bridge social and economic divisions among citizens. For both the privileged and the disadvantaged, the sorting of households into fragmented municipalities with radically different demographic profiles narrows civic identities, polarizes political interests, and dampens important forms of civic engagement. Simply put, highly segregated localities defy pluralist democracy.

SPRAWL

Segregation and stratification across metropolitan localities are not the only obstacles to a vibrant local civic culture. Civic activity is shaped by a variety of place-related factors besides demographic differences and jurisdictional boundaries. Sprawl itself may dampen civic engagement, as may other aspects of community design that emphasize the private over the public.[74] Many scholars argue that the physical design of suburbs—their dearth of public gathering spaces, greater reliance on automobiles, the absence of sidewalks and front porches—encourages people to withdraw from public life into a private world of family and work.[75] An influential school of thought called "new urbanism" maintains that sprawled suburban development creates an environment of "soullessness" and "placelessness" that eats away at community involvements.[76]

The idea that urban form can affect civic engagement has a long pedigree in the United States. The great landscape architect Frederick Law Olmsted argued that urban parks are necessary in a democracy so that people of different economic and social stations can rub elbows and establish trust.[77] Probably the best-known advocate for the salutary effect of traditional mixed-use urban design on civic engagement is Jane Jacobs. In her 1961 classic, *The Death and Life of Great American Cities*, Jacobs argued that city neighborhoods with relatively high population densities and mixed primary uses (residential, retail, and so on) generate social capital that carries over into the political sphere. As Jacobs famously observed, "Lowly, unpurposeful and random as they may appear, sidewalk contacts are the small change from which a city's wealth of public life may grow."[78]

Evaluating the impact of urban form on civic engagement is challenging. Not only is sprawl hard to specify because of its many forms, but isolating its impact from other factors associated with it, such as homeownership and community size, is extremely difficult. Scholars have employed two research methods: case studies and multivariate studies using survey data.

The case studies tell conflicting stories about the impact of urban form on civic engagement. Herbert Gans's study of Levittown, New Jersey, a quintessential bedroom suburb, concludes that suburbanites are not the lonely individualists they are often portrayed to be; they have rich social and political lives. Gans finds considerable civic activity in suburbs on account of the fact that large numbers of middle-aged, relatively well-off, and well-educated families with kids live there; he does not attribute this greater activity to the form of suburban life, but neither does he find suburban form to be an obstacle to engagement. Gans denies that urban form is a major shaper of social relations.[79] However, in a detailed historical study of New Haven, Douglas Rae shows how neighborhoods in the early twentieth century typified Jacobs's notion of diversity and supported a rich array of associations that nurtured civic engagement. In a nod to Jacobs, Rae calls this political system "a sidewalk republic." Rae's understanding of the sources of the rise and decline of urban civic life includes much more than physical form: "urbanism" declined, on Rae's account, in important measure because of deindustrialization and the loss of neighborhood retail establishments, jobs, and middle-class residents. We do not deny the importance of economic and technological change, and we agree with Rae that cities themselves have been hamstrung in their capacity to respond to these changes.[80]

More recently, scholars have employed survey data to test the effect of different physical environments on civic engagement. Eric Oliver concludes, for example, that land use, specifically living in single-use bedroom suburbs, has little independent effect on civic engagement.[81] In contrast, Robert Putnam finds that larger distances between home and work mean less time for civic activity. After controlling for individual variables, "each additional ten minutes of daily commuting time cuts involvement in community affairs by 10 percent."[82] Reinforcing this finding, studies have found that increasing the percentage of out-of-town commuters in a community reduces political participation and increasing the number of residents driving to work alone decreases neighborhood ties.[83]

The most extensive analysis of the political effects of sprawl using survey data has been done by Thad Williamson.[84] He finds that living in a central city, in an older neighborhood, in an area with fewer out-of-town commuters, and in an area with substantial pedestrian activity and the presence of public transit are each independently associated with higher levels of some forms of political participation, such as being a member of a political group or attending a political meeting. In suburban areas that do not share those characteristics, then, civic engagement is measurably lower. Other characteristics of suburban life, such as smaller city size and higher rates of homeownership, tend to *increase* political participation, but even so, as Williamson concludes, the cumulative impact of all these factors is a decrease in civic activity.

Overall, evidence concerning the ways in which urban form, specifically sprawl-related characteristics, influences political participation supports the sorts of trade-offs discussed in chapter one. Individuals who live in low-density bedroom communities, where private automobile use dominates, are less likely to participate in politics, especially in more contentious political activities such as attending protests, demonstrations, and partisan political events. At the same time, research consistently shows that suburban contexts are associated with higher levels of trust. Both findings make sense: living with other people like yourself in suburban environments where there are few opportunities to encounter strangers in public places should reinforce trusting relations, but citizens are unlikely to be mobilized for issue-driven political participation in homogeneous places that fence out much of the polity's diversity.

Place, Context, and Civic Activity

Changing patterns of metropolitan form affect the ways that citizens act in politics, although the influences may be subtle and complex. Our collective choices about the organization of the places in which we live, as we have seen, help to bring about particular kinds of political communities. Of course, individual choices matter—choices about where to live, with whom to associate, and whether and how to participate—but these private choices take place within contexts created by our collective decisions, and those contexts influence our civic opportunities and our political interests and choices. When rates of participation decline, when communities become increasingly segregated and stratified, we should think not only about market forces, technological change, and individual decisions; we should think also about how the created environment contributes to these outcomes. By doing so, we can better understand the degree to which the civic patterns we observe might be altered by different decisions.

Having described some of the ways in which changing patterns of metropolitan form affect local politics, we now consider the central avenues through which residents of metropolitan areas act to influence policies, solve public problems, and improve their communities. The menu of opportunities for local civic engagement begins with electoral politics, including voting, campaigning,

and running for office. It also includes various forms of participation in deliberation and policy development between elections, from service on traditional
city councils and school boards to an expanding array of other public committees, commissions, and panels that are receptive to citizen input. Many large
cities have developed innovative ways of bringing government closer to the
people by creating neighborhood councils, citizen advisory boards, and other
means for citizens to participate in policymaking and the provision of local
services. Beyond formal institutions, citizens often act through an array of nongovernmental institutions, committees, and organizations to influence political choices.[85] Although we emphasize in what follows that localities furnish a
great many opportunities for civic and political engagement, our aim is not to
argue for the maximum number of participatory venues or to suggest that
political design should constantly "ratchet up" the demands that civic life makes
on citizens. In the end, one important feature of political design is to "econo-
mize" on the demands that we make on citizens, who reasonably have a great
many interests and concerns outside of politics.

Engagement with Electoral Politics

Voting is the most common and arguably the least demanding form of citizen
participation at the local level. Local politics offers a prodigious array of opportunities to cast ballots. In 1992 there were 494,000 *locally* elected officials,
including not only mayors, city councilors, and school board members but also
a wide variety of other town, city, and county officers and a vast array of com-
missioners and board members. A remarkable 96.2 percent of the nation's
elected officials serve at the local level.[86]

Turnout in local elections is, however, notoriously low. In general, the lower
the level of election, the lower the turnout. Although 62 percent of eligible voters claimed in 1990 to have voted in all or most presidential elections since they
were old enough, only 54 percent claimed to have voted in all local elections.[87]
Actual voting rates are certainly much lower, as turnout figures acquired
through municipal records in cities over 25,000 in 1962 and 1975 put the
average turnout in municipal elections at 31 percent. This compares with an
average turnout rate in national elections of 59 percent during roughly the
same period.[88] A more recent study of 57 cities with populations between
25,000 and 1 million found average voter turnout between 1993 and 2000 to be
34 percent.[89]

Low levels of local turnout have not always been the rule, however. One
important study finds a steady and substantial decline in local turnout over
time, with voter participation falling from a high of more than 60 percent in

the mid-1930s.[90] As a consequence of the low turnout in local elections, a wide array of local elected officials—from mayors and council members to law enforcement and judicial officials—are selected by a very small fraction of the constituents they represent. Meager turnout may mean that localities are not serving as effective schools of democracy. Moreover, low turnout in local elections may depress the relative influence of particular groups within society, especially disadvantaged segments of the population.[91] Based on a study of the nation's ten largest cities as well as a much larger sample of nearly 1,700 localities, Zoltan Hajnal and Jessica Trounstine argue that low voting rates in local elections lead to "substantial reductions in the representation of Latinos and Asian Americans on city councils and in the mayor's office."[92] If more Latinos and Asian Americans were to vote, expressing the same preferences as those who do make it to the polls, they could change the outcomes of many elections.

Local elections provide city residents with the opportunity not only to vote but also to participate in campaigning and electioneering. Among the most important preelection civic activities are citizens' efforts to mobilize other citizens. As we emphasize in chapter two, scholars have convincingly demonstrated that mobilization increases political and civic engagement.[93] Getting someone to participate in public life is a bit like dating; it is a lot more likely to happen if someone asks, preferably in person. In a study of 30,000 registered voters in New Haven, Connecticut, for example, Donald Green and Alan Gerber find that personal, face-to-face contact substantially increases the probability that individuals will turn out to vote, while direct mail has only a slight effect on turnout and telephone solicitation has no effect at all.[94] In a later study of local elections in six cities, Gerber, Green, and David Nickerson find that face-to-face contact increases turnout as much as 14.4 percentage points.[95]

The goal of elections and campaigns is, of course, winning and holding elective office. Running for office is the most intense form of civic engagement available at the local level. An elected official has made the decision to run for office, solicited the support of others, and succeeded in that effort and subsequently participates in the exercise of public authority. Each of the nearly 500,000 local political offices represents considerable and recurrent collective political efforts, although the scope of the activities varies widely. The sheer number of local elected offices would seem inevitably to be a major spur to civic activity in America. Between 1974 and 1994, however, the number of candidates running for local offices dropped by 15 percent, despite increasing numbers of local governments.[96] And in a development that gives cause for deep democratic concern, some California localities recently canceled elections because of a dearth of candidates.[97]

Local elective offices are especially important to minority groups. Both African Americans and Latinos have had substantial and growing electoral success at local levels. By the most reliable estimate, the number of African American elected officials has increased nearly fivefold since 1970: with 9,101 holding office in 2001. The number of Latino public officials has also risen steadily.[98] Of these minority officeholders, approximately 70 percent serve at the local level, in municipal political offices or on school boards.[99]

One important reason for the increased minority office holding in cities and working-class suburbs is the implementation of the Voting Rights Act in 1965 and its expansion to include language minorities in 1975. Enforcement of the Voting Rights Act compelled many cities and towns that had "diluted" the votes of African Americans and Latinos through gerrymandering and the use of at-large elections to transform their electoral systems.[100] Because of actions taken directly under the auspices of the Voting Rights Act, cities such as Dallas, Houston, San Antonio, Chicago, Los Angeles, New York, and many others have experienced considerable increases in the number of African American and Latino local elected officials. As we discussed further in chapter two, political choices like the Voting Rights Act can facilitate the active participation of minority groups.

Another important factor in the rise of minority office holding is the outmigration of whites who, in the decades after World War II, chose to leave many central cities and working-class suburbs. As whites left, those who remained and moved in were often African Americans and Latinos. These demographic shifts helped minority candidates to win office in increasing numbers. This is only part of the story, however. Another part is the ability of minority candidates to build interracial coalitions. In the vast majority of cases in which blacks and Latinos have been elected mayor, blacks have not constituted the majority of the voting or general population. Black and Latino mayors have to appeal to members of their own race as well as to white and Asian voters in order to build a winning electoral coalition.

But these victories come with sobering challenges. The increase in black and Latino mayors coincided with the outmigration of retail as well as industrial businesses and the loss of jobs and tax revenue that was crucial to the maintenance of viable municipal economies. Moreover, as whites migrated from the cities to suburbs and federal government policies provided fewer funds to municipalities, the newly empowered black and Latino mayors often faced almost insurmountable difficulties in finding sufficient financial resources to meet the needs of the diverse constituencies that placed them in office.[101] As a result of the magnitude of challenges and the depressed economies of many urban areas, public office holding among blacks, Latinos, and Asians is sometimes described as a "hollow prize."[102]

Even in the face of these challenges, the substantial numbers of African Americans and Latinos who hold local elective office is a clear sign that a core of minority leaders is willing to undertake demanding forms of civic engagement. To the extent that local elective office serves as a training ground and springboard for leaders who go on to win higher elective office, local civic engagement in the metropolis may promote more inclusive forms of civic activity in the polity as a whole.

PROGRESSIVE-ERA REFORMS

While local electoral politics furnishes a cornucopia of opportunities for civic engagement, these activities are structured, facilitated, and constrained by local political institutions. The political reform movements that swept across many cities in the 1890s and early decades of the twentieth century transformed local institutions, including methods of filling many local government jobs (from patronage to civil service), election districts (from ward or district elections to more at-large elections), election ballots (from partisan to nonpartisan), the timing of elections (from concurrent with state and national election days to off-cycle), and types of executive (from elected mayor to appointed city manager). These reforms remain intact in many places today, and new municipalities often choose to adopt reform institutions.

There is no doubt that patronage and many types of corruption animated urban politics in the era of the machines. Reformers sought to curtail graft by replacing political machines and partisan politics with greater professionalism and businesslike efficiency, although many scholars argue that reformers also sought to curb the political power of recent immigrants.[103] Whatever the mix of intentions, research from the field of urban politics indicates that the changes were not without negative consequences for civic engagement. While the machines themselves eventually became entrenched power centers, so long as urban politics remained competitive they did a great deal to spur participation and incorporate immigrants into the political process. One of the leading scholars of cities argues that they were "a veritable school of politics for working-class and minority voters, compared with big-city reform."[104] Recent research demonstrates that the mobilizing efforts of machines dropped precipitously once the machines consolidated their power and attained local political dominance.[105] Still, even after periods of dominance, machine politics left a legacy of higher turnout than in cities that adopted reform institutions.[106]

The impact of reform institutions on civic engagement is difficult to sort out. Several classic as well as more recent studies suggest that some reform institutions—nonpartisan elections and council-manager forms of government—

decrease election turnout.[107] Partisan elections are, by definition, competitions between groups and ideas. The reform effort to clean up what was viewed as a sullied electoral system simultaneously dampened the participatory zeal of partisan mobilizers and obscured the real differences among political interests. Cities without partisan elections thus lack important catalysts for civic engagement; voters lack the important information (or "cues") furnished by party affiliations. In moving from mayor-council to council-manager systems, reformers eliminated another potential stimulus for political activity. Elected mayors have constituencies that are independent of city councils: the system thus involves political checks and balances. In contrast, city managers are typically selected by the local council or legislature: they have no independent political base. Because appointed city managers tend to work more closely and consensually with local legislatures, conflict is suppressed, and managers are far less visible to voters than are mayors. Mayors are more likely to be seen—rightly—by the public as important political actors who wield significant power.[108] As Curtis Wood puts it, "The mayor has more influence over policy and administrative matters, and voters will know whom to credit or blame for governmental performance."[109] Reformers' attempts to clean up corrupt city halls thus resulted in a system that mutes political conflict and eliminates important instruments of political mobilization. Because reform institutions have been popular with newer localities, especially the high-growth cities outside of the Northeast, these participatory weaknesses are widespread in contemporary metropolitan regions.

Reform institutions seem to dampen participation most especially among African Americans in the South, Latinos in the Southwest and West, and people of lower socioeconomic status, raising special concerns from the standpoint of democratic equality.[110] In addition, evidence from the 1970s shows that cities with a system for choosing a mayor other than through a popular election are less likely to have an African American mayor.[111] This correlation has important civic implications because the presence of a black mayor tends to increase rates of African American local participation.[112]

Another important progressive-era reform changed the timing of elections so that they would occur in "off years," or in the spring, rather than at the same time as higher-profile state and national elections.[113] The idea was to prevent campaigns for higher offices from overwhelming local races. Of course, putting another election on the calendar can depress turnout. We emphasized in chapter two that Americans are asked to vote a great deal more frequently than citizens of most other democracies and that the frequency of elections seems to depress turnout. Recent research shows that local elections held concurrently with state and national balloting have dramatically higher turnout rates. One study calls election timing the "single largest predictor" of municipal voter turnout, with concurrent elections increasing voter participation in cities by a staggering 29 percent.[114] Similarly, a study of California cities reports that local elections held at the same time as presidential elections are associated with turnout rates approximately 36 percent higher than those held off-cycle.[115] The lesson of these studies is clear: timing has a dramatic impact on voting rates in local elections. It is equally clear, however, that the increased numbers of voters who turn out to cast ballots in concurrent elections are not motivated primarily by local issues. As we emphasize in this report, the sheer quantity of participation is not our only goal.[116] While we are wary of the dangers of overburdening citizens, we cannot say definitively whether those citizens who turn out to vote in concurrent national and local elections are less attentive to or knowledgeable about local issues than the smaller numbers who vote in off-year local elections. Virtually no polling data speak directly to this question. (We do have reason to believe that those who do not expend the effort to go to the polls have less intense preferences.)[117]

Decisions concerning local political institutions are rife with difficult trade-offs among conflicting civic values. By shifting from neighborhood-based to citywide representation and by placing the powers of the chief executive officer in the hands of an appointed manager, reform institutions widen the distance between governing processes and ordinary citizens. By removing the cue of party labels and lessening neighborhood-based representation, they reduce the information available to citizens about candidates' positions and about how to get involved in politics.[118] At the same time, council-manager forms of government and governments in which some of the seats are elected at-large are associated with higher levels of trust in government.[119] Reforms aimed at curbing partisan politics may thus promote greater citizen trust in local government while at the same time decreasing engagement (although the evidence on these matters is thin).

Choices about institutional forms may also be important for immigrant incorporation. While higher levels of income, education, and homeownership increase the political activity of immigrants (just as they increase the civic activity of persons generally), the political and institutional contexts of immigrants and their communities are also critical to understanding their political behavior.[120] In a recent study of immigrants and blacks in Los Angeles and New York, for example, Michael Jones-Correa finds that responsiveness to immigrants' concerns is a function of institutional frameworks within the two cities.[121]

Institutional form matters, and we believe that progressive-era reforms tend to depress participation, but we need to be careful not to draw sweeping conclusions based on the published evidence suggesting that reform institutions depress turnout: some of that evidence focuses on an earlier era, and updating it would be useful. Research that demonstrates a link between some types of reform institutions and greater trust in government establishes that progressive-era reforms are not all bad. Moreover, any system can stop being competitive over time, resulting in low levels of mobilization and dampening civic engagement: where particular machines achieve political dominance, as already mentioned, they no longer act as mass mobilizers. The partisan governance model of elected mayors and district or ward-based councilors is not guaranteed to generate robust civic engagement: party competition is also crucial, and in this respect our findings here complement those of chapter two.[122] One reason for cities to experiment with new institutional designs is to break up ossified systems of power.

SPECIAL DISTRICTS AND AUTHORITIES

The reformist impulse also contributed to the formation of new governments insulated from partisan politics. Services previously supplied by municipal governments, such as water, sewers, and fire protection, are now frequently supplied by "special districts" and authorities. The number of special districts in the United States increased from 8,299 in 1942 to 35,052 in 2002.[123] These districts often overlap one another as well as municipal boundaries.

The tremendous growth of special districts represents, in part, an effort to take the politics out of municipal government. The formation of special districts and authorities may also be a strategy to overcome the tax and debt limitations of municipal governments, to provide services on a more regional basis, or to professionalize service delivery. In recent decades, however, corporations and real estate developers have been most successful at forming special districts, often via referenda that they succeed in placing on the ballot.[124] Once they are formed, special districts can become tools for developers to acquire access to powers of eminent domain and to tax-exempt revenue bonds to fund the infrastructure needed for private development—all with very little, if any, democratic oversight.[125]

The formation of these districts is a profoundly political act that has significant implications for civic engagement. Beyond the fact that they can be a source of tremendous confusion for ordinary voters trying to understand and influence local decisionmaking, special districts enable the private values of selected groups to dominate via obscure political structures that are nearly invisible to residents. Even if most residents remain unaware of them, special districts make important decisions, especially about spending, public indebtedness, and development.[126] Yet turnout in special-district elections (when they occur) is exceedingly low, usually less than 5 percent, compared with about 30 percent in municipal elections. Moreover, special districts can impose property qualifications for voting, and they are not required to follow the one-person, one-vote requirement placed on municipal governments.

Special districts do not take the politics out of municipal government; they only make it less visible and accessible to the average citizen. As Nancy Burns argues, "These local institutions . . . are created for reasons that often impair their ability to be democratic training grounds. . . . [They] discourage participation because . . . the information costs associated with learning even the names of the districts that govern a location are prohibitive."[127]

Political Engagement between Elections

Citizen participation in political and civic life should extend beyond voting, campaigns, and elections. The design of government institutions can either enhance or depress electoral turnout, in both national and local settings, and political choices similarly shape the opportunities for participation between elections. As we see in what follows, governments have created a great array of opportunities for direct citizen participation in the formation of policy at the local level. After policy is set, implementation also involves choices about values that cannot and should not be left entirely to technical experts or professional public administrators. Cities, towns, and neighborhoods provide many opportunities for direct participation by local residents in decisions that affect issues ranging from local development to environmental preservation, the operation of schools, and the character of local policing. All these opportunities for participation are especially important in large localities, where one's chances of knowing or regularly interacting with public officials are significantly reduced.

Of course, citizen participation between elections shapes and constrains the discretion available to public officials in fulfilling the duties of their offices. Some fear that direct citizen participation makes government slow and inefficient. Professional administrators worry that technical expertise will be cast aside by the emotional demands of uninformed citizens whose parochial views will ignore citywide or regionwide interests. Although it is true that citizen participation often involves trade-offs with other values, we do not believe that these trade-offs are written in stone. In some contexts, citizen participation can result in decisions that are more effective and efficient, more representative of the interests of all, and more legitimate. Citizen participation can force experts, who often approach policies from the viewpoint of their narrow functional specializations, to confront the broader implications of their policies.[128] *Decision-making may be slower, but policy is often more legitimate, and implementation is often faster and more effective when all the major stakeholder groups have been consulted in the process.*[129]

LOCAL BOARDS AND COMMITTEES

Beyond voting and holding office, millions of citizens continue to express their views to locally elected officials by writing letters, making phone calls, or attending public meetings. In a 1987 survey, for example, almost 25 percent of Americans reported having contacted a local official about an issue in the previous year, and in 1989, 14 percent reported attending a meeting of a local board or commission.[130] In the 2004 National Election Study, 27 percent responded that they had attended a meeting to address a community issue in the past twelve months. Millions of citizens also serve on local councils, commissions, and advisory boards.[131] In 1990, 3 percent of U.S. adults reported volunteering for an official local board or council in the previous two years.[132] But citizens appear to be using these traditional avenues of politics in declining numbers. One study found that between 1973 and 1994, for example, the percentage of people reporting that they had attended a public meeting on town or school affairs fell from approximately 22 to 12 percent.[133] Service on local boards and councils also seems to be declining.[134] These trends highlight the need to invigorate traditional avenues of engagement and to search for new and better opportunities for citizens to deliberate and help to decide local issues.[135]

NEIGHBORHOOD COUNCILS

Many promising participatory structures focus on neighborhood concerns, especially in large cities, where city hall is more remote. The neighborhood is where citizens may have the most to say about what government should do and how it should be done. Under the right conditions, government-mandated neighborhood-based structures for citizen input can stimulate engagement.

Historically, the federal government played a key role in the rise of neighborhood structures for citizen input into government. (There is no inherent contradiction between federal action and local empowerment; the two can be, and often are, reinforcing.) President Johnson's 1964 War on Poverty and its Community Action Program and Model Cities encouraged direct community involvement.[136] Community action agencies were created and charged with developing and administering poverty-reduction programs "with the maximum feasible participation of the members of the groups and residents of the area served."[137] Many urban neighborhoods participated, and the establishment of more than 1,000 community action agencies across the country made the Community Action Program a "vast incubator" of civic engagement.[138]

Critics have identified several major failings of these early efforts. Participation often produced frustration because local organizations frequently lacked the capacity and resources to accomplish their missions. Big-city mayors sometimes captured these efforts to advance their own political aims rather than to harness civic engagement for poverty reduction and community empowerment. The rhetoric and design of these programs sometimes generated a good deal of conflict within and between community organizations and local government.[139] Nevertheless, the "maximum feasible participation" mandated by the Community Action Program laid the groundwork for other forms of citizen participation in policymaking and changed expectations about what the process ought to look like.[140]

Following the federal government's efforts to promote neighborhood participation as well as the upsurge of community organizing in the 1960s and 1970s (something we take up later in the chapter), many city governments have tried to incorporate neighborhoods into the institutions of city government. Boston Mayor Kevin White set up "Little City Halls," New York created fifty-nine community planning boards, and St. Paul empowered seventeen district councils, just to mention three examples with widely varied powers and citizen involvement. In a 1993 survey of the 161 cities with populations over 100,000,[141] Carmine Scavo found that 60 percent used neighborhood councils: these cities reported an average of fifty-five neighborhood councils in their systems.[142] These councils vary widely in their power and viability, and many of these council systems are neither especially active nor well functioning.[143]

Cities continue to innovate in the area of neighborhood governance. For example, the Minnesota state legislature and the city of Minneapolis initiated a Neighborhood Revitalization Project in 1990. Through the project, neighborhood associations have implemented a host of projects for housing rehabilitation, construction, economic development, education, and public service improvement.[144] In 1999 Los Angeles revised its city charter to create what will become a system of more than 100 neighborhood councils: these may serve as a much-needed layer of intermediate civic associations between residents and city government. Although the expansion has proceeded in fits and starts, more than half of the neighborhoods in the city created representative associations within the first three years.[145]

Neighborhood councils address such issues as housing, the physical quality of the neighborhood, and public services. They vary widely in their powers, effectiveness, and methods for selecting representatives.[146] These bodies have received scant attention from researchers, so there is little evidence to report and few generalizations to be offered about the effects of different forms of neighborhood government on the quantity, quality, and equality of civic engagement in metropolitan areas. Ideally, the existence of neighborhood councils, associations, and similar bodies could increase the quantity of civic engagement by multiplying the avenues through which citizens can engage with each other and with local government. They would seem, at a minimum, to offer a first step on the ladder of civic leadership, as neighborhood councils are more accessible than many citywide institutions, such as city councils, school boards, or zoning board offices.

We cannot say with certainty, however, that neighborhood governance increases the level and improves the distribution of civic engagement. In the absence of neighborhood councils, issues might be brought directly to city councilors or agency officials. Neighborhood councils, furthermore, are subject to the same kinds of background inequalities that shape participation in other political venues. In particular, homeowners and wealthier and more educated residents participate far more actively than renters and low-income residents.[147] In addition, governments may co-opt neighborhoods and seek to control their organizing and advocacy efforts or fail to give them the resources necessary to address public concerns effectively.[148] Poorly designed systems of neighborhood councils could become another confusing layer in a burdensome array of local institutions.

Only one study has examined whether neighborhood governance increases civic engagement generally. Jeffrey Berry, Kent Portney, and Ken Thomson compare five cities with strong systems of neighborhood government to a group of cities without such institutions and find no significant differences in aggregate civic participation.[149] In terms of equity of engagement, this study also finds that the expected socioeconomic biases in participation (with greater activity exhibited by wealthier, more educated citizens) do not seem to diminish in cities with neighborhood governance structures. Berry, Portney, and Thomson are, however, more sanguine about the impact of neighborhood governance structures on the *quality* of civic engagement. They argue that well-designed neighborhood councils make government more responsive to residents and make those who participate more knowledgeable about public affairs, more tolerant of differences, and more confident that their participation can make a difference. Furthermore, residents of cities with robust neighborhood governance institutions are more likely to engage in a variety of more demanding forms of democratic participation.

CITIZEN DELIBERATION

Since the general assemblies of New England town meetings, Americans have experimented with various forms of direct citizen deliberation on public issues.[150] As we emphasized in chapter two, a growing movement promotes citizen engagement with public issues through face-to-face discussion. These efforts are consistent with a large and growing body of work within political theory about the importance of opportunities for citizens to come together and talk with one another about pressing public issues.[151] A number of these scholars and advocates argue that opportunities for "deliberative democracy" improve the quality and legitimacy of public policy, while also educating citizens.

Many localities have experimented with deliberative forms of citizen engagement and decisionmaking. Minneapolis, Portland, and Rochester are among the municipalities that have developed innovative participatory programs for neighborhood planning. Citizen deliberations may be organized through city hall or particular city departments, as with the Chicago Local School Councils and Alternative Policing Strategy.[152] Alternatively, they may be organized by nongovernmental institutions and civic groups, such as the National Issues Forums, America*Speaks*, or Study Circles Resource Center.[153]

Regardless of the sponsor, deliberative events can be a valuable addition to the formal institutions of local government, and public officials, seeking better ways to grapple with increasing heterogeneity and demands, are often willing to participate in them.[154] For example, the 2002 "Listening to the City" event, which drew some 5,000 participants to the Jacob Javits Center in Manhattan to deliberate about the plans to rebuild the area of Lower Manhattan around the former World Trade Center site, opened typically insular urban design and planning processes to public criticism.[155] Some promising evidence indicates that taking part in such forums for "discursive participation" can lead to significant increases in other forms of civic engagement as well.[156]

While there is growing empirical research examining deliberation in practice, more is needed. It is often not altogether clear, for example, how the results of deliberative efforts ultimately fare in the wider, adversarial decisionmaking process, where elected officials, bureaucrats, or others may have the final say. Although some evidence supports scholars' assertions that deliberative participation improves the process, the participants, and the product, there are stern voices of caution, and more systematic study is needed to understand fully the conditions under which local public deliberation succeeds both as a participatory opportunity and as a means to improve outcomes.[157]

CITIZEN "COPRODUCTION" OF PUBLIC SERVICES

Citizens should be not just *consumers* of public services but active participants in the *production* of those services as well. In his city survey, Scavo finds widespread use of coproduction strategies: 92 percent reported block watches, 39 percent used adopt-a-park programs, and 27 percent reported adopt-a-street programs.[158] Public safety is perhaps the most obvious policy area in which the involvement of citizens themselves is crucial for achieving the desired public goods. From providing "eyes on the street"[159] to forming block watches, citizen patrols, and anticrime marches and crusades, residents frequently engage in activities—sometimes with police and sometimes by themselves—to promote their physical security.[160] These forms of civic engagement are often essential to creating safer neighborhoods. In addition, fully 40 percent of the U.S. population is protected by volunteer fire departments (most communities with less than 50,000 residents are served by volunteer departments).[161]

With respect to schooling, parent-teacher associations used to be a widespread and important part of our common commitment to education, but they have experienced a huge decline in membership, "from a high in the early 1960s of almost 50 members per 100 families with children under eighteen to fewer than twenty members per 100 families with children under eighteen in the early 1980s."[162] Some of this decline has likely been absorbed by parent-teacher organizations, which, unlike parent-teacher associations, are not organized nationally.[163] Even if parents continue to be involved in their school districts, the fact that they are no longer doing so (to nearly the same extent at least) through organizations that are linked across school district boundaries is troubling, given the increasing homogeneity of school districts and the problem of metropolitan-wide fragmentation.[164]

The federal government sponsors efforts to involve citizens in local service provision. Programs such as AmeriCorps or Teach for America engage citizens in solving the problems of central cities and other disadvantaged places, and new federal initiatives promote faith-based service provision. We explore these topics in greater detail in chapter four.

With a few notable exceptions, citizen participation in the production of public services has escaped the attention of political scientists, who tend to focus on engagement in lawmaking and policymaking rather than on implementation.[165] However, many of the most salient encounters between citizens and government occur at the level of local program administration and service delivery. Here, individual engagement offers reasonable prospects for success. Citizens are crucial conduits of information and vital participants in the creation of public goods. Citizen participation in service provision, then, offers many of the benefits claimed for participation generally: more informed and responsible citizens, on one hand, and more accountable and responsive government, on the other.[166]

INFLUENCE AND EQUALITY IN PARTICIPATION

One lesson is clear from our review of institutions for citizen engagement with local governments between elections: sustained participation requires giving citizens authentic decisionmaking power. When we design institutions with this lesson in mind, reform efforts appear to overcome some obstacles that commonly hinder participation.[167] In any event, citizens want their engagement to make a difference, and it is hard to see why their activity matters unless it does make a difference. In some cases, such as the design of the World Trade Center site, public involvement appears to have had a significant impact on some elements of the evolving plan. Part of the attraction of deliberative participation and citizen involvement in the coproduction of public services is that these valuable forms of engagement promise greater opportunities for residents to make a substantial difference in their communities.

Of course, any measure that increases the access points for political influence to be exercised raises the worrisome possibility that participatory opportunities may be unequally distributed. Those who take advantage of these opportunities may be unrepresentative of the public as a whole: they may be motivated by intense private interests or ideological zeal.[168] Or participation in the new venues may simply mirror inequalities in more traditional forums.

Although it is true that many participatory initiatives have failed to draw participation from low-income neighborhoods and disadvantaged groups, certain designs seem much more successful in this regard. Contrary to what socioeconomic models of participation predict, for example, Archon Fung finds that attendance at police beat meetings across Chicago is not a function of income, education levels, or racial composition of the neighborhood. Instead, attendance is driven primarily by neighborhood crime rates. With respect to public schools, the number of parents who run for local school councils varies in part by the socioeconomic characteristics of the school, but turnout is higher in neighborhoods with higher proportions of black and Hispanic students. Fung suggests that the existence of public problems coupled with innovative participatory structures can spur civic engagement in communities that we might otherwise expect to be relatively quiescent.[169]

Moreover, it is clear that direct mobilization, including support for participation from cities themselves, can involve citizens in these various venues. As part of its community policing initiative, for example, the City of Chicago provided $3 million to a community-based group charged with deploying organizers throughout the city to recruit participants for neighborhood community policing meetings. They used door-to-door contacts, outreach to neighborhood forums, and other time-tested methods to generate substantial participation rates across most Chicago neighborhoods.[170]

These experiences suggest that both the equality of civic engagement—in particular, the extent to which less well-off citizens participate in the coproduction and cogovernance of public services—as well as its quality and quantity depend on the nature of the opportunities for participation. In particular, disadvantaged citizens participate when doing so confers influence to improve outcomes about which they care, such as neighborhood safety and local school quality. Nevertheless, additional systematic study is needed to understand fully the conditions under which participatory opportunities are successful.

Community Engagement through Nongovernmental Institutions and Groups

Opportunities for civic engagement in local settings are not limited to the formal access points that governments provide. Citizens who care about the issues facing their communities can find many other avenues of political action, including those provided by organizations that bridge the gap between citizens and the formal institutions of government. In some cases, these bridging efforts have become deeply enmeshed in government institutions, making it difficult to tell where one stops and the other begins. Often, these organizations work to mobilize different communities within the metropolitan region, including communities that share a common interest or a concern with a particular issue, communities of racial and ethnic similarity, and communities of geographic location, such as neighborhoods. In an age of rapidly growing and diversifying metropolitan areas, these institutions can play an especially important role in helping individuals, including the newest arrivals to our cities, to connect with their communities. We first highlight efforts to engage citizens by shared interest or issue and by demographic profile. We then turn to a discussion of citizen mobilization by neighborhood. Of course, to the extent that neighborhoods are fragmented and segregated, these distinctions are not clear-cut.

COMMUNITY ORGANIZING AND COMMUNITY ORGANIZATIONS

One branch of extragovernmental local community engagement is "community organizing." That phrase evokes for many the adversarial tradition of radical neighborhood organizing pioneered by Saul Alinsky in Chicago's Back of the Yards.[171] Since the 1930s, organizers in that tradition have sought to mobilize residents of poor neighborhoods along with local institutions such as churches and labor unions to demand concessions from city government and private corporations on issues such as employment, health, public services, and local amenities. This tradition remains significant in many cities today. Its hallmarks are the use of professional organizers who attempt to build lasting "power" organizations with indigenous leaders in low-income, typically minority communities. These organizations employ a variety of tactics, ranging from electoral mobilization to disruptive protests, to improve the quality of life in disadvantaged areas.

Community organizing efforts often take the form of reaching out to disadvantaged groups.[172] In cities, the settlement houses of the late nineteenth and early twentieth centuries provide an early example of efforts to engage immigrants and the poor. Established to address the economic, social, cultural, and intellectual needs of impoverished immigrant neighborhoods by mobilizing residents, these associations filled gaps in the larger civic and municipal political structure. The settlement houses drew public attention to the condition of impoverished areas and produced many activists who would later engage in broader reform endeavors.[173]

Community organizations may be part of larger national organizing networks. The largest of these networks—and the ones that have been most studied—are the Industrial Areas Foundation, Associated Community Organizations for Reform Now (ACORN), the Pacific Institute for Community Organizing (PICO), the Gamaliel Foundation, and the Direct Action Research and Training Center (DART).[174] There are no doubt thousands of less heralded organizations in cities and towns across the United States, dedicated to fair housing, community development, environmental justice, and school quality.[175]

It is difficult to estimate the general effect of this brand of populist, adversarial community organizing on the quantity or quality of civic engagement. No census of community organizing exists to reveal the number of persons involved.[176] It is similarly difficult to assess the quality of participation in these organizations. Surely they provide crucial avenues through which residents of disadvantaged areas can learn the skills and reap the benefits of collective action. But there are also reasons to view these organizations critically: the quality of democracy within them varies. Even highly sympathetic writers notice tendencies toward top-down control and paternalism within their organizing techniques.[177]

The effect of these groups on the distribution of civic engagement seems clearer. These groups create paths of sociability and collective action in precisely those communities that often lack the resources and connections to engage civically. They reduce the bias in civic engagement that stems from inequalities in material conditions, social status, and political privilege. Community organizing can lead directly to improved economic access, school quality, public and private investment, and public services.

Community empowerment and mobilization initiatives can have an especially important impact on African Americans, Latinos, and other segments of working-class urban communities.[178] Such organizing efforts may be even more critical for immigrants, who face unique obstacles to mobilization and engagement in many aspects of community life. Immigrants often confront statutory and bureaucratic obstruction, especially those who are not citizens.[179] In addition, many have limited English proficiency, and many fill lower-status occupations and receive correspondingly modest incomes. Immigrant incorporation is a pressing issue because migration to the United States is one of the leading factors driving the dramatic demographic changes in American metropolitan areas.[180]

IMMIGRANT POLITICAL EMPOWERMENT

A considerable range of new research investigates immigrant mobilization. Immigrants are likely to follow settlement patterns marked out by conationals who preceded them—hence the striking array of ethnic enclaves in which immigrants from particular "sending countries" live in close proximity. This residential concentration should make mobilization easier, but efforts by political parties to activate political participation among immigrants are sporadic at best.[181] The mobilizing work traditionally accomplished by political parties is now undertaken largely through civic organizations, labor unions, churches, and voluntary organizations in immigrant communities.[182]

Immigrant mobilization is influenced by particular features of gateway cities and their surrounding metropolitan areas, by differences across the states in political culture and election laws, and by the behavior of political parties and other mobilizers.[183] There have been some recent efforts to increase the turnout rates among registered voters in areas of high Latino population density but low Latino turnout. Preliminary research shows that live phone contacts can increase turnout in areas with a low propensity to vote. Evidence from a number of urban communities shows that personal contacts may be an especially effective strategy for increasing voter turnout.[184] Among the local contextual factors that are especially important for immigrants are the density of coethnic populations, the competitiveness and receptiveness of local political party structures to immigrants, the possibilities for cooperation in cross-group coalitions, and the tradition of balancing slates with ethnic groups.[185] For newer immigrant groups, one challenge is to find the most effective mechanism for becoming a part of the municipal governing coalition through collaboration, displacement, or the forging of new coalitions among immigrants that cross racial and ethnic boundaries.

Research on immigrant empowerment suggests that, even in the midst of difficult circumstances, immigrants are very much involved in nonelectoral political activities, including labor union organizing and participation, church-related activities, national-origin mutual aid societies, social movements, women's organizations, and other nongovernmental organizations. In order to find such instances of engagement, political scientists must be willing to look beyond electoral participation.[186] We still have much to learn about existing patterns of civic engagement among immigrants and the ways in which they might be empowered to participate more. Latin American immigrants, for example, may be engaged simultaneously in churches whose activities focus on lived realities in the United States and in "hometown associations" that maintain ongoing links with their home country.[187]

NEIGHBORHOOD ORGANIZATIONS

For nearly all Americans, from the newest immigrant to the well-established homeowner, neighborhoods can be fertile ground for community engagement, and our discussion of neighborhood councils has shown ways in which government institutions can connect with neighborhoods. But even in the absence of formal institutions of neighborhood governance, many Americans have strong neighborhood ties and cooperate with their neighbors to pursue collective aims on a regular basis. Efforts to mobilize along geographic lines have included both rich and poor neighborhoods and have attempted to accomplish a variety of aims.

Neighborhood-based social service providers can be especially important in disadvantaged areas.[188] Consider, for example, the Grand Boulevard neighborhood on Chicago's South Side, which was studied by a research team at Northwestern University. This is a high-poverty neighborhood of 36,000 residents in which fully 82 percent of the children grow up in families living below the poverty line. Yet even in this very poor neighborhood, a block-by-block inventory revealed 319 "face-to-face organizations" where volunteers do the bulk of the work. About 100 of these nonprofits were churches or religious groups.[189]

Indeed, for blacks, urban churches not only administer the Gospel but also encourage political action by grooming political leaders, contributing to political campaigns, mobilizing parishioners, and imparting crucial political skills that, in turn, facilitate political participation. Moreover, black churches have become key players in community development, as they partner with municipal governments to transform inner-city communities into more livable neighborhoods.[190] Churches and other social service organizations can empower citizens and provide an important link between residents and city hall. We elaborate on these efforts in chapter four.

Other neighborhood-based organizations could do more to promote effective citizen engagement. Community development corporations, or CDCs, are one such example. CDCs are nonprofits with a primary focus on housing and are governed by their own independent boards of directors. The federal government played a crucial role in the rise of CDCs by providing financial support. The number of CDCs grew from a handful in the 1960s to an estimated 200 in 1980 and to around 3,600 in 1999, with over half in urban areas.[191] Through the ability to adapt and coordinate grant programs to the norms and needs of neighborhoods, as well as the ability to leverage voluntary contributions, such as sweat equity in housing, CDCs hold great democratic promise. Critics argue, however, that CDCs are preoccupied with bricks-and-mortar development to the detriment of community organizing and advocating for their neighborhoods.[192]

As vehicles of citizen engagement and empowerment, the performance of CDCs varies widely across the country. The ability of CDCs to realize their democratic potential has much to do with how they are treated by the local political regime.[193] Barbara Ferman shows how CDCs in Pittsburgh were incorporated into the governance structure of the city, sitting at the table when city government decided how to spend its federal Community Development Block Grant funds. By contrast, in Chicago, where CDCs were viewed as rivals to the Democratic Party organization, they had little direct input into housing policy.[194] Across many cities, CDCs have lost the élan and grassroots orientation that characterized the early years of the movement and are increasingly being driven by contracts and grants.[195]

Neighborhood-based mobilization may be especially important in poor or disadvantaged areas, but it is also frequently found among residents of middle- and upper-class neighborhoods, who are especially likely to organize their neighborhoods to preserve the value of their homes or promote the quality of local public goods (and thereby to enhance the value of their homes). Most sizable towns and cities in America contain dozens, if not hundreds, of neighborhood improvement associations, block clubs, neighborhood corporations, and residential community associations.

In the national 2000 Social Capital Community Benchmark Survey led by Robert Putnam, 20 percent of respondents claimed to participate in a neighborhood association.[196] Those with a college education were almost three times as likely (32 percent responded affirmatively) as those with a high school education or less (12 percent responded affirmatively) to participate in such an association.

Other studies have found different relationships between neighborhood participation and socioeconomic status. Nearly a quarter century ago, Richard C. Rich identified 167 neighborhood associations in the consolidated county of Indianapolis-Marion, Indiana.[197] Rich found *no* associations in the wealthiest quarter of neighborhoods, 10 percent of the associations in the poorest quartile, and 90 percent in the middle half. More recently, Matthew Crenson argues that participation tends to be highest in middle-income neighborhoods and considerably lower in both poor and wealthy neighborhoods (or, as political scientists would say, there is a *curvilinear* relationship between socioeconomic status and neighborhood participation). Eric Oliver finds a similar relationship between different communities' median household income and a host of other local participatory acts.[198] If this is correct, neighborhood participation operates in ways quite unlike other forms of political engagement, such as voting, working in political campaigns, and contributing money to campaigns, all of which tend to be lowest among the poor and less educated, higher among the middle class, but higher still for the better-off and better educated.[199]

HOMEOWNERS ASSOCIATIONS

One increasingly widespread type of neighborhood organization, especially common among middle- and upper-income Americans, raises concerns about civic engagement. Homeowners associations have grown dramatically over the past forty years. In 1964, there were fewer than 500 homeowners associations. By 2003, 8,000 new associations were forming each year, and an estimated 50 million Americans—almost one out of every five—lived in association-governed communities.[200] Established by covenants attached to the deeds of residential property, homeowners associations are "private governments" that have taken on many of the roles traditionally assumed by local governments. They collect mandatory fees, similar to local taxes, to finance their operations, which include management of property held in common, trash collection, and snow plowing. Perhaps their most important role is the enforcement of covenants and rules that regulate the behavior of residents, such as pet ownership, home improvement, and parking. In addition, they usually hold a public meeting once or twice a year and elect a governing board that supervises business between meetings.[201]

Because they are self-governing and lobby local government, homeowners associations seem generally to stimulate civic participation. Indeed, they might be viewed as "small republics," the epitome of grassroots democracy, where residents closely identify their own personal interests with the interests of their community. The proliferation of these sorts of associations gives citizens much greater choice among residential communities, which facilitates the sorting described by Charles Tiebout. However, both the quality and equality of the participation generated by homeowners associations are problematic. They nurture a sense of shared fate among residents, but at the expense of connections to the larger political community. Accompanying their rise has been the growing prevalence of gated communities, where physical walls make real the separation of homeowners associations from the broader community.[202]

Despite their growing numbers, few, if any, homeowners associations serve residents of low-income or subsidized housing.[203] As exclusively middle- and upper-middle-class homeowner enclaves, homeowners associations reinforce income segregation and may thereby reinforce racial segregation.[204] The reluctance of prosperous homeowners, whose services are provided by their association, to contribute to public coffers may also leave fewer resources to meet the needs of those outside their neighborhood, attenuating the possibilities for redistribution and the promotion of other inclusive public goods within the public sector. Homeowners associations can thus exacerbate place-based inequalities.

In addition, despite the semblance of direct and representative democracy, the governance structures of homeowners associations do not encourage norms of healthy political engagement. For example, renters do not have a vote, meetings are not subject to sunshine laws, free speech and other constitutional guarantees are not protected, and many decisions are delegated to hired professionals and contractors, leading to a system that, in the words of one author, "attempts to replace politics with management."[205] The underlying rationale for limiting participatory decisionmaking is that the community is a voluntary association and residents are free to leave if they do not agree with the services that are provided and the rules of behavior that are enforced.[206] It is further assumed that everyone agrees on the goal of protecting property values, so there should, in theory, be few conflicts. If those assumptions are met, management might replace politics because most values are agreed on, and those who do not agree are free to move.

In practice, though, the governance of homeowners associations is characterized by a combination of widespread indifference along with recurrent nasty conflicts of interest and value. Many associations have trouble mustering a quorum for their meetings or filling board seats. More than half of the respondents to a 1988 survey of homeowners association board members characterized their members as "apathetic."[207] Much of this nonparticipation is probably due to the fact that members are basically satisfied with the services provided, perhaps because the dissatisfied have moved away. But when conflicts do arise, usually over enforcement of association rules, the private decisionmaking process, or managerial model, of homeowners associations is poorly suited to resolving these conflicts. Members are forced to go outside the association to the courts, using expensive and time-consuming lawsuits to address their grievances. Homeowners association litigation is a thriving legal specialty, and association boards increasingly resort to eviction or foreclosure to enforce rules or collect fees.[208]

Homeowners associations can stimulate citizen participation in the larger community and, in fact, have become increasingly effective lobbying organizations. However, they usually become politically active when residents perceive that a proposed action, such as a commercial development or a landfill, threatens their property values. According to research based largely on case studies, homeowners associations "are in the vanguard of the NIMBY (Not In My Back Yard) movement across America."[209] In contrast to renters and low-income homeowners, homeowners associations have the resources, networks, and, often, the paid legal assistance to effectively direct patterns of land use around their neighborhoods.[210] They have every right to organize and lobby the government, but their capacity to "mobilize bias," to use E. E. Schattschneider's term, tilts the playing field of metropolitan development in the direction of these well-financed and well-organized property interests.[211]

Homeowners associations clearly provide avenues for civic engagement for their members, but it is a narrow form of civic engagement, aimed at advancing the particular interests of well-defined, homogeneous groups. They seem to exemplify the dangers of small scale and homogeneity: the weaknesses of small and insular communities that do not serve as effective schools for civic engagement appropriate to a large and diverse society.

What Is to Be Done?

As we say at the outset, metropolitan regions have experienced dramatic change—most notably growth, decentralization, and diversification, coupled with increasing economic stratification and persistent segregation. These changes have had profound and complex effects on the quantity, quality, and equality of civic engagement in cities and their suburbs. We also emphasize two central trade-offs, even dilemmas, of civic engagement in the metropolis. One is the dilemma of size: small scale serves in many ways to spur civic activity by keeping government accessible to citizens. But small communities are liable to be narrow and exclusive in their outlook. In addition, the political fragmentation that creates smaller political communities in many of America's metropolitan areas facilitates the social stratification that undermines our capacity to address broad and important public problems, such as concentrated poverty, environmental pollution, and traffic congestion.

There is also a challenge of diversity or heterogeneity: the personal encounter with diversity is essential to democratic citizenship in a vast heterogeneous republic such as ours, and this diversity may spawn productive conflict over meaningful political issues, thus drawing some citizens into political activity. But evidence suggests that more heterogeneous places, irrespective of size, are less trusting and also, quite possibly, less apt to nurture engagement. Homogeneous communities thus promote social trust and ease of social intercourse, while simultaneously organizing key issues out of politics.

OVERVIEW: MANAGING THE TRADE-OFFS

The presence of trade-offs could easily make one pessimistic about the prospects for metropolitan reforms to improve civic engagement. If improvements on one dimension automatically lead to offsetting harms on another dimension, then nothing we can do will really make us better off. Two points need to be made, however, about the trade-offs we have identified. First, the existence of these trade-offs highlights the need to make value judgments about the kinds of cities and civic engagement we want to realize. In general, we believe that metropolitan development and governance in the United States has tilted too far in the direction of localism and segregation, with negative effects for both the quality and the equality of citizen participation. To address this, we recommend, among other things, creating broader, more diverse decisionmaking arenas in metropolitan areas, even if this has some negative effects for trust and local community participation.

More important, the trade-offs we have identified are not fixed; they can be managed in better and worse ways. In certain circumstances, we can transcend the conflict between values and pursue multiple goals at once or at least alter the nature of the trade-offs. It is possible, for example, to have small and quite homogeneous communities that foster high levels of interpersonal trust, while at the same time requiring them to recognize the diverse claims of other communities in wider public settings. Such insights are part of the genius of American federalism.

There is no simple formula for managing difficult trade-offs or for improving their terms. But such opportunities exist, we believe, and a central task for research is to identify them. These recommendations, which seek to enhance the quantity, quality, and equity of civic engagement in metropolitan regions, address state and federal, as well as local, policymakers; because cities are highly constrained political entities, fostering metropolitan civic engagement requires deliberate and concerted action at all three levels. We recommend four kinds of actions.

First, it is important to reduce concentrations of rich and poor within metropolitan areas as well as the segregation of races and ethnicities. Geographic separation that reinforces political, economic, and social divisions undermines the quality of our civic life.

Second, new institutions of metropolitan governance should be explored that enable citizens and their political representatives to address problems that cannot be addressed adequately or effectively within the ambit of current local institutions. The challenge here is to devise structures that overcome the fragmented nature of many metropolitan areas without suppressing opportunities for local political engagement or overburdening citizens with excessive demands.

Third, the scope for organized politics, popular engagement, and political conflict in local and metropolitan government should be widened by reconsidering the progressive-era reforms that attempted to insulate the operations of local government from political conflict.

Finally, we must encourage citizens to participate directly in decisions that affect their lives, including decisions about neighborhood planning, local school governance, public safety, and local economic development. The challenge here is to create new institutions—and reinvigorate old ones—that invite public engagement and deliberation beyond the formal electoral process.

We must enter one final caveat. As we have said before, political scientists have not paid sufficient attention to many aspects of metropolitan life and local political institutions. We wish we knew more about how political institutions and human interactions might best be structured to promote government that is wise and capable because all of its citizens are actively engaged. We hope that our efforts may stimulate others to turn their attention to these matters. In the meantime, however, and in contrast with the discussion in chapter two, we venture to speak here without nearly as much evidence as we would like and without the confidence that we hope future research will supply.

Therefore, to manage the trade-offs, we recommend the following:

▌ Reduce concentrations of rich and poor within metropolitan areas as well as the segregation of races and ethnicities.

▌ Explore new institutions of metropolitan governance.

▌ Expand the scope for organized politics, popular engagement, political conflict, and public collaboration in local and metropolitan government.

▌ Encourage citizens to participate directly in decisions that affect their lives.

MAKE COMMUNITIES MORE DIVERSE

Local political communities in America too often reflect and reinforce the most significant divisions among citizens, including divisions of class and race. We recognize that diversity can be a source of conflict and that creating trustful and cooperative relations among people who are different is a challenge. Nevertheless, vital aspects of the democratic experience are short-circuited when local communities erect barriers that create exclusive enclaves of privilege: the political agenda is artificially constrained, and those who are excluded are denied equal opportunities.

The fragmentation of local political communities and their subsequent stratification according to class and race undercut their ability to serve as effective training grounds in the skills of politics. The social and political marginalization of racial and ethnic groups creates unequal opportunities for meaningful civic and political engagement. These engines of systematic material and political inequality, which some critics have called an "American apartheid," enervate metropolitan civic engagement.[212] Immigrants face high hurdles to political incorporation. Many immigrant groups are rarely mobilized, and they face additional obstacles to full participation, such as language barriers and naturalization requirements. Political scientists must do more to understand the dynamics of civic and political engagement among new immigrant communities. We also recognize that there are deep disagreements about the extent to which noncitizens should be fully incorporated into the political system.

We recommend several policies to enhance the political capacity and engagement of racial minority and immigrant groups and to foster engagement that bridges racial and economic divides.

First, municipalities should be encouraged to provide a mix of housing that meets the needs of the people who work in the area. Madison, Wisconsin, for example, recently passed an inclusionary zoning law that requires all new development to include affordable housing. Zoning laws that exclude apartments or require all houses to be built on large lots are usually not in the public interest. Federal and state governments should consider a variety of more ambitious housing policies for economic integration, such as tying grants to "fair share" affordable housing plans, encouraging inclusionary over exclusionary zoning, and fully funding housing voucher policies that facilitate geographic mobility. Legislatures and courts should explore ways to encourage municipalities to provide housing choices that reflect the broad range of households in the metropolitan area. We know that the political pressures here are intense, but if courts or state legislatures require suburbs to meet "fair share" housing requirements, then suburbs will be more comfortable building affordable housing, knowing that neighboring suburbs are required to do the same and that they will not be overwhelmed with subsidized housing.[213]

Second, we need to enforce fair housing laws. Vigilant enforcement of fair housing laws already on the books would help to ensure that all Americans have the same opportunity to live in desirable neighborhoods. Increasing racial and social integration would, in turn, inject diversity and pluralism into experiences of local engagement.[214]

Finally, we need to lower the formal barriers to the political participation of immigrants. At the federal level, we should investigate the consequences of easing paths to naturalization. Some cities and towns have expanded the local political franchise. Takoma Park, Maryland, for example, permits noncitizens to vote in school board elections; this is at least worth considering, although it raises too many questions for us to endorse it now.[215]

Therefore, in an effort to make communities more diverse, we recommend the following:

▎ Encourage municipalities to provide a mix of housing that meets the needs of the people who work in the area.
▎ Enforce fair housing laws.
▎ Lower the formal barriers to the political participation of immigrants.

GOVERN THE METROPOLIS CIVICALLY

We began by noting the complex relationship between civic engagement, size, and diversity. The conflicting values we face in addressing trade-offs between more and less centralized decisionmaking are indeed vexing.[216] Other things being equal, taking decisionmaking authority out of the hands of local governments, and putting it in regional bodies, undermines civic engagement. But "other things" are not always equal.[217] Increasing the authority of regional institutions can, in some contexts, enhance the power of local governments. The ability of a local government to make effective decisions depends not simply on being left alone by higher-level governments but also on their relationship to other local governments and to the private market. Greater local autonomy does not always mean greater local control. Isolated and weak institutions are at the mercy of more powerful forces. If a local government is resource poor or locked in competition with its neighbors, it will not be able to exercise its formal authority effectively. Regional reforms that impose limitations on local governments can, in effect, free them to address problems of sprawl and segregation that they otherwise would be reluctant to address. Civic engagement may be improved—certainly the quality of governance may be enhanced—if important problems that are now effectively off the public agenda can be brought onto it, albeit at the regional or state level. It may, moreover, be possible to respond to some pressing problems only by moving governance to higher levels: individual communities are not likely unilaterally to forgo exclusionary zoning practices, nor are individual suburban governments likely to invest adequately in affordable housing initiatives. State or federal initiatives in this area are not at all popular, as we well know, but political action at higher levels is essential for assuring local communities that everyone will bear their fair share of collective burdens. Moreover, while the politics of metropolitan governance may seem hopeless, Myron Orfield argues that, in many metropolitan areas, inner-ring suburbs are experiencing fiscal problems similar to those of older cities. This creates the possibility for an effective coalition of support for reform uniting cities and inner suburbs.[218]

Ideally, metropolitan political institutions should foster participation and engagement at the local level in ways that encourage citizens of localities to transcend their parochial interests and identities in favor of more encompassing and inclusive political perspectives that span boundaries of race, class, and locality. Although there is no consensus among social scientists or policymakers regarding the institutional arrangements that best combine public engagement with the capacity to confront pressing metropolitan challenges, some approaches are worthy of further study.

Local government scholars David Barron and Gerald Frug, for example, argue for legal and institutional reforms that would allow citizens and representatives of localities to address common concerns and conflicts in new metropolitan political arenas.[219] These reforms have two prongs. First, state laws that define the powers of local governments should compel them to take seriously the effects of their actions on other localities and create incentives for cooperation on regional problems.[220] Second, state legislatures should create representative regional institutions that allow municipalities to address common issues by forging enforceable agreements with one another.[221] Such regional institutions would have supermajority requirements, perhaps modeled on the European Union, to forestall problems of the tyranny of the majority. We cannot with confidence endorse this or any other particular proposal, but the approach is promising and merits more research and experimentation.

At present, there are few, if any, metropolitan-wide institutions that are elected by the population they serve and fewer still that purport to represent the individual municipalities that make them up.[222] Still, a few metropolitan areas—most notably, Portland, Oregon—have established successful regional institutions or patterns of effective cooperation without weakening local civic participation.[223] Nevertheless, one study that directly examines the effect of metropolitan-wide governance in Indianapolis finds sharp declines in electoral turnout after consolidation, although the researchers attribute these declines to a lack of party competition in the consolidated jurisdiction.[224] These and other examples of metropolitan governance are worthy of greater study from the perspective of their effect on civic engagement, both quantitatively and qualitatively.

We believe that regional reforms that address metropolitan-wide issues can, under the right circumstances, enhance civic engagement. The challenge for future research is to determine what these circumstances are. Given the urgency of the problem of metropolitan governance, but the absence of consensus on any solution, it is appropriate to embark on a course of institutional innovation and experimentation in which metropolitan regions become laboratories of democracy and civic engagement.

First, state and local policymakers should experiment with a range of institutions that alter municipal powers and create arenas that encourage citizens from different localities and their political representatives to engage with one another around issues of metropolitan concern. New regional forms should include civic engagement as a critical goal. They should recognize that whatever institutions are created will affect civic engagement, for better or worse. When possible, they should strive not to override local decisionmaking but rather to create incentives that align local and regional aims.

Second, social scientists should develop a comparative metropolitan politics that illuminates the variety of institutional arrangements under which metropolitan regions can be governed. Which of these are better and worse for civic engagement and other aims of regional governance? Such a social science would inform policy experimentation.

Finally, social scientists should seek to understand the conditions under which individuals pursue highly parochial aims without regard to the consequences for other neighborhoods, towns, and the region as a whole. When, conversely, do residents embrace more encompassing identities or wider concerns for equity, welfare, or environment?

Therefore, to improve civic governance, we recommend the following:

▌ Experiment with a range of institutions that alter municipal powers and create arenas that encourage citizens from different localities and their political representatives to engage with one another around issues of metropolitan concern.

▌ Develop a comparative metropolitan politics that illuminates the variety of institutional arrangements under which metropolitan regions can be governed.

▌ Endeavor to understand the conditions under which individuals seek highly parochial aims without regard to the consequences for other neighborhoods, towns, and the region as a whole.

REVITALIZE POLITICS IN LOCAL GOVERNMENT

In the first part of the twentieth century, urban reformers instituted political reforms to combat corruption and enhance the professionalism of public agencies. These reforms, including at-large systems of representation, city-manager forms of government, and professionalized agencies that insulate themselves from political "interference," had the effect of depoliticizing many activities of city government and dampening civic engagement. Mayoral campaigns can spur civic engagement, and party labels provide voters with much-needed information. Moreover, elected mayors have the political clout to stand up to elected city councils. They also have a far greater incentive to stand up to city councils than unelected managers who are chosen by and beholden to those councils.

While local partisan politics seems more conducive to civic activity, local political organizations tend to become entrenched around settled institutions. There may be virtue in reforms that dislodge and unsettle dominant parties.

We believe that partisan competition can and should be revitalized at the local level (although we wish we had more evidence to rely on). Conflict can be healthy, especially when it brings new voices and perspectives into the arenas of public discussion and decision. While conflict associated with racial and economic diversity may turn some citizens off to politics and cause them to feel less connected to their localities, it may also foster new patterns of political mobilization and help local politics to take up important but neglected issues. Furthermore, enlarging the scope of politics invites not just conflict but also the give-and-take between political and civic interests and organizations that can result in innovative collaborations that thicken the relationships between government and civic groups and among civic groups themselves. We also recognize that, while increasing conflict in local government will mobilize some, it will prove distasteful and difficult for others. We suspect that widespread aversion to conflict and compromise highlights the need for more and better education of citizens about the centrality of disagreement and debate to democratic political life.

Finally, special-purpose governments should be more open and transparent. Corporations and real estate developers have used special districts to confer benefits on a few and impose burdens on the many in ways that are almost invisible to the public at large. Special-purpose governments should allow meaningful input from citizens and prevent private interests from pursuing their goals hidden from public scrutiny. They should be required to coordinate and balance their functions with other special districts and general-purpose governments.

Therefore, we recommend the following:

▌ Reconsider progressive-era reforms at the city level, including council-manager governance, at-large city council districts, and nonpartisan elections.
▌ Make special-purpose governments more open and transparent.
▌ Work to understand which municipal institutions promote more and better civic engagement.

EMPOWER PEOPLE TO PARTICIPATE BETWEEN ELECTIONS

As we emphasize throughout the report, improving the overall amount, distribution, and quality of civic engagement holds out the promise of more legitimate public policy that enjoys the support of a broader array of stakeholders, more capable and active citizens, improved public policy as a consequence of broader discussion, and greater fairness insofar as the range of relevant voices heard is widened.

Political scientists should seek a more systematic understanding of the conditions under which direct citizen participation creates inclusive deliberative encounters and improved public policy. Conversely, we must also understand the conditions under which participation falls short of these aims by excluding particular groups or perspectives or by hobbling the policy process. Although we do not fully understand the conditions under which citizens are likely to participate, we believe that the most successful of participatory and deliberative reforms exhibit several features. First, citizens are more likely to participate when they are asked to do so: personal contact that seeks to mobilize citizens to act in politics is vital. Second, participation is more likely when it makes a difference: citizens must see that their efforts influence decisions and shape policies. Third, residents should not merely be allowed to express their opinions, which officials may then consider or dismiss, but should have the opportunity to work directly with elected officials and agency staff and to have a say about the shape of proposals at an early stage in decision making.

Institutions can be designed so as to discourage or invite greater participation: we recommend inviting more direct, broader, and more consequential input from citizens. These recommendations are not directed exclusively at governments. Indeed, many problems can be addressed by citizens acting on their own through voluntary associations and nonprofit organizations. Many public policies are now implemented in partnership with nonprofit and voluntary organizations. Just as government should be opened up to citizen participation, so civic and community organizations can be structured in ways that invite greater direct involvement by those who are affected by the actions of associations and organizations. This theme is at the center of chapter four, but we touch on it here as well.

First, local governments should enhance opportunities for citizens to become involved in issues they care about. All government agencies should explore methods to involve citizens in shaping and administering policy through advisory boards, public meetings, and greater citizen involvement in what we call the coproduction of public goods and services. Large cities should make extra efforts to ensure that local government is brought close to the people through means such as neighborhood governance and administrative decentralization. As much as possible, citizens should be involved "up front," before the agenda has been set, rather than late in the process when most important decisions have already been made.

Second, citywide systems of neighborhood councils should be strongly encouraged. The best models for such systems, like the structures in Minneapolis, Minnesota, and Portland, Oregon, are those where every neighborhood of the city has at least one officially recognized neighborhood association. City governments should devolve some significant responsibilities onto their neighborhood councils, including zoning powers and the distribution of some government funds. Although each neighborhood council should be run by volunteers from the catchment area, city hall should provide modest support in the form of liaison staff.

Third, community and neighborhood organizations should be structured in ways that foster greater citizen engagement. They should envision their missions not simply as providing services but as engaging residents in efforts to improve their communities. The governing and advisory boards of CDCs, for example, should involve more residents, and these organizations should invite residents to participate in a wider range of activities. Government programs that provide funds to neighborhood organizations should require that a majority of the governing board resides in the neighborhood.

Fourth, cities should invest and engage in direct mobilization, especially to support new and promising avenues for civic engagement. These efforts should supplement the important mobilizing activities of political parties and other community organizations. Even in cities with a system of neighborhood councils, the local government should do what it can to facilitate the mobilizing activities of political parties and other community organizations. At the same time, we recognize that getting government involved in community organizing has the danger of furnishing public officials with a new instrument of partisan politics. We are mindful of this concern and seek ways of addressing it.

Finally, political scientists should seek a more systematic understanding of the relationship between engagement and good governance. In particular, what kinds of engagement make governance more deliberative, accountable, effective, and legitimate? Conversely, what sorts of engagement polarize, facilitate capture, or, as our colleagues have long worried, overload government with the demands of special interests?

Thus we offer several recommendations in the area of direct political participation and citizen empowerment:

- Enhance opportunities for citizens to become involved in local governments to address issues they care about.
- Encourage citywide systems of neighborhood councils.
- Structure community and neighborhood organizations in ways that foster greater citizen engagement.
- Ensure that cities invest in and engage in direct mobilization.
- Seek a more systematic understanding of the relationship between engagement and good governance.

Conclusion

The features of the metropolitan landscape that shape civic engagement are the result of many factors. New technologies, especially the automobile, have played a major role in shaping the places where people live and work—the spreading out of the American metropolis, the separation of home from work and other functions, and the sorting of population along economic lines.[225] But technology has not worked this transformation without the significant and ongoing influence of political choices at all levels of government.

Local communities often cannot undertake the necessary actions alone. Cities remain, as Douglas Rae and Paul Peterson argue, weak players in the mix of actors that shape the future of the nations' metropolitan areas. Federal policies—governing programs, including interstate highways, Federal Housing Administration loan guarantees, and the deduction of home mortgage interest and property taxes—have contributed to certain patterns of residential organization by encouraging suburbanization and segregation.[226] Although it was inevitable that cities would spread out, it was not inevitable that this new development would be governed by hundreds of local governments. Local governments are not mentioned in the U. S. Constitution; states are the source of city authority, determining cities' revenue streams, often limiting their ability to annex their suburbs, and frequently preventing regional governance and cooperation.[227] Although cities and other local governments are often relatively weak players, they do have policy options at their disposal, including zoning codes, economic development incentives, and the way they deliver local services.

The institutional arrangements that organize our metropolises are not incorrigible facts of nature. We often choose to live with the consequences they produce: dramatically unequal opportunities for civic engagement, local governments that too often are dammed off from popular influence rather than being channels that facilitate self-government, and balkanized enclaves that deprive us of opportunities for encounters with those who have different life experiences and perspectives. But we can and should reject these consequences in favor of other institutions and politics that are more worthy of our democratic ideals.

Serious reform requires hard work from public leaders, citizens, and social scientists. Here in particular, the challenge demands not just action but greater knowledge. Scholars and researchers also have a crucial role to play, for we have yet to adequately understand the vexing dilemmas and problems we have described, let alone find ways to repair metropolitan civic life.

- *Each year, 84 million Americans volunteer.*

- *Private charitable giving is estimated at $200 billion a year.*

- *Approximately 1.5 million nonprofits are registered with the federal government, including close to 1 million public charities or 501(c)(3)s.*

- *The United States has 70,000 foundations, with collective assets of $450 billion.*

- *Americans are drawn to worship in a total of 350,000 religious congregations, which represents approximately one congregation for every 850 people.*[1]

4

Associational Life and the Nonprofit and Philanthropic Sector

A T THE HEART OF CIVIC ENGAGEMENT IS ASSOCIATIONAL LIFE. Modern mass democracies need associations to organize communities, link neighbors to one another, integrate neighborhoods in cities and towns, and forge bonds between people across geographic distances. Associations are classrooms for citizenship and building blocks for broader political movements of all kinds. Obviously, formal political institutions and public agencies can do some of these things as well, but there has long been a widespread consensus that associations play a crucial civic role, and we agree. Associations can help to mobilize and organize individuals and groups within the polity, sometimes directly for political purposes and sometimes mainly for nonpolitical purposes, but often with appreciable civic side effects. This chapter focuses on the role of associations in nurturing civic engagement and on the ways in which public policy enhances or inhibits the opportunities for associations and their members to participate in civic and political affairs.

Associational life in the United States is extraordinarily diverse and diffuse, including phenomena as transient, local, and small as getting together socially with neighbors and organizations as enduring, extensive, and large as the major religious denominations. Associational life includes civic associations, community groups, sports teams, religious organizations, workplace associations, political movements, issue-oriented advocacy groups, and more. A comprehensive account of associational life and its importance for citizenship, encompassing the entire array of organizations that individuals create and join, is a hopelessly broad task, far beyond the scope of this chapter. Instead, we examine an important sphere of activity and an important segment of associational life that we believe are vital to civic engagement.

Much of what we discuss in this chapter appears to buck the declining trends in civic engagement documented by Robert Putnam, Theda Skocpol, and others. The sheer number of charitable organizations has grown tremendously, as has the amount of resources they have at their disposal. Religious organizations remain healthy for the most part and may grow in importance by taking over more of the government-funded social service provision. However, unions have experienced a precipitous decline in membership as well as a weakening of their historic role in encouraging civic engagement.

We focus first on volunteering in American life and then on associations within what is sometimes called (perhaps misleadingly) the "independent sector," a catchall term that refers to nonprofit organizations and philanthropic foundations (we sometimes say simply "nonprofit sector"). While our focus on volunteering and the nonprofit sector narrows the scope of our subject matter somewhat, this chapter still covers much ground. Volunteering is an expansive category, encompassing a wide range of activities from baking cookies for a school fundraiser to committing a year of service to the poor as a member of the Jesuit Volunteer Corps. Similarly, this sector includes the extremely diverse assortment of nonprofit organizations that fall outside of government and for-profit businesses. For our purposes, three types of these organizations merit special attention because they historically have had a large and significant influence on civic and political life: charitable organizations (especially ones that provide social services), religious organizations, and labor unions.

We have selected this focus for three reasons. First, nonprofits and philanthropies account for a large percentage of those groups in associational life that possess a formal structure; second, the institutional and regulatory environment that stimulates (or deters) volunteering and governs the independent sector is well developed and complex and exerts a wide influence; and third, the rules governing nonprofits and philanthropies specifically restrict their ability to engage in overtly political behavior such as lobbying or campaigning. In this chapter, we ask and answer questions about how public policy can improve the potential of associational life generally, and the nonprofit and philanthropic sector specifically, to enhance our civic life. We also consider the ways in which government policy can enhance the volunteer experience by making volunteer opportunities more widely available and by linking them more directly to citizenship and civic capacities.

We believe that volunteering and the nonprofit sector generally strengthen democracy, especially under favorable conditions. Here, as in earlier chapters, we seek to advance an argument: we can significantly foster or inhibit individual and collective involvement in public life through the regulation of associational life and the independent sector. Here, as elsewhere, the characteristics of individuals—their level of education, socioeconomic status, and age, among others—influence the decision to get involved, with whom, and on behalf of which causes. But the institutional environment in which people associate with others in collective activity is important too. By adjusting or revamping institutional and regulatory frameworks, policymakers can enhance the civic role played by associations in American life and, in the process, enliven the civic and political capacities of individuals.

Scholars and commentators often overlook the extent to which law and policy shape associational activity. For example, when those interested in civic engagement look back to Alexis de Tocqueville's canonical account of the importance of groups and associations to democracy, pride of place is often given to individual freedom and to mores or culture. Scant attention is paid to the ways in which, as Tocqueville emphasized, a healthy civic life depends on sound policy choices and well-designed institutions. True enough, Tocqueville argued that freedom helps to give rise to association: "Better use has been made of association and this powerful instrument of action has been applied to more varied aims in America than anywhere else in the world."[2] In his rhapsodic descriptions of American life, citizens organize at the slightest pretext: "If some obstacle blocks the public road halting the circulation of traffic, the neighbors at once form a deliberative body."[3]

But this great observer and theorist of democratic life also emphasized the crucial role of institutional design and policy choice in establishing the conditions for an active citizenry. A federal political structure, administrative decentralization, a strong public commitment to education for all, and the expectation of jury service are among the ways in which political design calls forth the civic energies of free individuals.[4] Not only did Tocqueville usefully emphasize the importance of laws and institutions to the behavior and attitudes of free individuals, he also argued that individual freedom—understood as the right to lead one's own life and make one's own decisions—is complemented and sustained, not threatened, by involvements in associations, groups, and practices of self-governance. Indeed, our attempt to reinvigorate political and civic involvement is, in important measure, an effort to elaborate, refine, and bolster Tocqueville's insight.

Associations and Civic Engagement

We first describe the relationship between associational life and civic engagement. Some associations may act directly in politics to advance the shared political interests of members, and others facilitate public-private partnerships that deliver social services to citizens. In these cases associations clearly organize individuals for political involvement. Many other voluntary associations are, however, oriented toward particular goals and activities that have little directly to do with civic and political affairs. Why should we think that associational life generally is of concern to politics?

The recent interest in the importance of associational membership was spurred in part by Robert Putnam's discussion of the civic by-products of social interaction among participants in groups and social activities of all sorts. Putnam argues that these general by-products, often referred to as social capital, highlight "the fact that civic virtue is most powerful when embedded in a dense network of reciprocal social relations."[5] The social networks at the heart of associational activity tend to stimulate civic activism: "Volunteering fosters more volunteering, in both formal and informal settings. Organizational involvement seems to inculcate civic skills and a life-long disposition toward altruism."[6]

The notion that there is a positive connection between associational participation and civic engagement is amply supported by Sidney Verba, Kay Schlozman, and Henry Brady, whose influential book, *Voice and Equality*, highlights the political impact of what they call the "non-political institutions of adult life—the workplace, voluntary associations, and churches."[7] These institutions and organizations are frequently schoolhouses for civic and political information and skill development. They provide, for instance, opportunities to learn about the political world and to develop politically relevant skills— from learning to give a talk to learning how to negotiate—that can be transferred to other realms. Putnam, for instance, notes that "churches provide an important incubator for civic skills, civic norms, community interests, and civic recruitment" because churchgoers often learn to run meetings, speak publicly, negotiate disagreements, and acquire managerial or administrative skills.[8]

One of the greatest civic virtues of associational involvement is that it can contribute to one's sense of political efficacy: the conviction that one is capable of influencing policymakers or that one's voice counts. In their study of neighborhood associations in cities, Jeffrey Berry, Kent Portney, and Ken Thomson conclude, "Community participation makes people feel better about their own political effectiveness and about the ability of the local government to respond to them. It contributes to the amount of political knowledge people possess."[9]

It seems clear, therefore, that civic associations and the nonprofit and philanthropic sector contribute in a host of direct and indirect ways to the quantity, quality, and equality of civic and political engagement in a democratic society. Even apparently "apolitical" associations bring individuals together in cooperative relations and social networks and thereby enhance the opportunities and willingness of members to engage in civic or political activity. Groups and associations are "mediating structures" in large, complex societies, and by linking individuals to others in cooperative relations, thereby creating and deepening social networks, they can encourage wider forms of civic and political involvement. In a variety of ways, therefore, voluntary associations are training grounds and laboratories of citizenship. Against the background of a civic playing field tilted toward the relatively wealthy and better educated, it is especially significant that membership and involvement in groups appear to furnish additional and distinct resources for civic engagement. Nonprofits, in particular, can play a role in nurturing the civic skills and behavior of the least advantaged members of our society.

Here, as elsewhere in this report, we must acknowledge that not everyone agrees with our claims. Miriam Galston, for example, has surveyed the evidence and concluded that there is little support for the claim that associations are "critical for cultivating moral values and public spiritedness in individuals or promoting attitudes and practices conducive to reflective self-governance."[10] In general, she argues, associations harness and direct, though perhaps also strengthen, existing moral and public-spirited attitudes. In addition, if we examine the effects of participation in a voluntary association on a political measure of special importance—voter turnout—the strength of the connection is unclear.[11]

As even the most fervent modern-day Tocquevilleans acknowledge, associational activity is not always an unambiguous good. Particular groups can be insular, exclusive, and self-protective in ways that harm the larger community and even their own members. Homeowners associations are sometimes thought to act against the larger public interest, a possibility we discuss in chapter three. More obvious, paramilitary and racist organizations, such as the Ku Klux Klan, clearly are harmful.[12]

Moreover, we know that the character of many associations has changed over time and that not all associations live up to their potential as schools of citizenship. Theda Skocpol shows that a significant portion of associational life has been transformed from mass membership organizations, in which individuals actively participate and come into contact with others, to professionally managed organizations, in which individuals are passively involved (by writing a check, for instance) and rarely meet other people. Citizens today are more frequently "doing for" than "doing with." The result, she claims, is a diminished democracy.[13]

It is the task of public policy—and our aim in this report—to craft policies and institutional structures that encourage the good and deter the bad of associational life. Even so, we acknowledge that sorting out causal connections and determining the civic benefits of different kinds of voluntary associations are difficult tasks, and we cannot settle all of the controversies here. Nonetheless, we believe that the weight of current evidence supports the general claim that active participation in voluntary associations enhances people's civic capacities and leads to more and better participation in political life.

We join Putnam, Skocpol, and many other students of associational life in being troubled by the decline of many groups and associations. If our associational life atrophies, so too will our democracy. Yet we also see crosscurrents and even some encouraging signs with respect to citizens' group involvements. By volunteering and participating in nonprofits and philanthropic activity, Americans in vast numbers escape the pull of "bowling alone." In contrast to the general downward drift of associational life, the apparent vigor of these sectors offers hope. These developments may not fully compensate for the deterioration of other aspects of civic life, but they represent important, vital, and widespread channels of civic education and engagement.

Moreover, the nonprofit and voluntary sectors are especially amenable to the influence of policy design. Public policy might do little to change the number of bowling leagues, but it can do quite a lot to effect changes in volunteering and in the nonprofit and philanthropic world. Thus, after examining these two promising trends in detail, we analyze how the civic and legal context of each may be reshaped to enhance their contribution to the vitality of American democracy.

We consider several significant features of the regulation of nonprofits: first, the treatment of tax-deductible contributions made to public charities, or 501(c)(3)s, as they are called because of the tax code section that defines them; second, restrictions placed on the political engagement of public charities; and third, the rules regarding nonprofit accountability and governance. We then turn to two particular types of nonprofits: we examine the continuing health of churches and their important contribution to civic life as well as the declining role of workplace unions and the unfortunate consequences for political representation and mobilization of working people. Finally, we consider significant recent initiatives to bolster volunteerism in the form of national service programs.

Two Positive Trends: Volunteering and Growth of the Nonprofit Sector

In terms of sheer numbers, volunteering is one of the most popular forms of civic engagement. Nearly as many adults volunteer as vote. A survey conducted by Independent Sector, a national coalition of nonprofits, foundations, and corporations that conducts research and advocacy on behalf of nonprofits and foundations, estimates the number of adult volunteers (twenty-one and older) at 83.9 million in 2000.[14] Because significant numbers of high school and college students volunteer, the actual figure is even higher, perhaps approaching the number of people who vote. The same survey indicates that the average time volunteered is 3.6 hours a week. It would not be overly cynical to wonder if there is some exaggeration in these self-reported figures. Because volunteering is universally considered to be virtuous, it is surely the case that some over-reporting occurs—just as people overreport their participation in elections. Still, even after discounting for some reasonable deflator, the figures remain impressive.[15] The most popular arenas for volunteers are religion, education, youth activities, and social services. The economic value of volunteering is staggering. The total dollar value of volunteer time, based on the average hourly wage for nonagricultural workers, was $239 billion in 2000.

Consistent with the findings of Putnam, the presence of social networks is an important predictor of who volunteers: individuals who are asked to volunteer are significantly more likely to do so (71 percent of all volunteers) than individuals who seek out a volunteer position on their own (29 percent).[16] Most important, the rates of volunteering, among both adults and youth (whose volunteering is not captured in the data just offered), rose in the 1990s.[17] This rise, most believe, is attributable to the increased professionalization of how volunteer time is managed and to changes in public policy that encourage volunteering, especially among youth.

Particularly notable among these public policy efforts is the proliferation of private and public programs designed to increase youth volunteering and public service. City Year and Teach for America, both created in the 1980s, are but two of the more visible efforts to direct the energies of recent college graduates to the problems of the disadvantaged. Campus Compact, a national coalition of colleges and universities that promotes community service among students, grew from twenty-five to 900 campuses between 1985 and 2003. At the federal level, each of the past few presidents has emphasized the importance of volunteering. George H. W. Bush endorsed the creation of the Points of Light Foundation in 1990; Bill Clinton created AmeriCorps and the Corporation for National Service during his tenure; and George W. Bush has followed with Freedom Corps and Citizen Corps, created in the wake of September 11, 2001. These efforts have paid real dividends: the long-standing survey of incoming freshman students at the University of California, Los Angeles (UCLA), indicates that more than 83 percent reported having volunteered in their senior year of high school in 2003, up from 66 percent in 1989.[18] We applaud this important and successful presidential leadership.

Putnam recognizes this promising trend, acknowledging that volunteering is "sailing . . . boldly against the tide of civic disengagement."[19] Yet he cautions against generalizing from recent patterns. His careful statistical analysis also uncovers a disproportionate amount of volunteering from older Americans—the "greatest generation," whose experiences with or memories of the depression and World War II have given them a distinctive inclination toward many forms of political activity and civic engagement. It remains to be seen whether the impressive levels of volunteering among the young presages the sort of sustained commitment to civic activity that has long characterized the greatest generation.

The quality of volunteer experiences appears to vary a great deal. Political scientist Jeffrey Brudney notes that many organizations devote scant resources to the appropriate staffing, training, and supervision of volunteers. According to a survey commissioned by United Parcel Service that asked 1,000 respondents about their volunteer experiences, roughly 40 percent of volunteers indicated that they had stopped going to a position because they were dissatisfied with the way their program was managed. Their most frequent complaints were poor use of their time, poor use of their skills, and poor definition of their tasks.[20]

Some worry that volunteerism and nonprofit association activity tend to bring into politics and public life values that are private, sectarian, or conflictual, such as religious convictions or particular ideological visions. Some worry that for these reasons volunteerism (or some forms of it at least) will weaken norms of consensus building, inclusiveness, and tolerance. Others laud volunteer efforts through churches and other nonprofits precisely because these may present an ideal blend of private values and initiative with public action in ways not available to public institutions alone. E. J. Dionne characterizes nonprofits as an engine of empowerment and social cohesion, connecting important conservative aspects of our public culture (including religion) and liberal aspects of our public culture (including traditions of popular political action and the empowerment of all citizens).[21] In Dionne's view, nonprofits tend to help bridge important social divisions and are, in effect, consensus builders.

Volunteerism appears to have qualitative properties that distinguish it from other modes of civic engagement, such as political activity. On the one hand, volunteer service activity tends to be local, particular, direct, and ameliorative: serving a hungry person a meal, caring for the injured, or rebuilding local playgrounds, for example. On the other hand, civic engagement involving partisan or mobilizing work, such as campaigning for food subsidies, raising money for particular causes, or organizing a low-income community food bank, tends to be more systemic: aimed at transforming law or policy or altering the general conditions of society. This reveals different aspects of the multifaceted role of the citizen. Straightforwardly political activity calls for participants to shape the laws and policies that govern all and, hence, holds out the possibility of broad-gauged public solutions to social problems. In volunteer activities, however, we typically join with others to address directly a common and particular problem: to help the poor or make a neighborhood safer or cleaner. We do not disparage either sort of activity—to the contrary, we think both are necessary and applaud each—but they are different sorts of activity, and it is worth asking how they tend to be related.

What, in particular, do we make of the fact that volunteering has been growing, while the more political forms of civic engagement, such as voting and party involvement, have been stagnating or declining? Perhaps volunteering and more directly political forms of engagement are, in fact, inversely related: volunteering might be a substitute for political action, a relationship that would link the promotion of volunteer activities to a disparagement of politics. Aggregate-level evidence of such inverse trends exists and is especially striking among the young. A UCLA study of incoming freshmen, which documents rising levels of volunteering, also shows, for example, steadily declining levels of interest and activity in political party involvement. This suggests that volunteering has become a de facto substitute for citizenship: not a bridge, but an alternative to those forms of engagement most closely associated with politics.[22]

Moreover, it is unclear exactly how much of the increase in volunteering among the young reflects their increased interest in such activity. Many high schools now require volunteering in order to graduate. Service learning—the integration of community service activity with academic learning in the classroom—has blossomed over the past generation. Even in the absence of required volunteer hours or service learning courses, many students may view volunteering as a necessary form of résumé building, believing that universities and colleges expect to see evidence of community service in the application of successful students. So what should we make of the evidence of increased volunteering among the young?

As we mention briefly in chapter two, we should be optimistic, not pessimistic, about the connection between volunteering and political engagement. The individual-level evidence to date shows that people who volunteer, including youth, are more, not less, likely to engage in political activity and that volunteers are less likely to feel alienated from public institutions.[23] For example, the 1998 National Assessment of Educational Progress Report Card indicates that students who engage in any kind of community service—through school or on their own—have higher scores in civic knowledge than those who do not volunteer. After a review of the scholarly literature, Diana Owen concludes that service learning programs can be effective in fostering political participation.[24]

Whether service learning programs do foster political engagement depends in large part on their design. The hallmarks of successful service learning programs are by now well known: they consciously engage teachers and students in civic outcomes and not merely academic performance; they allow students to work on public policy issues; they give students a choice about their community service; they help them to see results within a reasonable amount of time; they provide regular opportunities for reflection on their service work; and they allow students to pursue explicitly political projects and outcomes. Thoughtful service learning programs that satisfy these criteria appear to be very promising vehicles for forging positive links between volunteering and increased political engagement.[25]

Like associational life in general, nonprofits provide opportunities for individuals to move beyond solitary, familial, and self-interested pursuits. Lester Salamon captures this dynamic:

> Like the arteries of a living organism, [nonprofits] carry a life force that has long been a centerpiece of American culture—a faith in the capacity of individual action to improve the quality of human life. They thus embody two seemingly contradictory impulses that form the heart of American character: a deep-seated commitment to freedom and individual initiative and an equally fundamental realization that people live in communities and consequently have responsibilities that extend beyond themselves. Uniquely among American institutions, those in the nonprofit sector blend these competing impulses, creating a special class of entities dedicated to mobilizing *private initiative for the common good.*[26]

Philanthropies and charitable nonprofits (which include civic associations, churches, many hospitals, schools, and cultural institutions) are among the principal means through which Americans try, in conjunction with others, to do good in this world.

Consider the size of the nonprofit sector. It employs almost 11 million people (or more than 7 percent of the American workforce), enlists another 5.7 million as full-time volunteers, and accounts for about 6 percent of the national income.[27] The vast majority of volunteers (about 75 percent) serve in nonprofits. Most of the remaining quarter work for government, although this figure does not adequately convey government's massive and growing dependence on volunteer labor.[28] Nonprofits have become the foot soldiers of social service provision, and this raises important issues for civic life.[29]

Nonprofit organizations are the recruitment agencies and entry points for the volunteer activities of many individuals. Some people sit on the boards of nonprofits and devote time to governing these organizations and mobilizing our communities around their goals. A large percentage of nonprofits provide social services; these often rely on public funding, thereby linking citizens and government. Beyond service delivery, many nonprofits engage in policy advocacy, bringing public attention to any number of social, political, environmental, and other concerns. Finally, a very large percentage of Americans (89 percent) make charitable donations, another form of care for the community; these must be directed to a certain class of nonprofits if they are to qualify for a charitable tax deduction.

People seeking to volunteer have a wide variety of options because many parts of the nonprofit sector have experienced dramatic growth over the past generation. The sector as a whole has come to include a vast array of organizations.[30] Peter Frumkin notes, "The nonprofit and voluntary sector is home to such a wide range of organizations that grouping them together into one entity is highly problematic."[31] This domain includes, for instance, half of hospitals, over a third of health clinics, more than a quarter of nursing homes, and 80 percent of individual and family service agencies. It also includes churches, charities, foundations, institutions of higher education, museums, operas, orchestras, theaters, think tanks, youth groups, social service organizations, neighborhood associations, parent-teacher associations, civic associations, arts councils, community development corporations, unions, trade associations, or any number of other types of organizations that fall outside the sphere of for-profit business or government. For purposes of this chapter, we pay special attention to nonprofits that provide social services. We do this for two reasons: first, along with religious organizations they are the largest class of nonprofits in the United States, and second, they have the potential to address the equality dimension of civic engagement. Nonprofit service providers can offer their poor and disadvantaged clients an avenue to become more engaged in civic life.

Public policy has played a large role in spurring the growth of nonprofit social service delivery in America. Given the growing pressure on government over the past quarter century to appear "lean and mean," it should come as no surprise that many ostensible government functions have been subcontracted to nonprofits, what Paul Light calls the "shadow of government."[32] As welfare policy has turned more and more away from income maintenance and toward social services, nonprofits have become increasingly important. The passage of welfare reform in 1996, designed to "end welfare as we know it," shifted even more responsibility to nonprofits. Temporary Assistance for Needy Families set strict time limits on eligibility for welfare and required many recipients to enroll in job training programs. This, in turn, led to more government support for nonprofits providing services to the disadvantaged. This shift in domestic policy broadened the ability of nonprofits to offer civic education and engagement opportunities to clients who may be poorly tied to their community. For example, when Chicago's Bottomless Closet offers a program of skill development, training for job interviews, and clothes to wear at work, it initiates a process that not only educates its clients but also begins to connect them to the outside world. With the increase in government funds available for training and social services, private sector organizations are increasingly competing with nonprofits for government contracts in some select areas such as child care and home health care.[33]

There can be no doubt that the United States possesses one of the most robust nonprofit sectors in the world. In comparison with other developed countries and measured by percentage of all employment, the United States has an atypically large share of its labor force working in the nonprofit sector. When volunteers are added to paid nonprofit employees, the United States stands out even more. At the same time, the share of nonprofit revenue provided by the government is considerably less in this country than it is in other industrial nations.[34]

America's growing reliance on the nonprofit sector affects how individuals relate to government. Nonprofits have the potential to play an increasingly significant role in engaging and mobilizing citizens, but their capacity to play a role in bolstering civic and political engagement depends on the rules under which they operate.

How Policy Creates and Regulates Nonprofits

Crucial to the formation of the nonprofit sector is the dual-prong preferential tax treatment that the federal government provides to one subset of nonprofits, namely, public charities, or the so-called 501(c)(3)s, a moniker derived from the section of the federal tax code defining and governing them.[35] In order to qualify for 501(c)(3) status, organizations must be "operated exclusively for religious, charitable, scientific, testing for public safety, literary, or educational purposes."[36] The first tax advantage is shared by all nonprofits: exemption from federal taxation on income (for example, fees from services, such as tuitions collected at universities or payments at nonprofit hospitals). The second tax advantage is limited to 501(c)(3) organizations. Since 1917, federal income tax law has offered tax deductibility for contributions to 501(c)(3)s because they are organizations that, presumably, do work so beneficial to the public good that they deserve this subsidy. Tax-deductible charitable donations are a subsidy because they result in a loss of tax revenue to the government, money that otherwise would be collected and allocated or distributed in accordance with the collective democratic decisions of citizens and their representatives.

Consider what the charitable deduction means in concrete terms for a would-be donor. The mechanism of a deduction from taxable income creates a subsidy at the rate at which the donor is taxed. Thus a person who occupies the top tax bracket—currently 35 percent—would find that a $1,000 donation actually "cost" her only $650. The government effectively pays $350 of her donation by subtracting this amount from her tax burden. Because the government is involved in paying, albeit indirectly and only partially, for the charitable donation, these deductions may be thought of as a tax expenditure, something on a budgetary or fiscal par with a direct expenditure. Such tax expenditures are common devices deployed to funnel funds to specific activities or to encourage certain kinds of behavior; the mortgage deduction is perhaps the best known such expenditure.

Close to one million 501(c)(3)s are registered with the Internal Revenue Service (IRS).[37] It is very difficult to gauge the level of activity of these organizations, as most are small and run entirely by volunteers—the threshold for registering is just $5,000 in annual income. The threshold for having to file a tax return is $25,000 in annual income, and just under 250,000 nonprofits surpass that threshold. All religious organizations are exempt from IRS filing requirements, regardless of their size.

These organizations are the face of charity in the United States. The 501(c)(3) nonprofit has become the organizational template of choice in community life, and their tax-exempt status and ability to offer tax deductibility to donors confer enormous legitimacy and decided advantages on them. Entrepreneurs wanting to form a group to address neighborhood problems have every reason to establish their new organization as a public charity.

Although charities and other nonprofits make up what is often labeled the "independent sector," these organizations arise and operate within a thickly textured skein of law. The federal government regulates nonprofits in at least four ways (and there are state laws analogous to the federal laws, too numerous to catalog here). Some regulations promote transparency, integrity, and accountability, like campaign finance or lobbying disclosure rules. Other regulations referee participation, such as labor union organizing rules or standing requirements for litigants. A third type of regulation shapes incorporation by drawing certain types of groups into the policymaking process. Laws like the Federal Advisory Committee Act and the Negotiated Rulemaking Act are important means of bringing citizen groups into bargaining forums where administrative regulations are written and revised. Finally, the government sometimes acts to promote and even subsidize associations. A well-known example is the Department of Agriculture's nurturing of farm groups in the early part of the twentieth century. As we saw in chapter three, the focus on urban problems in the 1960s brought about community action programs, and, today, community development corporations (CDCs) are able to take advantage of unique financing opportunities designed to promote them as middlemen in neighborhood development.

The many nonprofits that deliver social services interact regularly with state and local governments and public officials at all levels, and some participate in politics via hearings, meetings, comment periods, advisory panels, reporting requirements, and so forth. The staffs and volunteers of nonprofits are vital conduits of information between public agencies and those who need social services: nonprofits thus respond to important social needs and are natural participants in the process of making and assessing public policy. As important as their actual and potential role is, they also face significant restrictions on their capacity to participate in politics.

Regulations governing nonprofits can affect the quantity, quality, and equality of their general activity and their participation in politics more specifically. Particularly striking evidence of the relationship between law and nonprofit activity comes from the comparison between growth rates of 501(c)(3) nonprofits and those of other types of organizations. Between 1987 and 1997, 501(c)(3) nonprofits grew by 64.2 percent.[38] By comparison, during the same period, the 501(c)(4) nonprofits, which include avowed citizen advocacy groups and are not entitled to offer donors tax deductibility, grew by just 2 percent. Hence, the lion's share of the growth in this area is concentrated among nonprofits that are limited in their capacity to mobilize civic activity among their constituents and clients to influence policy.

In other ways as well, public rules influence the health of organizations and their capacity for political voice—and thereby the distribution of participation across the population. Unions often have been important schools of instruction to working-class men and women. Many scholars are concerned about the declining proportion of the workforce that holds membership in a union, although too few study the complex web of rules and limitations that govern union activities. In contrast, business associations, despite some regulations particularly in the area of campaign finance, have plentiful opportunities to participate in public policymaking and to involve their members. We discuss the rules affecting labor unions later in this chapter.

Over time, government has cut back on formal opportunities for citizen participation through public involvement programs mandating various types of hearings and meetings with members of the community. Nevertheless, it has shown increasing skill in learning how to work with citizen groups critical of its programs. In their recent study of "mega-projects," Alan Altshuler and David Luberoff find that recognizing the legitimate interests of citizen groups and demonstrating a commitment to negotiating seriously with them are critical to the successful siting of very large and disruptive public works projects.[39] In her comparative study of growth politics in Pittsburgh and Chicago, Barbara Ferman documents the advantages of a process that emphasizes cooperating with citizen groups rather than confronting them.[40] Clarence Stone and his coauthors advance similar arguments: local governments' capacity to govern depends on "civic capacity," which means the ability of local stakeholders, including business groups and community leaders, to mobilize and coalesce on behalf of reforms.[41]

The broader point is simple: citizen organizations, including nonprofits, matter in promoting successful and legitimate self-governance, including the formation of social policy and the delivery of social services. These organizations should help to organize, express, and represent the interests of important segments of the population, including those who need public services. Public incentives shape the formation of civic groups of one sort or another, and government policy may also hinder or encourage political communication and advocacy, thereby influencing the quantity, quality, and equality of political and civic activity.

Reshaping the Civic Context for Associations

A wide range of public policy measures affect the ability of associations to become involved in public affairs and, in turn, to involve and educate their members. We seek to discern ways of reshaping public policy and redesigning institutions in order to facilitate volunteering, expand philanthropy, link citizens to government, promote community involvement in neighborhood problem solving and government policymaking, and, in sum, build better citizenship.

We take up six important areas of public policy involving associations and civic engagement, focusing on the rules affecting participation. We begin with an examination of the incentives relating to philanthropy, then move on to laws regulating public charities and voluntary associations that may involve lobbying, followed by analyses of issues pertaining to accountability and governance of nonprofit organizations and foundations, the question of charitable choice (the public funding of faith-based organizations that deliver social services), the role of unions in civic engagement, and national service programs. Each of these topics involves current debates about the role of associational life and the nonprofit sector in the larger civic life of the United States.

INCENTIVES AND PHILANTHROPY

Large numbers of Americans donate money, time, goods, and services to charitable causes. Public policy encourages this activity through federal and state tax laws: donations to charities are generally tax deductible. Monetary and asset donations are the easiest to measure. In 2003 total charitable gifts in the United States amounted to over $240 billion, of which almost 75 percent came from individuals (the remainder from foundations, corporations, and bequests).[42] A remarkable 89 percent of American households made a charitable contribution in 2000, a striking level of participation.[43]

The total amount of giving has grown in recent decades, even when adjusted for inflation. However, it is notable that, despite the growth in philanthropy, individual giving as a share of personal income has declined over the past generation. And this decline has been largest among the richest Americans. Compared to 1980, taxpayers earning more than $1 million gave 70 percent less in 1994, taking into account increased wealth in constant dollars.[44]

Many extol the virtues of the charitable tax incentive because it funds private, innovative approaches to social problems as an alternative or supplement to government programs. Indeed, President George W. Bush announced that, although he would seek fundamental reform of the federal tax code, the charitable tax deduction was inviolate. Still, there is recognition that governmental incentives to give may need adjusting. Only those who itemize receive the deduction for charitable donations, and most low-income taxpayers take the standard deduction. Moreover, the vehicle of a tax deduction for donations results in what has been called "upside-down subsidies": the rate of the subsidy rises with the tax bracket of the donor and, thus, higher-income earners gain larger subsidies for their donations. Congress has debated (but has not yet passed) a charitable tax deduction of up to $250 for persons who do not itemize. A proposal along these lines in the 108th Congress would have increased the tax-deduction cap for the charitable contributions of corporations. The expansion of the charitable tax deduction to those who take the standard deduction or the creation of a flat-rate tax credit for charitable contributions might enlarge the pool of donors and could be a step toward greater civic engagement for those lower on the income scale. Another simple regulatory change that many believe would increase giving would be to allow tax filers to itemize and deduct in the prior tax year any charitable gifts made up through the April 15 deadline for filing federal income tax returns; a similar approach is used for contributions to individual retirement accounts.

On the important issue of stimulating more charitable contributions from wealthy individuals, the current debate over permanent elimination of the estate tax assumes great importance. The 2001 Tax Act gradually lifted the amount exempted from estate tax from $675,000 in 2002 to a total repeal of the estate tax in 2010. Congress will have to decide whether to make the increasing levels of exemption, or the total repeal, a permanent feature of the tax code. The estate tax has been assumed to provide wealthy individuals with a powerful incentive to make charitable contributions prior to their death; the rising exemption rate is thought, therefore, to decrease the incentive for donations. The Congressional Budget Office concludes that a repeal of the estate tax would decrease overall charitable contributions by 6 to 12 percent.[45] More concretely, these estimates indicate that, had the federal estate tax not existed in 2000, charitable giving would have decreased between $13 billion and $25 billion, a figure that represents more than the total amount that all corporations gave to charity in 2000. Doing away entirely with the federal estate tax has the strong potential, therefore, to worsen the distressing trend of less giving (as a percentage of income) among the wealthy.

PUBLIC CHARITIES

Public charities enhance our civic life and provide opportunities for citizen engagement in many ways. They are, however, limited in their ability to engage in political campaign activity and lobbying. For those who are concerned about the ability of nonprofits to act in politics—to express the political interests of clients and to mobilize those individuals who work and volunteer for nonprofits—the most pernicious regulation is the limitation on legislative lobbying and grassroots mobilization by 501(c)(3) nonprofits.

One problem is a simple lack of clarity. The law governing public charities says that nonprofits may not lobby to any "substantial" degree, but what constitutes "substantial" lobbying in this context? No IRS guidance elaborates on this standard, and the few judicial decisions on this question are also unclear. In practical terms, this means that nonprofits are left in the dark as to what proportion of their resources can be spent on trying to persuade legislators, how much of their leaders' time can be spent meeting with legislators they are trying to influence, or what kinds of grassroots campaigns may get them into trouble.

Compounding this lack of clarity is ignorance on the part of nonprofit leaders about what the law actually says. A high percentage of nonprofit executive directors believe the law is far more restrictive than it is. As a result of this misunderstanding, the advocacy of their organizations is much more limited than it needs to be.[46]

Here we must get a bit technical. In particular, and unbeknown to many 501(c)(3)s, there is an alternative to the ambiguous "substantial" standard for allowable direct lobbying and grassroots mobilization. The so-called "H election" permits most 501(c)(3) organizations to devote up to 20 percent of their budget to legislative advocacy.[47] And the H-election regulations offer clear and explicit definitions of what counts toward the lobbying limits. Further, many activities associated with lobbying, such as research, do not need to be counted toward the limit. Thus few 501(c)(3) nonprofits would bump up against the limits even with significant advocacy efforts. Most important, H electors do not lose the most precious asset of 501(c)(3) status: the right to offer tax deductions to contributors.

In spite of all of these advantages, only about 2 percent of 501(c)(3)s take the H election, largely because they remain ignorant of it or misunderstand it. The IRS deserves blame for not publicizing this option more widely, and nonprofit infrastructure organizations—those that train other nonprofits—should do more to bring the H election to light. Regardless of where the fault lies, it is clear that a high percentage of nonprofit executive directors believe the law is far more restrictive than it is.

Research by Jeffrey Berry and David Arons demonstrates that the law on public charities has a profound chilling effect on participation of nonprofits in public policymaking, reducing advocacy across a range of activities.[48] Companion interviews with the executive directors of a variety of nonprofits reveal a pattern of excessive caution in dealing with government: they worry that any transgression in this area will lead to an IRS revocation of their charitable status.

Although the most significant civic benefits of nonprofits involve the mobilization of clients and constituents, it is also significant that the professionals employed by nonprofits often represent the interests of clients through their own advocacy efforts. We would be remiss to ignore the work of nonprofits in representing their constituents in ways that do not directly involve them. This is especially significant because many nonprofits work with the most disadvantaged members of American society: the frail, elderly, immigrants, mentally retarded, children, battered women, the disabled, those without medical insurance, and the mentally ill. For some Americans, their connections to government and community affairs are going to be indirect at best. For these Americans, it is crucial that the organizations with an interest in representing them are not significantly restricted by the regulatory environment. Nonprofit political activity holds out the possibility of redress for some of the class-based participatory inequalities discussed earlier. And yet under current regulations, as Jeffrey Berry puts it, "Enron and the Teamsters Union have more rights in our political system than the Susan G. Komen Breast Cancer Foundation or the Children's Defense Fund."[49]

Nonprofits working on behalf of disadvantaged constituencies may also offer the disadvantaged a first step toward civic engagement. Our conception of engagement must be elastic enough to cover incipient steps toward participation by those who face real obstacles to personal involvement. Nonprofits in health and human services provide clients with a link to government in a number of ways. For the poor and many other disadvantaged constituencies, nonprofits are the source of government-sponsored services, thus making them a face of government to many of their clients.[50] Fully half of all nonprofits large enough to be required to file a tax return work in the area of health care or human services (see figure 4-1). Nonprofits can do a lot just by having service providers make it clear to clients where funding for services comes from: by accepting services from a nonprofit receiving government grants, a person is in effect interacting with the state. Beyond this, nonprofits can take concrete steps to convey civic and political information and assist in certain kinds of mobilization. For instance, the Codman Square Health Center in Boston registers voters, provides skill-building courses in its facilities, and even encourages clients to contact their legislators (along with providing information about how to do it). Those who are poor are not by definition apathetic, and our knowledge that the poor participate less than others should not become an assumption that they will not participate at all.[51]

No one would suggest that nonprofits should be able to do whatever they want with charitable donations; government regulation of 501(c)(3)s is entirely appropriate. Public charities should not be overtly partisan political organizations, and the ban on partisan electioneering should remain intact. Because federal and state governments provide a significant amount of funding for nonprofit organizations, especially for those that deliver social services, the question arises regarding the extent to which these public funds should be permitted to support legislative lobbying. We do not argue that nonprofits should make advocacy their central mission. Many 501(c)(3)s believe that they do not have sufficient resources to become involved in public policymaking or regard it as a low priority. Nevertheless, at a minimum, nonprofits should understand their rights under the law. The unnecessary uncertainties of the IRS rule barring "substantial" nonprofit lobbying, including grassroots mobilization, inhibit the capacity of nonprofits to involve and educate members, clients, and constituents. As it currently stands, the lobbying restrictions of section 501(c)(3) of the Internal Revenue Code are an enormous barrier to expanding civic engagement in America by the most disadvantaged and underrepresented Americans. We encourage the Internal Revenue Service to offer a specific definition of "substantial," to publicize the "H election" as a viable alternative to the substantial standard, and to offer nonprofits a choice between the two standards when an organization applies for 501(c)(3) status. As it is now, new nonprofits fall under the "substantial" criterion by default and have to seek out information on the H election and file a separate form requesting a change after qualifying as a public charity.

FIGURE 4-1 Proportion of America's Nonprofits, by Sector[a]

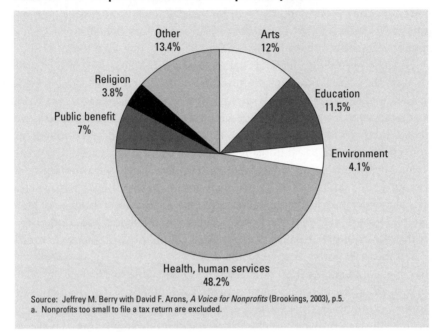

Source: Jeffrey M. Berry with David F. Arons, *A Voice for Nonprofits* (Brookings, 2003), p.5.
a. Nonprofits too small to file a tax return are excluded.

ACCOUNTABILITY AND GOVERNANCE

Discussions of nonprofit accountability—the integrity and transparency of their operations—have become pervasive; so too have discussions of nonprofit management, administration, and governance. These issues may seem disconnected from political and civic engagement. Yet these matters affect people's decisions regarding whether to donate or volunteer as well as how much to do so. They can affect the perceived legitimacy of nonprofits as providers of critical social services. Of course, we recognize that overly intrusive regulation may have a chilling effect on philanthropic activities.

Two types of accountability concern us here: financial and democratic. By financial accountability we refer to whether nonprofits spend their dollars wisely. The increased popularity of models of businesslike efficiency—expressed in the language of outcome measures, deliverables, and benchmarks—make this kind of accountability the most familiar and the most prominent within the independent sector. Democratic accountability refers to the means available to funders, clients, government officials, and the public at large to examine nonprofit operations: to make nonprofit operations transparent to the public. Unlike government officials who are subject to a number of important mechanisms of democratic accountability, nonprofits are largely exempt from such requirements. They are not even required to hold public board meetings. Sunlight does not seep into the windows of many nonprofits.

In recent years, foundations, in particular, have been subject to increased scrutiny of their operations, especially the transparency of their finances.[52] With close to 70,000 foundations in the United States and the number continuing to grow, the federal government has rightly instituted some guidelines governing accountability and the yearly amount, or payout, that each foundation is required to disburse every year. Many foundations remain tightly controlled by the families and corporations that created them, sometimes raising suspicions about their financial operations. Support has emerged in Congress for a revision of the payout rule, effectively raising the share of assets (currently set at a minimum of 5 percent) that must be expended each year. Such legislation reflects the widely held concern that foundations are too autonomous, spend too much on administrative overhead (costs that currently may be included in the 5 percent minimum annual payout), and are more interested in private gain or enrichment than in philanthropic endeavors for the public good.

A small number of well-publicized scandals have put the nonprofit world on the defensive. The post–September 11 revelations that the Red Cross was intending to use for general administrative expenses some of the money it raised for helping the victims' families resulted in furious denunciations of the organization. Financial improprieties by the president of the United Way more than a decade ago also raised real and embarrassing questions about accountability to donors.[53] There has been no shortage of exposés of small family foundations where boards of directors have enriched themselves at the foundation's expense, made unconscionably small payouts after expenses, and otherwise abandoned their fiduciary responsibilities.[54]

There is no question that scandals at foundations and other charities have eroded confidence in the integrity of philanthropies. Important legislators have displayed frustration with the independent sector because it is so unaccountable. At the same time, they know the challenge of passing legislation that would effectively protect against dishonest behavior by nonprofits. This only adds to their frustration. At a hearing on abuses in the charity world in June 2004, the chair of the Senate Finance Committee, Charles Grassley (R-Iowa), made little effort to restrain his anger: "It's obvious from the abuses we see that there's been no check on charities. Big money, tax free, and no oversight have created a cesspool in too many cases." Making the attack bipartisan, ranking member Max Baucus (D-Montana) added that the abuses among foundations and other nonprofits "are immoral and inexcusable—and threaten to taint the reputation of all charitable organizations."[55]

If hyperbole is evident here, so too is recognition of a serious problem. Even though it is surely the case that only a small percentage of charities has skirted or ignored ethical or legal boundaries, what has been uncovered is disturbing. The lack of confidence in the nonprofit and philanthropic sector voiced by policymakers has also been fueled by the defensiveness of nonprofit leaders who resist government regulation. Adam Meyerson, president of the Philanthropy Roundtable, called a Senate report completed by Grassley's committee a "spectacular overreach." Melissa Flournoy, head of the Louisiana Association of Nonprofit Organizations, criticized lawmakers as well: "By only focusing on the bad behavior of a few actors, this could lead to a dramatic overcorrection and overregulation."[56]

The ultimate consequence of unethical behavior may yet be federal legislation or new regulatory measures. Particularly striking is the lack of a federal nonprofit analog to the Sarbanes-Oxley law, passed in 2002 in the wake of scandals involving Enron, WorldCom, and other major corporations, which aimed to strengthen the audit and accountability requirements of corporations. There is a strong movement among nonprofits to voluntarily comply with some of the fundamentals of Sarbanes-Oxley. The most common steps are developing or strengthening conflict-of-interest prohibitions, internal financial controls, and codes of ethics. Establishing separate and independent audit committees, as required by Sarbanes-Oxley, is common as well. A recent survey has found that half of nonprofits have strengthened their corporate governance.[57] Some states, including California, have recently passed legislation to increase the accountability standards of nonprofits.

The reaction of government is but one worry. If the public continues to read about abuses in the nonprofit world, the level of charitable giving could be affected across the sector, as it has for individual organizations whose integrity has been questioned. Just as damaging would be a drop in volunteering. Community leaders and activists will not turn apathetic, but those who stretch the hours in the day may decide to serve on one less board, to take on one less responsibility. The newly rich, some of whom have worked to develop new philanthropic projects and start their own foundations rather than just donating to the usual suspects, may decide that such efforts are not worth their valuable time. This would be a terrible loss, and for that reason, the negative publicity concerning small family foundations remains a serious and ongoing concern for American philanthropy.

In addition to strengthening policies to assure the integrity and transparency of nonprofit operations, we should take general steps to improve nonprofit leadership and management. Leadership development in the nonprofit sector is often deficient, as has frequently been recognized.[58] During the 1980s, the Fund for the Improvement of Postsecondary Education sponsored innovative educational practices for volunteer training through leadership organizations such as the Red Cross, the Girl Scouts of America, the Junior League, the YWCA, the National Council of Negro Women, and the Lutheran Social Mission Society.[59] Such efforts need continuing public support because volunteerism and nonprofit performance can strengthen democratic fundamentals.

Millions of volunteers serve on nonprofit boards, and this is a vital form of civic engagement in every American community. Boards are, of course, instrumental in raising money, but they are used for many specialized tasks beyond this. Approximately 40 percent of nonprofits have at least one advisory group beyond their board of directors.[60] Given their duties, it is not surprising that nonprofit board members tend to be community elites. Laws requiring citizen participation in various government-sponsored nonprofit programs sometimes mandate that a significant portion of boards must come from the community. This is understood to mean that the board must include those with low incomes and reflect the ethnic and racial diversity of the neighborhood or city. Federal regulations, for example, require that at least 50 percent of the boards of community health centers be composed of patients.

Like most other organizations, nonprofits select their own boards. It is not uncommon for small foundations to be dominated by family members of the donor or family agents chosen for their loyalty. In neither case do citizens have any formal point of access for participation, even though the operation of nonprofits and foundations so frequently touches their lives in direct ways. For example, a trio of foundations in Pittsburgh decided in 2002 to suspend grantmaking to the Pittsburgh public school district and to withhold $3 million of a $12 million prior commitment. Their stated aim was to prod the district into making important structural reforms. This private decision had serious repercussions for all public schoolchildren in Pittsburgh: the foundations' money was directed at reading and literacy programs, teacher training, and technology support, and some of the district's government grants were contingent on receiving foundation money. Yet in spite of the broad public impact, citizens had no role in this decision.[61]

Important questions about accountability and governance of 501(c)(3) nonprofits in general also merit attention. Their favorable tax status and significant levels of direct government grant support might argue for the appropriateness of significant public oversight. One helpful mechanism for such oversight is the fact that 501(c)(3) organizations must make their tax returns public, and these IRS Form 990 tax returns typically are available online. Generally, however, the accountability of nonprofits to the public is highly attenuated and indirect. Aside from regulations on finances and political activities, there are few public requirements to which nonprofits and foundations are held. The boards of nonprofits are supposed to be the public's accountability mechanism, but nonprofit boards do not always function effectively and many are used primarily for fundraising. If nonprofits are not accountable to the public, neither are they accountable to clients. The clients of social service organizations in particular—the disproportionately marginalized and dispossessed—are rarely in a position to demand better performance.

Another bar to effective collaboration between nonprofits and public agencies is weakness in the national capacity to monitor and evaluate public policies coproduced by these organizations. As program implementation increasingly devolves to nonprofit organizations, we risk the loss of centralized record keeping and data gathering, which are necessary for measuring performance. There is a conspicuous need for a national survey focusing on nonprofits and volunteers analogous, say, to the National Election Studies Series, which has produced high-quality data on voting, public opinion, and political participation for more than five decades. If better information is needed, so too is better leadership education. Increasingly, the graduate programs in public administration and in nonprofit management are recognizing the degree to which public goals are now met through coproduction—operating partnerships of nonprofit organizations and the public sector—and are introducing into their curricula attention to training on both sides of this relationship.[62] We endorse this trend.

The issues of nonprofit accountability and governance are important and complex. It is central to the dynamism of the sector that individuals and small groups be able to form nonprofits or establish foundations that are dedicated to the inventive and even eccentric ideas of their founders. A great virtue of the nonprofit sector is that it operates in the public interest without the larger bureaucracy of government agencies and their attendant regulatory burdens. However, as nonprofits and foundations have assumed a larger role in society and increasingly influence the lives of Americans, there is greater reason to hold them accountable, to insist on transparency of operations, and to encourage forms of democratic governance. We cannot answer the question of where the balance should be struck, but the guiding principle can be expressed in simple terms: although nonprofits of all sorts, especially foundations, want to protect their ability to promote the aims they favor, there should always be a role for broad, sustained, and meaningful community participation in the oversight and assessment of their operations.

CHURCHES

Places of worship are central to the civic life of America, playing a dual role in civic education and engagement. They are, at their core, among the most common and enduring forms of associational life. Beyond serving as a gathering place for the faithful, churches also have long played a central role in the delivery of social services to needy citizens, and the issue of public funding for social service provision by faith-based organizations has recently become a prominent feature of public policy debate.

It is important to recognize that religious organizations vary a great deal. It is no exaggeration to say that churches are as diverse as the country itself in their demography, theology, and ideology.[63] Some embrace political involvement, others skirt the edges of it, while still others avoid it studiously. Some go so far as to encourage their members to withdraw from the public square altogether. On balance, however, churches do more to push their members into civic life than to pull them out of it.

Although there is considerable variation by individual congregation and denomination, churches provide individual churchgoers with the skills, opportunities, and motivations for participation in political activity. Churches offer opportunities to learn the skills necessary for effective political engagement, such as running meetings, giving speeches, and writing letters.[64] For many low-income Americans whose educational background and jobs have not provided training in such skills, churches play a valuable role in equipping them to make their voices heard in the public square. Churches do more than just teach skills, however. They also foster social networks and, thus, are also important venues for political mobilization.[65]

Among African Americans, churches have long served as a primary conduit for the rise of a cadre of black leaders and also for the mobilization of voters, who, in turn, have facilitated their election to public office. There is a reason so many candidates for office—black and white—regularly visit black churches during the campaign season. Politicians recognize the role of churches as political mobilizers within the African American community.[66] Beyond their mobilization efforts, in the post–civil rights era, black urban churches are performing yet another civic function: taking the sanctuary to the streets to engage in collective efforts of community development aimed at revitalizing the economic, social, and political conditions of inner-city neighborhoods.[67] Similarly, churches are often the central civic association within Latino communities and thus provide an important channel for Latinos' full participation in the nation's civic and political life.[68] Churches often successfully partner with other organizations to accomplish civic ends. Organizations like the Industrial Areas

Foundation are able to leverage the institutional resources of churches and other faith-based institutions in promoting the activism of racial minorities and the disadvantaged.[69]

In addition to equipping individuals to express themselves in the political process, many churches, particularly in urban areas, also contribute to their community by providing social services to the disadvantaged. For example, in a recent national survey of congregations, Mark Chaves and William Tsitsos find that 58 percent of churches provide some type of social service. Although this is a lower percentage than suggested by some other sources, it still represents a huge investment in assistance to people in need.[70]

At the same time, the level of commitment to social services by individual congregations is far more modest than the "58 percent" figure suggests. Chaves and Tsitsos also note, "Only 6 percent of congregations have a staff person devoting at least 25 percent time to social service projects."[71] Some confusion arises because a considerable amount of denomination- and congregation-based service provision comes not from churches but from separate nonprofits created for that purpose. Organizations like Catholic Charities and Jewish Family Services obtain government funding for various programs they administer, and no controversy exists over such support. Little government support goes directly to the nation's religious congregations—only 3 percent of which receive any government funding.[72] A significant number of churches disavow government funding for social service delivery or any other purpose because they believe that accepting such funds will lead to government influence over them.

The movement toward expanding the role of churches and religiously affiliated 501(c)(3) organizations in the delivery of social services received a major boost with the passage of welfare reform in 1996 and the "charitable choice" provision included in it. Charitable choice was designed to clear obstacles making it difficult for churches to receive government funds for social service programs. On taking office, President George W. Bush expanded the effort to direct federal money to social service providers with a religious character by establishing the White House Office of Faith-Based and Community Initiatives and related offices in five federal agencies.[73] The initiative has now been extended to ten federal agencies. These offices are designed to promote the role of faith-based organizations in social service delivery, help them to understand grant procedures, and aid them in navigating the bureaucracy.

We do not attempt here to offer an account of the most effective and appropriate way of delivering social services or to settle the many questions surrounding President Bush's faith-based initiatives. We believe that policymakers can fashion appropriate policies that allow for broader participation of faith-based nonprofits in social service delivery, while not engaging in affirmative action for faith-based organizations. The efforts of government grantmakers to aggressively pursue and assist religious groups, but not others, are ill-conceived, as they tilt what should be a level playing field. Religious organizations are a vital and enduring source of civic engagement, and ways can be found to enlist their energies further while still respecting the fairness toward all that underlies our constitutional principles regarding churches and the public sphere. Members of churches and participants in faith-based organizations are to be applauded for the massive contributions they are making to political and civic mobilization and to efforts to address a host of social ills. America's civic landscape would be far poorer without the crucial role played by people of faith.

UNIONS

Churches are the most common form of associational involvement for Americans. But the workplace is yet more pervasive, and associations tied to the workplace, such as occupational and labor organizations, can similarly foster civic skills and engagement. Indeed, labor unions are famous for their efficacy in political mobilization.[74] Participation in a union, like active membership in a church, may help citizens to acquire civic skills and resources, including civically useful connections, and thereby lead to many forms of participation and engagement. There is some evidence of a relationship between rates of union membership and electoral turnout; one study claims that "each percentage point of the workforce organized elevates turnout by 0.4 percent ... [and] every percentage point decline costs just under half a percentage point of turnout."[75] This figure may be exaggerated, but it is certainly true that major associations like the American Federation of Labor-Congress of Industrial Organizations (AFL-CIO) do a tremendous amount of outreach to members leading up to elections: these efforts aim to register voters, disseminate information, and mobilize people to turn out to vote.[76]

It is also important to remember that organized political interests are liable to be more influential than unorganized interests: unions represent the interests of important segments of the population and hold out the possibility of partly redressing the significant class imbalance in many forms of political participation (the now-familiar fact that wealthier Americans participate at much higher levels and also contribute far more in campaign contributions). However, unions no longer represent as great a percentage of the workforce as they once did.

In 1954 more than one-third of wage and salary workers belonged to unions, despite the fact that public sector employees were still excluded from the right to bargain collectively under the umbrella of the National Labor Relations Act.[77]

(Agricultural workers still are today.) Despite the huge growth in public sector unions since the 1960s, union membership in 2003 constituted only 12.9 percent of all wage and salary workers, and the decline has been especially precipitous among private sector workers.[78] Whereas 37.2 percent of public sector workers belong to unions, only 8.2 percent of private sector wage and salary workers are union members.[79] Just since the 1970s the overall rate of union membership has fallen by half. Whereas increasing proportions of better-educated Americans belong to professional societies, there has been a sharp decline in blue-collar trade union membership. As some of our colleagues have put it in their report *American Democracy in an Age of Rising Inequality*, "The already privileged are better organized through occupational associations than the less privileged."[80] Union decline is worrisome with respect to its consequences for the amount as well as the distribution of both civic activity and political influence.

Union decline has many causes. It partly reflects the decline in manufacturing jobs and the increase in service sector jobs, traditionally the hardest to organize. It partly reflects a decline in the demand of potential members for unions and perhaps also a lack of commitment by many unions to engage in serious organizing. The cost of organizing additional workers may be high. But it is at least partially the result of the outdated legal framework in which unions must organize. The National Labor Relations Act (1935) and the more restrictive Taft-Hartley Act (1947) and Landrum-Griffin Act (1959) are still the reigning laws, and they create numerous obstacles to organizing. This is particularly clear when we compare American labor regulations with those in many European countries.[81] New rules could help unions to grow, as we suggest below.

Not only do unions have links to fewer people than in the 1950s and 1960s, they also are not, arguably, educating or mobilizing members (and their families) as effectively as they once did. There were once labor pages in the daily newspapers and reporters dedicated to the labor beat; the first is long gone and the second is almost nonexistent. Union halls and newspapers used to be far more important places for imparting political knowledge than they currently are, and central labor councils used to be much more integrated into local politics.[82] On the positive side, the AFL-CIO has developed intensive civic and economic education for its membership, and this has been carried out at the local level throughout the country. The AFL-CIO has also enhanced its lobbying efforts and ability.

David Greenstone famously argued that, by the late 1960s, the AFL-CIO had become a powerful campaign organization for the Democratic Party at the state and local level.[83] This remains true in a few cities and states, but most union-based lobbying, pressure politics, and get-out-the-vote campaigns were weak or moribund at both the national and local level by the mid-1990s. In addition to mobilizing, traditional union lobbying efforts have focused primarily on legislation that will significantly affect their members. Since John Sweeney and the "New Voices" team took office in 1996, the AFL-CIO has renewed its emphasis on conducting social justice campaigns, mobilizing voters, and influencing the outcome of elections through votes, ad campaigns, and contributions—and with some increased success.[84] The labor movement often joins with other social justice groups to push for changes in government policies and laws that will affect migrants, the unemployed, and others who are not necessarily dues-paying members. Organized labor has been a key partner in living wage campaigns and antisweatshop campaigns around the country.[85] Unions are important organizations for representing the interests of the less privileged, and we support the efforts of unions to foster civic participation by amplifying the voice of working-class people.

We acknowledge that unions often have not fulfilled their civic potential. Internally, unions have not lived up to their democratic promise: they have tended to be oligarchical and dominated, at the leadership level, by white males. There are far too many examples of racism, sexism, corruption, and xenophobia, at least among some unions some of the time. They have often lagged in organizing minorities and women. Nevertheless, unions are one of the few forces that speak out for workers and provide a countervailing force to better organized business interests.

There are still approximately 15.8 million union members. Many of them are young, poor, and people of color. Certainly the 2004 presidential campaign revealed a significant labor presence in grassroots mobilization (as it did for churches as well). The labor movement may have declined in its potential to provide civic education and voter turnout, but it remains an important mobilizing organization with the potential for doing more. We identify ways of reinvigorating the role of unions as civic mobilizers in our recommendations at the close of the chapter.

NATIONAL SERVICE

Although volunteerism remains widespread in America, we hear frequent calls to increase or enhance it, especially among young people. Among the more ambitious are proposals to provide opportunities for, or even to require, a sustained period of service, which many believe can be a life-changing experience.

The federal government has promoted various forms of service. Most significantly, military service is often regarded as a powerful instrument of civic education; at least as implemented during World War II, it is credited with creating bonds among citizens of widely different social classes, regions, religions, and ethnicities. Similarly, the Civilian Conservation Corps, instituted by President Franklin Roosevelt during the depression, gave "500,000 jobless young men the opportunity to live and serve in the nation's parks and forests."[86] John Kennedy established the Peace Corps as an opportunity for Americans to serve abroad. Lyndon Johnson created a domestic service program, Volunteers in Service to America (VISTA), as part of the War on Poverty. Although the number of Peace Corps volunteers never reached much above 15,000, idealists in this era argued that some significant period of citizen service should be the common expectation for all Americans.

Early in his first term in office, President Clinton proposed a national program of voluntary service in exchange for modest stipends and college aid. AmeriCorps, as the program was dubbed, would be a domestic Peace Corps, mainly but not exclusively for the young. Among the goals were "getting socially important work done, instilling an ethic of sacrifice, helping troubled youths turn their lives around, reducing the barriers between different races and classes, and reinvigorating an assortment of civic virtues."[87] Clinton hoped for a program that would enroll 500,000 volunteers for a cost of $8 billion a year; what he got when the bill finally passed Congress was $300 million for the first year, which was enough to fund 20,000 volunteers.[88]

In return for a year of full-time service, AmeriCorps contributes $9,700 toward an enrollee's living allowance (which can be supplemented from other sources). A year of service also entitles an enrollee to an education award of $4,725. Some AmeriCorps volunteers have worked in federal environmental agencies, but most work with local voluntary groups, community youth and after-school programs, and nonprofits such as Big Brothers/Big Sisters and the YMCA. Members of Teach for America and City Year also receive AmeriCorps funding.

In addition to AmeriCorps, President Clinton created the Corporation for National and Community Service, which manages a portfolio of federal government grants to organizations that promote volunteering (including the National Senior Service Corps, the Retired and Senior Volunteer Program, and the Foster Grandparents Program), and Learn and Serve America, which provides grants to schools to develop service learning programs.

Critics often fasten on the ideas of paid service and of government aid to charities and nonprofits. Government support for charitable work will make charities dependent on government assistance, critics charge, and vulnerable to political and bureaucratic whims. AmeriCorps, in particular, could give the federal government a "management position" in the social service sector. Service is a vital force in America because it is decentralized and privately organized.

With government aid comes government regulation of various sorts, and charitable institutions could lose their moral and religious anchors and eventually their ability to attract the energetic engagement of volunteers. Indeed, paid national service transforms the notion of freely given service arising from personal duty into work that is paid for by the government.[89] Martin Anderson indicts "paid volunteerism" as an oxymoron.[90]

So why, then, do we advocate "paid volunteerism"? Why not leave community service to purely volunteer efforts and the professional staffs of not-for-profit organizations? In many ways, this is the nub of the issue. AmeriCorps volunteers appear to fill an important "in-between" need for many organizations. The typical charitable organization must depend on two types of personnel: volunteers who give a limited amount of time, along with a small number of full-time paid professionals. AmeriCorps volunteers are neither paid professionals nor pure volunteers. Training is provided by the service agency in which they are employed, and there is an expectation of at least one year's full-time service. The idea is that AmeriCorps members will have some of the staying power and expertise of professionals, along with the energy and commitment of volunteers.

Worries about government attempts to promote or even mandate voluntary activity are worth taking seriously, but there is little evidence that government involvement has seriously compromised the integrity and independence of nonprofit organizations. Many nonprofits receive significant funding from the government. Although they are certainly cautious in taking actions or stands that might offend their funding agency, there is little evidence to support the idea that long-standing government aid has sapped the spirit of public charities.

While funds and broad guidelines come from Washington, a serious effort has been made to preserve the spirit of local initiative. AmeriCorps is administered largely by state commissions that allocate funds on the basis of proposals submitted by local agencies and organizations, including religious organizations (although funds may not be used for religious purposes). Thus the program tries to ensure that initiatives come from the local level.

In the wake of the terrorist attacks of September 11, 2001, President George W. Bush called for a renewal of citizenship in the form of service. In his 2002 State of the Union Address, "Bush called for 4,000 hours—or two years—of service by every American and asked for a doubling of the Peace Corps and a 50 percent increase in AmeriCorps in one year, from 50,000 to 75,000 members."[91] He reorganized AmeriCorps into Freedom Corps, a new umbrella organization to coordinate the range of federal service programs, including Senior Corps and the Peace Corps. Bush asserted that Freedom Corps "provided the answer to the post–September 11th question: 'What can I do to help?'"[92] However, in the face of the yawning budget deficits that followed his tax cuts and the economic downturn of 2002, Congress changed course and proposed not an increase but a substantial cut in the national service budget.

We applaud well-designed national service programs such as the Peace Corps, AmeriCorps, and Senior Corps. More research needs to be done on the lifelong effects on civic engagement of participation in such programs. We know that volunteering tends to increase political participation, but little is known about the additional effects of national service. Are the people who join national service programs already active and engaged citizens? Several studies on Teach for America, for instance, document a small increase in civic engagement after the years of service. Researchers also identify a phenomenon called "compassion fatigue," in which service providers refrain from engaging in voluntary activities directly following a period of service. In short, prior to recommending a massive expansion of national service programs, especially one that would be mandatory rather than voluntary, much more research is necessary.

Even so, the existing programs are clearly doing a wealth of good and at relatively low expense. Federal efforts to make some form of service an expectation for all Americans, across all ages, are to be encouraged, as many in both major parties have long recognized.

What Is to Be Done?

We believe that associational life strengthens democracy and that this realm of civic engagement is promoted and constrained by government regulation. Policymakers have the ability and the opportunity to shape the regulatory framework governing nonprofit organizations in ways that encourage their creation, enhance their longevity, increase their transparency, and promote a citizenry that is more politically active and engaged. To be sure, we should be encouraged by the rising number of volunteers in this country as well as by the growth of the nonprofit and philanthropic sector. But we should also be troubled by the well-documented trends in declining associational life—the civic decline described by Robert Putnam and others—as well as the replacement of mass membership organizations with professionally run groups that do not require active participation by their members.

We recognize that there is considerable disagreement among scholars about how to counteract some of these more troubling trends and how to build on the more promising trends, but we have attempted to make recommendations based on the best available evidence and scholarship. We have divided the recommendations according to the types of organizations that they affect.

PHILANTHROPY AND PUBLIC CHARITIES

The Internal Revenue Service should clarify vague rules that unnecessarily discourage advocacy by nonprofits afraid of losing their tax-deductibility status. It should, in particular, offer an explicit definition of what constitutes a "substantial" amount of lobbying for legislative and grassroots advocates. We have no specific recommendation for that definition, but the guidelines governing the H election are certainly satisfactory. In the absence of any such action by the IRS, we encourage nonprofits that are interested in advocacy to take the H election, which permits them to devote up to 20 percent of their budget to legislative advocacy while maintaining their right to offer tax deductions to contributors. The IRS should also do more to make nonprofits aware of the H alternative. With respect to individual charity, we believe that the expansion of the charitable tax deduction to those who take the standard deduction or the creation of a flat-rate tax credit for charitable contributions might enlarge the pool of donors and could be a step toward greater civic engagement for those lower on the income scale. In addition, the government should permit individuals to take deductions up until April 15th.

To review, then, our recommendations are threefold:

■ The Internal Revenue Service should offer an explicit definition of the "substantial" standard for legislative and grassroots advocacy and do more to make nonprofits aware of the H alternative.
■ Congress should consider permitting those who take the standard deduction to also deduct charitable contributions or to afford them the opportunity of a flat-rate tax credit for some contributions.
■ The IRS should permit individuals to take deductions for their charitable contributions made through April 15.

NONPROFIT ACCOUNTABILITY AND GOVERNANCE

We encourage nonprofits of all types to maximize the transparency of their finances and governance to increase the confidence of both the public and policymakers in the nonprofit and philanthropic sector. For example, they should develop or strengthen conflict-of-interest prohibitions, internal financial controls, and codes of ethics. They should also consider establishing separate and independent audit committees. We also encourage all nonprofits, especially foundations, to ensure that their boards of directors are broadly representative of the communities they serve, thus allowing for some form of citizen input into organizational oversight. Selection to boards should not be insular and, to maximize public accountability, the actions of boards should be as open as is practical. Another obstacle to effective oversight of nonprofits is the weakness in the national capacity to monitor and evaluate public policies coproduced by public and nonprofit organizations. The fact that more and more nonprofits are administering government programs means that record keeping and data gathering are less coordinated and less centralized. The federal government should initiate efforts to better evaluate public policies coproduced by nonprofits. In addition to maintaining better data, public agencies and schools of public administration should devote more attention to training administrators how to manage relationships between public and nonprofit agencies.

In brief, we recommend the following:

- Maximize the transparency of the finances and governance of all types of nonprofits.
- Ensure that the boards of directors of nonprofits are broadly representative of their communities.
- Initiate efforts on the part of the federal government to better evaluate public policies coproduced by nonprofits.
- Train administrators in public agencies and schools of public administration to manage relationships among public and nonprofit agencies.

CHURCH AND STATE

We applaud the involvement of churches in civic engagement and believe that religious organizations have an important role to play in civic engagement and in the delivery of social services. As a result, we should continue to encourage the important work of faith-based nonprofits, while still respecting the separation between church and state. We do not favor affirmative action for any category of nonprofit. Faith-based nonprofits that seek and obtain public funding should have the same opportunities and responsibilities as other nonprofit organizations.

In short, we offer the following recommendations:

- Find ways to encourage the work of faith-based nonprofits, while still respecting the separation between church and state.
- Ensure that faith-based and nonsectarian nonprofits that seek and obtain public funding play by the same rules.

UNIONS

We are troubled by the civic effects of the decline of unions, which have been important political mobilizers of working people. It is difficult for us to venture recommendations here because most important features of the American labor regime involve matters that take us far afield from our focus on civic engagement.

A possible relevant candidate for reform is the set of requirements that workers face to organize a union in the first place. To organize a new union requires an election at the workplace, which gives employers opportunities to intimidate workers and organizers, even to the point of engaging in illegal behavior. Penalties for firing or intimidating workers who support unionization are minor. The arbitrating institution, the National Labor Relations Board, is often ineffective in ensuring fair and open elections: it has been too slow to respond to complaints, and its technical rules and rulings have (at least some of us believe) been unreasonably hostile to unions.[93] Changing the rules so that a majority of workers could show support for a new union by signing cards or petitions could help to solve this problem. It might be preferable to strictly enforce laws prohibiting intimidation by employers. The process of participating in an election to decide whether to organize a union is itself an educative experience, after all, with possible spillover effects into civic engagement beyond the union. But we believe that decades of experience have shown that there is no way to prevent employers from intimidating workers or setting up unfair hurdles under the current laws.

The entire framework within which labor unions operate seems to inhibit their effectiveness as well as their ability to attract the support of workers, thus hampering their capacity to mobilize political activity among workers. In the United States, national labor law ensures that bargaining is generally decentralized and localized. The American labor regime insists on collective bargaining by specific unions in specific workplaces (bargaining units) rather than in whole firms or occupations or industries. Many European countries, in contrast, have centralized and coordinated bargaining, which correlates highly with higher union density, national labor movements, and unions far more engaged in the political process and in mobilizing voters among their membership.[94] With different laws in place, American unions might well increase union membership and their reach and role in encouraging workers to become engaged citizens. We acknowledge, however, that the connections between labor laws and civic activity are indirect and complex. Changes in the rules governing collective bargaining are worth considering, but we do not offer specific recommendations on this matter.

We recommend that the government should undertake the following:

▌ Ensure that workers can make the decision whether or not to unionize in an atmosphere that is free of harassment and intimidation.

NATIONAL SERVICE

Governments at all levels can provide opportunities for citizen and voluntary service. Most important, we call on the federal government to adequately fund a national service program. Various options are worth exploring. For some, service could be a rite of passage between high school and college, as it is for many better-off youngsters in the United Kingdom. Another option is a year or two of service after college, as is typically the case with AmeriCorps volunteers. We favor a variety of options for service, ranging from full-fledged military service to shorter fifteen- or eighteen-month enlistments—a "citizen soldier" option—involving such noncombat assignments as peacekeeping or humanitarian missions or homeland security. Regardless of the type of service, programs created to promote volunteerism should be designed to enhance rather than ignore the connections between service and citizenship. We also suggest considering tying student aid and other public benefits to public service, although this makes service more appealing to (or obligatory for) poorer Americans. We acknowledge that making service mandatory is one way of promoting fairness and reciprocity for all: if everyone benefits from public institutions, everyone should play a role in sustaining them. Nevertheless, most of us believe that, absent a national crisis, conscription is unjustified and possibly counterproductive.

Our recommendations, then, are several:

▌ Adequately fund a national service program that offers a variety of options for service, concentrating especially on the service of young Americans.
▌ Consider tying student aid and other public benefits to public service.
▌ Design policies that promote volunteerism and service learning programs so they enhance rather than ignore the connections between service and citizenship.

Conclusion

The importance of a vibrant associational life to the civic health of a country has attained the status of an unimpeachable axiom of democracy. While many scholars have documented a distressing decay in associational patterns—more bowling alone—we have reported here on two trends in associational life that are quite positive: healthy and increasing levels of volunteering and a generally robust and growing independent sector of nonprofits and philanthropy. These positive trends stand in contrast to the worrisome trends in electoral participation and metropolitan life that were the subject of chapters two and three.

We believe that the political institutions that buttress the nonprofit sector and provide incentives for volunteering could nevertheless do more to foster civic and especially political activity. In general, public policy should seek to improve political engagement by tapping into the energy of the millions of individuals who are active volunteers and who participate in nonprofit organizations. There is a fine line to walk in pursuing such policies, however. The trust that Americans place in nonprofit charitable organizations cannot be compromised by encouraging or permitting these entities to become wholly partisan enterprises. The independent sector will lose its distinctiveness and independence if it is unduly burdened by state regulations or remade into a mere instrument of narrowly partisan advocacy.

The recommendations here—for increasing opportunities for individuals to make charitable contributions, for increasing nonprofit governance and transparency, for clarifying rules about permissible political lobbying by nonprofits, for providing public funding and oversight of faith-based social services while respecting the separation of church and state, for better enabling unions to organize, and for increasing the range of national service programs— successfully navigate this fine line, we believe. We recognize, however, the possibility of disagreement on this score.

The goal of improving civic engagement confronts us with a variety of options and possible trade-offs. We have focused here on the civic benefits of associational life, charitable giving, and volunteer activities outside the direct control of public agencies. Tax breaks for charitable giving provide powerful incentives, indeed subsidies, for this range of activities. But some would emphasize that these subsidies may come at the cost of publicly funded government programs that promote important aspects of national citizenship. Scholars, including Suzanne Mettler, Andrea Campbell, and Theda Skocpol, argue that federal programs can positively influence citizens' identities and patterns of civic engagement. Mettler shows, for example, that the notable commitment to civic life of the so-called "greatest generation" of Americans who came of age during World War II was profoundly influenced by the G.I. Bill; veterans who took advantage of the bill's education and training provisions subsequently participated in political activities and civic life at a far higher rate than those who did not.[95] Similarly, Campbell argues that the Social Security program transformed senior citizens, especially low-income seniors, into a politically active and powerful group.[96] While tax breaks for charitable giving reduce the federal government's ability to support large-scale and inclusive programs like the G.I. Bill and Social Security, they may also undermine its capacity to promote important aspects of national citizenship.

The historical tendency of Americans to form associations, to volunteer, and to make charitable contributions represents a distinctive vision of civic engagement: citizens joining together to confront common problems directly. The astonishing extent of the resources commanded by America's vast array of nonprofits and philanthropic organizations is partly the consequence of the incredible success of this Tocquevillian vision of direct citizen action. These resources and activities are not simply the consequence of private action, however: they are underwritten and encouraged by publicly provided incentives and government policies. Like the local political and civic activity we described in chapter 3, moreover, associational and nonprofit life is shaped pervasively by laws and regulations. The task now is not only to enhance levels of volunteer and associational activity and the resources of nonprofit organizations, but also to create a framework within which associations and voluntary and charitable activities tend to promote rather than undermine the country's most inclusive political ideals.

5

Conclusion: Assessing Our Political Science of Citizenship

MANY CONSIDERED A REPUBLIC OF SELF-GOVERNING CITIZENS to be impossible on the extended scale of the American nation in 1787. The Anti-Federalist opponents of the Constitution complained about not only the excessive size but also the excessive diversity of the consolidated thirteen states. In so vast and various a polity, the remote national government would not have the confidence of the citizens; neither would it be possible to keep government accountable to the people as a whole. The national legislature would be composed of "such heterogeneous and discordant principles, as would constantly be contending with one another."[1] Finally, the Anti-Federalists argued that an extended and commercially oriented republic would not provide an appropriate educative setting in which to nurture the virtues of good citizenship. Instead of the mutual confidence and public spirit on which self-governance should rest, and might rest in a smaller and more homogeneous community, the consolidated government of America was fated, argued an Anti-Federalist writing under the pseudonym Brutus, to engender a politics of distrust, animosity, and conflict:

> In a republic, the manners, sentiments, and interests of the people should be similar. If this be not the case, there will be a constant clashing of opinions; and the representatives of one part will be constantly striving against those of the other. This will retard the operations of government, and prevent such conclusions as will promote the public good.[2]

Citizens would neglect their public duties, narrow and clashing interests would distract attention from the public good, distinctions of wealth would create destructive disparities and corruption, elites would gain disproportionate power, and tyranny would eventually result.

The Anti-Federalists were only the first in a long-running tradition of critics who have warned of the shortcomings of democracy in America, often with good reason. We have become vastly larger and, in some respects at least, considerably more diverse in the time since the nation was founded. Constitutional institutions have survived, liberties have been expanded, the nation's military might is awesome, and America prospers. And yet the anxieties of those who have doubted the reality of rule by and for all the people as a whole were not, and are not, simply misguided. Keeping government accountable to all, including minorities, fairly negotiating differences among more and less powerful groups, and hammering out workable solutions to pressing national problems amid the vast heterogeneity of America remain formidable challenges in the face of which we have often fallen short. In America today, as we have seen throughout previous chapters, citizens often vote at low levels compared with those in other countries and exhibit little political knowledge, in spite of sharply rising levels of wealth and education; political activity and power are distributed unequally across important groups within society; and our political institutions foster polarization and rancor when they should bring us together and encourage reasoned discourse. If there were a "report card" on American democracy, it would be difficult to argue that we are earning "A's."

In the following section, we recap the main grounds for our conviction that American democracy is not all that it should be. Next, we reprise our principal recommendations. Finally, we consider, and respond to, several lines of criticism that could be leveled at the argument we have advanced.

America's Democratic Deficit

One problem with democracy in America, we argue, is the overall *amount* of political participation and civic engagement. Voting has declined by most standards since the 1960s, and it has declined steeply among the young since the early 1970s. But voting is only the most visible and easily measurable form of engagement: many other political activities have declined far more steeply, as we describe in chapter two, as have levels of attention to and interest in politics. Political knowledge has stagnated, and many forms of engagement have declined considerably in spite of vastly higher levels of wealth and schooling.

Local institutions also circumscribe the amount of engagement and attention to politics. Progressive-era reforms favored expertise and managerial forms of governance over popular involvement and the virtues of competitive politics. Special districts and public authorities allow important decisions to be made with incredibly low levels of public scrutiny and involvement. In spite of the fact that many public goods—safety, health, education—are "coproduced" by public agencies and citizens, our means of involving citizens are often primitive and undeveloped.[3]

We also describe the participatory *inequalities* that plague American politics. There are vast differences between rich and poor Americans with respect to a wide range of political activities. While participation among African Americans increased considerably in the wake of the civil rights movement, differences in education and income continue to foster great disparities in political activity and influence, and African Americans are disproportionately poor. The political consequences of lower participation based on low levels of education and income are amplified by the astonishing decline in union membership, outside of the public sector, since the 1950s. Immigration status is also associated with lower levels of participation, and we have seen surging numbers of new arrivals who need to be prepared to take part in civic life.

America has vibrant voluntary and nonprofit sectors, as we detail in chapter four, but public policy inhibits the positive impact that these organizations might have on political and civic activity. Nonprofits might redress some civic inequalities by giving voice to the interests of those who stand in need of social services—the sick, the poor, the aged, and others—but public rules inhibit the capacity of nonprofits to articulate and represent the interests of these groups. We describe a growing movement toward voluntarism, especially among the young, but also point out that "service learning" programs in schools rarely prepare students for the great office of citizenship.

In addition to substantial concerns with the overall levels and distribution of political and civic activity in the United States, we see a variety of shortcomings in the *qualitative* dimensions of these activities. Perhaps the most striking problem is the degree to which our politics has become polarized. This is surprising in many ways, since evidence suggests that most Americans remain firmly "middle of the road" in their political views; we are a diverse country, but there are few ideological extremists on either left or right, and the population as a whole is still dominated by political moderates. Nevertheless, our politics and polity are considerably more polarized than they once were in several important respects.

First, there is ample evidence of ideological polarization among political elites: members of Congress, for example, are far more polarized than the electorate. As recently as the late 1970s and early 1980s, there were many members of the House and Senate who were "cross-pressured" and prepared to work across party lines to solve national problems. There are now far fewer such legislators. Our politics has become far more rancorous, and this not only makes it harder to legislate but also turns off moderate voters, while arousing the passions of those at the ideological extremes (precisely the opposite of what our political institutions should do as a general matter). A politics of excessive and unnecessary contention distracts from efforts to work together to solve shared problems.

There is a second and perhaps even more destructive way in which we have become more polarized: by place. We live in political communities that continue to be racially segregated and that are strikingly and increasingly stratified based on class differences. In chapter three, we describe how cities were once far more mixed by race and class than they are today. The great migration to the suburbs has been spurred in substantial part by white middle- and upper-class flight away from urban problems and residents. Tens of millions of disproportionately minority urban residents live amid levels of concentrated disadvantage that are civically debilitating for many. Suburbs on the whole have become more diverse based on race and income, but much of this diversity is across rather than within suburbs.

Local institutions are vital to democracy: keeping government close to the people encourages participation. However, a peculiar and civically pathological combination of localism and poorly structured private choice—the freedom of the wealthy to set up and maintain exclusive local communities—has encouraged racial and economic sorting and created separate and unequal political communities. Local politics should help to realize, not undermine, larger ideals of a common citizenship based on equal liberty for all. So long as local communities and public services (including schools) reflect the grossly unequal resources, both financial and human, associated with concentrations of privilege and disadvantage, many children will receive inequitable and inadequate preparation for the office of citizenship and the opportunities of democratic freedom.

Another aspect of the problem directly relevant to the quality of civic engagement is that the sorting of people into political units defined by these hierarchies circumscribes the range of our fellow citizens whose interests we are obliged to consult when considering political questions. Thus political boundaries reinforce and exacerbate divisions among citizens. Those with whom we share a political community are, or should be, coparticipants in the production of public goods of all sorts, including health, safety, recreation, and the education of the next generation. When we think about our stake in those goods, we are obliged to consider these others. Where local political communities are segregated and stratified, however, political processes that should broaden individuals' interests and political identities instead sharpen and polarize them.

We believe, finally, that our politics is not as deliberative as it should be. A more thoughtful and reflective politics, we argue, would be one in which citizens come to better understand the reasons that underlie their own political positions and the positions of others, a politics in which citizens become capable of offering one another reasons and perhaps even finding mutually acceptable compromises. As things stand, too little attention is given to the articulation and exchange of reasons and evidence; politics presents too few opportunities for citizens to articulate their own arguments and to encounter and grapple with the reasonable arguments of others. There are many ways in which local politics could do more to elicit the input of citizens and to establish regular exchanges among citizens and public officials. At the level of presidential campaigns, an absurdly long and episodic primary and selection process also discourages sustained attention and learning.

If this reprise of complaints seems severe, we would do well to remember that the project that falls to us—to sustain and improve self-governance in a vast national republic, while guaranteeing everyone's basic liberties and equal dignity—was never expected to be easy. None of the founding generation—neither those who supported nor those who opposed the Constitution—expected it to be easy to sustain an actively participatory, inclusive, deliberative democracy on the vast scale and amid the astonishing diversity of a continental, commercial republic of nearly 300 million people. Jefferson's warm support for democracy was joined with the conviction that states and localities should enjoy political preeminence, a preeminence we now understand to be at odds with the extent of national power needed to secure equal liberty for all.

American democracy should, we argue, be judged by standards of achievement commensurate with our increasing collective capacities. We should expect no less than continual improvement, no less than to be a model for others. Improvement here depends on heeding the most enlightened critics of American democracy and seeking to discern how we can do better.

Our Agenda for Reform

Unlike many who address themselves to the shortcomings of democratic practice, our aim is not principally to excoriate Americans for being bad citizens. This book is not an exercise in "finger wagging." This is not to say, however, that we do not care about civic virtues: the character traits possessed by good citizens. Citizens make choices, and families, churches, and schools can and should play a greater role in awakening a sense of civic duty, combating prejudice, and instilling concern for all our fellow citizens.

But citizens make choices within a framework of laws, institutions, and policies and within a context of social groups and norms that are themselves shaped to some degree by the laws. Institutions are educative: they shape patterns of behavior, encourage broad or narrow interests, and even help to form citizens' identities. Faulty design may either fail to draw citizens into politics or place excessive demands on them. To a great extent—how great an extent can be determined only by observing the consequences of reform—people are inactive, bored, and turned off by politics because we have designed politics to bore, annoy, and frustrate even conscientious citizens. Our primary emphasis, therefore, has been on how the institutions that we, as Americans, have collectively established shape our nation's patterns of participation and engagement. We have argued that political life is a political artifact and that improved institutional design can improve citizenship by enhancing the formative context of political activity, interests, and identities.

Our main aim is to criticize faulty political design and suggest improvements. We explore how electoral institutions as currently constituted turn citizens off in various ways and how they foster polarization. We describe how poorly designed metropolitan institutions encourage citizens to sort themselves into stratified and segregated communities. These structures do not render enlightened and virtuous politics impossible, but they make it harder to achieve. Our analysis does not render appeals to the "better angels of our nature" superfluous, but it furnishes tools for shaping an environment more apt to elicit admirable forms of political and civic activity.

How well do we succeed in proposing ways of increasing the amount of civic activity as well as its quality and distribution? Political scientists have studied the extent of participation most thoroughly, its distribution and equity somewhat less so, and its quality least of all. Nevertheless, we offer a considerable practical agenda as concerns all three of these dimensions of political and civic activity. We believe that some of our recommendations could "add up" in positive ways, complementing and enhancing one another. Of course, we also know that all calls for reform are likely to have some unintended consequences. Many of our reforms may result in productive synergies, but some may work at cross-purposes, and we try to be alert to this. Let us, therefore, recap some of our principal recommendations, with an emphasis on the ways in which they could complement one another. We discuss, in turn, some of the main ways we recommend to enhance the quantity, quality, and equality of civic and political engagement. Although we find it useful to distinguish these three dimensions of political and civic engagement, particular recommendations have multiple consequences, and the ordering of what follows is by necessity messy. (Measures to increase political competitiveness, for example, seem likely to enhance both participation and learning, which could be considered contributions to quantity and quality.)

INCREASING THE AMOUNT OF POLITICAL AND CIVIC ENGAGEMENT

Our principal suggestions for reforming elections and voting aim to increase participation by making political contests more competitive, more engaging, and more effective learning experiences. One of our most important recommendation concerning elections is to require that the periodic adjustment of political districts be done in a less partisan fashion. Allowing party leaders to deliberately craft noncompetitive election districts to protect incumbents has a highly detrimental impact on voters' engagement and consequently on democratic governance. States should use methods such as nonpartisan commissions to establish new political boundaries for congressional and state legislative districts. Furthermore, they should *not* redistrict multiple times in a single decade. Such reforms would have multiple beneficial consequences for the amount as well as the quality of participation. More competitive districts should make politics more interesting and should, thereby, increase attention to political contests and, along with it, turnout in elections. With more competitive congressional elections, citizens might also learn more about public policy and the positions of the two parties.

And consider a complementary recommendation: our proposal to spread competition in presidential races across the country by altering the way we allocate electoral college seats. Under the current winner-take-all rule that applies in forty-eight states, the candidate who wins the popular vote within a state takes all of its electoral college votes. This means that presidential candidates have no incentive to campaign in states now considered "safe" for either side. Their campaigns thus focus almost all of their energy on the handful of "battleground" states, while most Americans barely see political advertisements, much less the candidates themselves. We should alter the process of allocating electoral college votes by giving two electoral college votes to the statewide winner in each state and one vote to the winner of each congressional district; we believe this change would encourage presidential candidates to campaign and compete across a much wider swath of the country.

Add to redistricting and electoral college reform our proposal to shorten the presidential primary process. The current system is absurdly long and drawn out, and the front-loaded nature of the typical primary cycle means that there is a long hiatus between the early contests in Iowa, New Hampshire, and "Super Tuesday" in early March (when the result is often decided) and the conventions, which occur in late August or even September. As things stand, by the November election citizens are bound to forget much of what they learned in February and March. Shorten the presidential selection process and more citizens will pay attention from beginning to end. They may also learn more, which will, in turn, improve the quality of their participation as well as increase the number of citizens who vote.

These three reforms—in combination with other commonsense policy changes such as making election day a national holiday and mailing sample ballots and polling place information to voters—have the potential not only to increase participation, but also to promote more sustained voter interest and learning. Campaigns are supposed to be educational experiences for voters, and they could be if we organized them with that in mind.

In chapter three, we also discuss a number of respects in which electoral institutions and democratic structures in metropolitan areas should be reformed so as to increase participation and make local power more responsive to the people as a whole. Progressive-era reforms from the early decades of the twentieth century have inhibited popular political activity. We do not romanticize the old party political machines, and we do not seek a return of the old urban "bosses," but we do believe that excluding the people from important aspects of local governance makes government less accountable and less responsive to the interests of all. To invigorate politics and make local governments more accountable to the people, we recommend that cities reconsider progressive-era reform institutions, including council-manager governance, at-large city council districts, and nonpartisan elections. These institutional forms depress participation, especially minority participation, and they limit the healthy checks and balances provided by a strong elected mayor and an elected city council.

We also endorse a whole variety of ways in which local public agencies and service providers can furnish additional opportunities to improve governance and accountability by enhancing civic engagement. Many local services, including education, public safety, and public health, depend on citizens playing an active role in what we call the "coproduction of public goods and services." All government agencies should explore methods to involve citizens in shaping and administering policy through advisory boards and public meetings. Large cities should make extra efforts to ensure that local government is brought close to the people through such means as neighborhood councils and administrative decentralization.

In addition, special-purpose governments—the ubiquitous if shadowy public "authorities" and special districts that allocate vast resources and shape patterns of growth across metropolitan regions—should be more open, transparent, and accountable to the people. Corporations and real estate developers use these anonymous entities to confer benefits on a few and impose burdens on the many, in ways nearly invisible to the public at large. Special-purpose governments should create meaningful opportunities for citizen input and prevent private interests from pursuing their goals invisibly.

We also argue that states should experiment with different forms of regional governance in order to make it possible for the citizens of regions to address more effectively issues (such as development and sprawl) that currently spill across the boundaries of political communities. There are a number of promising possibilities for a new regional politics, but we do not recommend a particular form because more experimentation and study are needed with respect to regional governance.

Here, then, is an interlocking set of institutional reforms concerning ways of enhancing national, local, and regional democracy. We also offer other less dramatic recommendations concerning the electoral process, including various ways of making voting, and information relevant to voting, more easily accessible, and, of course, we emphasize that Americans are asked to vote too frequently, often in staggered elections for local and national offices. Holding local elections concurrently with state and national elections may not create more interest in local politics and may exacerbate the problems associated with uninformed voters. Nevertheless, a strong case can be made for reducing the burden of too-frequent elections. By increasing competitiveness at the national and the local levels, by making campaigns more interesting, by creating new forms of local and regional governance to enhance transparency and popular control, and by making voting less demanding, our recommendations would, we believe, significantly increase political activity and make government more accountable to the people.

The principal recommendations highlighted so far address ways of enhancing levels of political activity and democratic accountability. In chapter four, we discuss ways of enhancing civic activity that would further support these democratic institutional reforms. We argue that, while associational life remains vibrant, especially volunteering and nonprofit and philanthropic activity, public policy could encourage "even more and better" civic activity. Poorly designed public rules and policies governing 501(c)(3) tax-exempt organizations impede the pathway from associational activity to political participation. We need to unblock this vital connection.

We urge that the federal government adequately fund national service programs endorsed by Republican and Democratic administrations over the past sixteen years. These programs provide a period of extended service that holds out the promise of enhancing the quality of American democracy. A variety of opportunities for extended periods of service should be made more widely available. We also recommend considering tying student aid and other public benefits to public service. Another central plank in our recommendations is that the incredible energies represented by the millions of Americans engaged in voluntary service and charitable work on a daily basis should be linked more directly to practices of citizenship. Service learning programs in schools and programs that promote volunteerism can and should be designed to enhance the connection between service and citizenship.

Whether one thinks that political and civic engagement in America has decreased, increased, or remained stagnant, the fact is that public rules and the design of institutions shape levels of political and civic activity in profound (if sometimes obscure or complicated) ways. We seek to cast some light on these influences, and we hope that our recommendations provide the beginnings of an agenda for civic renewal.

ENHANCING THE QUALITY OF ENGAGEMENT

At least as important as the overall amount of political and civic engagement are the quality and distribution of these activities. Those who would reform democracy must think not only about *how much* popular political activity there is but also about *who* is participating and *how* they participate.

Some of our proposals to increase the amount of political and civic engagement in the previous section refer to qualitative aims as well. Indeed, there is no hard line of separation between quantity and quality: campaigns that promote *more political learning* increase both dimensions, for example. New participatory opportunities at the national and local levels should be crafted with the quality of participation in mind: we discuss, for example, a variety of promising deliberative reforms connected with the electoral process in chapter two and several deliberative opportunities connected with the delivery of local services in chapter three.

Quantity, quality, and equality can interact in surprising ways. So consider, for example, the complaint that our politics is excessively polarized. One aspect of this is that, while voters as a whole are moderate, there is too much rancor and unproductive conflict among political elites. This decline in bipartisan cooperation alienates voters and, understandably, makes them trust the intentions of politicians less. one way of ameliorating this trend in representation may be to ensure that representatives come from districts where they face healthy electoral competition, encouraging them to moderate their views in the interest of electoral success. Allowing incumbents to use ever more sophisticated technology to draw district lines that protect their interests is highly unlikely to promote this type of competition. Nonpartisan methods of redistricting have the potential, therefore, of contributing not only to more participation but also to a more constructive—less polarized and less contentious—system of government: a process of governance more worthy of popular confidence.

Moreover, reforms that have the effect of increasing voter turnout could also reduce this rancor by making the actual voters more representative of the views of the electorate as a whole. When rates of turnout are low, we have reason to think that those who do turn up tend disproportionately to be ideological zealots.[4] If rates of participation increase, we can expect that greater numbers of moderate and independent voters will reenter the political process. The need to appeal to these voters may further moderate the ideological polarization among elites and make the ideologies of elected politicians more representative of the people as a whole, and this would help to make governance less bitter and more constructive.

Another form of polarization that is also of great concern to us is the increasing fragmentation and segregation of the places in which citizens live, our principal focus in chapter three. The polarization of places in America is constituted by continuing racial segregation, especially in areas of concentrated disadvantage, and ever-worsening class stratification across the separate political communities that compose the metropolitan region. We believe that the quality of collective governance is seriously undermined when the citizens of a diverse republic sort themselves into different political communities that reinforce hierarchies of privilege and disadvantage. The problem of polarized places is deeply rooted. America's strong tradition of localism has long been considered a jewel in our democratic crown: we are a vast extended republic, but we also keep government close to the people via intricate networks of local governance. However, this combination of localism and poorly structured freedom—the freedom of the wealthy to set up and maintain exclusive local communities—has resulted in substantial racial and economic sorting and created separate and unequal political communities. We worry not only about the cumulative effects of concentrated advantage and disadvantage—for schooling, safety, and health—but also about the civic effects of living in stratified and separate communities that circumscribe citizens' interests and identities.

Housing segregation is the underlying problem, and our most significant recommendation here is to enact "fair share" housing laws that deny local communities the right to exclude all but wealthy families. Municipalities should be encouraged and even required to provide a mix of housing that meets the needs of the people who work in the area. Exclusionary zoning laws should be curbed, and federal and state governments should consider a variety of more ambitious housing policies for economic integration, such as tying grants to having a "fair share" affordable housing plan, encouraging inclusionary over exclusionary zoning, and fully funding housing voucher programs that facilitate geographic mobility. Legislatures and courts should explore ways to encourage municipalities to provide a mix of housing choices that reflects the broad range of households in the metropolitan area. We are not so naive as to underestimate the political hurdles faced by "fair share" housing, but we urge courts and other political actors to work to overcome the class-based exclusion and racial stratification that defy our most basic ideals of equal citizenship.

Clearly, the "quality" of political participation is not a simple property: it encompasses a variety of features that we value in political activity. We propose various ways of increasing valuable qualities of participation at all levels; these include ways of making citizens better informed, providing more opportunities for the exchange of reasons and arguments in deliberative settings, reducing elite polarization and with it rancor and unproductive conflict, and finally making political communities more inclusive.

REDUCING INEQUALITIES OF POLITICAL AND CIVIC ACTIVITY

Throughout this book, we point out various inequalities in political and civic activity that constitute obstacles to the realization of democratic ideals of rule by and for the people as a whole. Ensuring equality in civic engagement is likely to affect both the quality and quantity of participation as well, once again demonstrating that the three dimensions of civic engagement overlap: the democratic process is improved—it is more legitimate and more likely to produce outcomes that promote the good of all—if all major groups in the community are heard from.

Some ways of redressing participatory inequalities are obvious, though not without controversy: reenfranchisement of ex-felons could bring greater numbers of relatively poor and disproportionately minority citizens back into politics. In our discussion of localities in chapter three, we argue for lowering the formal barriers to the political and civic participation by immigrants. In addition, governments could increase participatory equity by targeting particular measures at disadvantaged groups: by making special efforts to supply voters with information in neighborhoods with relatively low turnouts, for example, and certainly also by making sure that voting places are as convenient and safe in poorer as in wealthier neighborhoods.

We note in chapter two that voting among younger people has declined notably since the early 1970s. Schools should provide instruction in the mechanics of voting to high school students and place greater emphasis on the teaching of civics and government as well as the inculcation of a sense of civic duty. And, of course, schools can help to redress participatory inequalities based on disadvantage by paying special attention to effective civic education in poorer neighborhoods and in places with high numbers of recent arrivals.

Our recommendations to address place-based polarization—the geography of class and race—could also have the effect of addressing some other participatory inequalities. Those who live amid concentrated disadvantage are far more likely to experience substandard schools, health care, safety, and access to steady employment; all of these create special obstacles to obtaining the skills and resources that support political and civic participation.

We emphasize in chapter four that important sets of organizations, especially nonprofit service providers and unions, could do more to help equalize opportunities for political voice, but their capacity to articulate client interests (in the case of nonprofits) or worker interests (in the case of unions) is inhibited by unnecessary regulations and impediments to free association. Nonprofits of all types should furnish avenues for community input and maximize the transparency of their finances and governance.

Nonprofits are inhibited in their capacity to speak out on behalf of the interests of their clients on account of various public provisions, including Internal Revenue Service (IRS) rules, that encumber their political speech. This inhibition not only blocks a pathway from civic engagement to political engagement but does so in a way that impinges most specifically on those who depend on social services: the old, the sick, and other disadvantaged populations. The IRS, we recommend, should change or at least clarify rules that inhibit the capacity of nonprofits to articulate and represent their clients' interests. Reducing these inhibitions on the ways that nonprofits may represent the interests of their clients could help to redress some participatory inequalities. In addition, the precipitous decline in union membership has undoubtedly undermined an important avenue of mobilization among working people. A decline in union membership would seem inevitably to exacerbate participatory inequalities based on economic status. We urge that laws should be strengthened so that workers can make the decision whether or not to unionize in an atmosphere that is free of harassment and intimidation.

There are no simple ways to cure the deep inequalities that affect our political system, but we believe that our recommendations would make a significant contribution.

SUMMARY

The foregoing represents a partial summation of our major recommendations: ways of increasing civic and political engagement, ways of increasing various qualities of civic engagement that we prize (including making political and civic activity better informed, more deliberative, and more inclusive with respect to the differences that divide Americans), and ways of promoting greater equality of political activity and influence (see box 5-1 for a recap). There is surely far more that can be said about the possibilities for enhancing political and civic

BOX 5-1 RECAP OF RECOMMENDATIONS

Registration and voting

▌ Mail polling place information to registered voters prior to election day.

▌ Mail sample ballots to voters.

▌ Employ election-day registration wherever possible.

▌ Reauthorize the voting materials provision of the Voting Rights Act.

▌ Continue efforts to register college students, including full implementation of the 1998 Higher Education Act.

▌ Restore the right to vote of felons who have served their complete sentence.

▌ Consider restoring the right to vote to felons on parole or probation.

▌ Encourage face-to-face contacts urging voter turnout.

▌ Provide more opportunities for deliberative engagement.

Districting and the Electoral College

▌ Prohibit states from engaging in redistricting multiple times in a single decade.

▌ Use nonpartisan commissions for establishing new political boundaries for congressional and state legislative districts.

▌ Give two Electoral College votes to the statewide winner and one vote to the winner of each congressional district.

▌ Recognize that deliberately crafting noncompetitive election districts has a detrimental impact on voters' engagement.

Schools

▌ Place greater emphasis on the teaching of civics, government, and civic duty, providing future citizens with an "owner's manual" on how they can and should be active in politics.

▌ Provide school-based instruction in the mechanics of voting to high school students.

▌ Encourage recognition of a young person's "first vote" as a significant rite of passage.

▌ Encourage greater use of newspaper reading and other in-depth news sources among high school students.

Metropolitan diversity

▌ Encourage municipalities to provide a mix of housing that meets the needs of the people who work in the area.

▌ Lower the formal barriers to the political participation of immigrants.

▌ Encourage public school officials to reach out to the parents of immigrant children.

▌ Enforce fair housing laws.

Revitalizing local politics

▌ Experiment with a range of institutions that alter municipal powers and create arenas that encourage citizens from different localities and their political representatives to engage with one another around issues of metropolitan concern.

▌ Make special-purpose governments more open and transparent.

▌ Develop a comparative metropolitan politics that illuminates the variety of institutional arrangements under which metropolitan regions can be governed.

▌ Seek to understand the conditions under which individuals seek highly parochial aims without regard to the consequences for other neighborhoods, towns, and the region as a whole.

▌ Reconsider progressive-era reforms at the city level, including council-manager governance, at-large city council districts, and nonpartisan elections.

- Work to understand which municipal institutions promote more and better civic engagement.

Enhanced local participation

- Enhance opportunities for citizens to become involved in local governments to address issues they care about.
- Encourage citywide systems of neighborhood councils.
- Structure community organizations in ways that foster greater citizen engagement.
- Ensure that cities invest in and engage in direct mobilization.
- Seek a more systematic understanding of the relationship between engagement and good governance.

Philanthropy and public charities

- Have the Internal Revenue Service offer an explicit definition of the "substantial" standard for legislative and grassroots advocacy and do more to make nonprofits aware of the H alternative.
- Have Congress consider permitting those who take the standard deduction to also deduct charitable contributions or to afford them the opportunity of a flat-rate tax credit for some contributions.
- Have the IRS permit individuals to take deductions for their charitable contributions made through April 15.

Nonprofit accountability and governance

- Maximize the transparency of the finances and governance of all types of nonprofits.

- Ensure that the boards of directors of nonprofits are broadly representative of their communities.
- Initiate efforts on the part of the federal government to better evaluate public policies coproduced by nonprofits.
- Train administrators in public agencies and students in schools of public administration to manage relationships among public and nonprofit agencies.

Churches and unions

- Find ways to encourage the work of faith-based nonprofits, while still respecting the separation between church and state.
- Ensure that faith-based and nonsectarian nonprofits that seek and obtain public funding play by the same rules.
- Ensure that workers can make the decision whether or not to unionize in an atmosphere that is free of harassment and intimidation.

National service

- Adequately fund a national service program that offers a variety of options for service. concentrating especially on the service of young Americans.
- Consider tying student aid and other public benefits to public service.
- Design policies that promote volunteerism and service learning programs so they enhance rather than ignore the connections between service and citizenship.

engagement in each of the areas we discuss. Moreover, the three broad sets of institutions on which we train our attention—electoral institutions, metropolitan areas, and voluntary and nonprofit organizations—represent only some aspects of the overall framework of institutions within which we live. For example, we say little about the family or the workplace—institutions that can exert great influence on the capacity of citizens for involvement.[5] There is far more to be said about the ways in which public policy and institutions offer opportunities for reinvigorating our public life; this is only a start.

We believe that were these policies to be implemented—and we acknowledge that some require further study and refining—rule by the people as a whole would become more of a reality and confidence in the project of collective self-rule would be invigorated. As we emphasize throughout, we do not envision a democratic utopia. Increased participation and more capable participation will not in themselves solve most of our problems. We do, however, believe that more, better, and more equitably distributed political and civic activity would improve our capacity to address fairly and effectively many of the issues that face us as a society.

We conclude by considering some of the possible criticisms of our project, including our analyses and recommendations. What follows is, indeed, an account of some of the worries that concern us.

Pitfalls of Our Political Science of Citizenship

There are those who will tend to view our project of enhancing civic participation as naive or even misguided in various ways. We do not here repeat the general criticisms of democracy that we raise and begin to answer in chapter one. Rather, in what follows, we state and respond briefly to several grounds for possible skepticism about the particulars of our project: Do we ignore the important role of citizen virtue and exaggerate the role of institutional and policy reform? Insofar as we seek to change citizens' incentives, interests, and identities, are we being manipulative and paternalistic? Do we make unrealistic or "utopian" assumptions about the likelihood of citizens' taking a greater interest in politics, given our recommended reforms? Is our report objectionably partisan? We believe that saying something about each of these charges will help to put our argument in proper perspective.

WHAT OF CIVIC VIRTUE?

Some might suggest that we are overly optimistic about the prospects for success. As we touch on in chapter one, a long-standing objection to calls for expanded democracy is that citizens are not up to the task. We readily grant and have repeatedly pointed to deep concerns about levels of political knowledge and interest. We cannot here recap the entire history of the long-standing debate within political science about citizen competence, but for our purposes, the fundamental problem is what to do about disturbing levels of ignorance and apathy among ordinary citizens. One important response to this problem is a call for greater civic virtue.

In focusing on the ways in which institutions and policies can and should be reformed, we have, to a considerable extent, followed Jean-Jacques Rousseau in taking "men as they are and the laws as they might be" in order to improve the quality of democracy in America.[6] But does our emphasis on institutions and policy structures shortchange the role of individuals as agents? If citizens are not active enough, nor well-informed enough, nor adequately concerned about our most encompassing and inclusive political interests, should not the focus be on improved citizen character or civic virtue? Do we exaggerate the role of political institutions and policies in shaping civic life?

We believe that our approach affirms the importance of civic virtue and civic education. We emphasize that schools, while not the primary focus of our work, play an important role. We would like to see a greater emphasis in schools on civic education that emphasizes civic duty and empowerment: young Americans need to learn not only how to think about political forces, causes, and effects but also about what they can do and the conditions under which they can make a difference. Our focus on institutions other than schools is meant not to discount the role of schools but to redress the balance.

Classic accounts of civic virtue, moreover, share our concern with the educative, formative impact of institutions and policies quite broadly. Plato and Aristotle certainly emphasized the importance of moral education as a prelude to political activity, but they equally insisted that education is neither principally a matter of "schooling" nor confined to one's early years. Our characters, interests, identities, and activities are formed by the contexts within which we act. In designing institutions and large-scale policies, we should pay attention to the formative impact on civic life. The point is not to discount the role of individual choice and virtue but to draw more people toward the sorts of activities we have reason to regard as valuable.

But do we exaggerate the role of institutions and policies in shaping or even "constructing" patterns of civic life and even political interests and identities? We certainly allow that cultural factors shape our political lives, and they operate with some independence from particular policies and institutions. Likewise, the interests, preferences, and convictions of citizens are not altogether politically constructed and (more to the point) are certainly not altogether reconstructable based on the sorts of reforms we have advocated here. We allow, as well, that technological changes such as the invention of the train and the automobile produce enormous transformations of the political and civic fabric. Nevertheless, precisely which consequences transpire depends partly on the choices we make collectively about laws, institutions, and policies. The form taken by suburbanization in the United States, for example, "has been as much a governmental as a natural process."[7] The foremost historian of American metropolitan life, Kenneth T. Jackson, puts it well when he argues that the particular type of man-made setting in which we live "is a function of the interrelationship of technology, cultural norms, population pressure, land values, and social relationships, but even within rigid environmental and technological restraints a variety of physical patterns is possible."[8]

We should be realistic about the political obstacles that lie in the path of reform, but that same realism also requires acknowledging and understanding the manifold ways in which the patterns of behavior we observe are shaped by collective choices of all sorts.

EXPANDING DEMOCRACY: A UTOPIAN FANTASY?

But a focus on institutional incentives and opportunities for engagement provokes another important concern—the danger of overburdening citizens by placing unrealistic expectations on them. It could be argued that multiplying the opportunities (or demands) for participation could be not merely futile but also dangerous: it could worsen our politics by enhancing the power of an unrepresentative few. After all, one problem is that only a few will show up at the public meetings, but another problem is that the few who do show up are liable to be unrepresentative of the wider public. They participate either because they have some special personal stake or because they are unusually motivated by intense convictions. Which is to say that participatory democracy tends to be dominated by activists who are motivated by special interests or ideological purity or both, and this is part of the reason why ordinary people do not like participatory politics.

Morris P. Fiorina advances an especially acerbic version of this argument. He charges that the problem becomes even worse when government activity broadens and concerns more aspects of our lives, because then the influence of activist zealots can become toxic for politics:

> The expansion of the scope of government created myriad new opportunities for those with particular issue concerns to become active in politics. There have always been people who felt extraordinarily strongly about the height and color of neighbors' fences, the contents of children's textbooks, the serving of foie gras in restau-

rants, and so on, but in times past they were called cranks or busybodies and were generally ignored or left to settle their conflicts informally. Today they are called activists, and they demand government action to enforce their views.[9]

Are our assumptions about citizens' willingness to become involved unrealistic and dangerous? Political activity, as scholars of public choice have repeatedly emphasized, is costly, after all. Will our ardor for expanding civic capacities and opportunities turn off ordinary citizens as the zealous few participate more and more?

There is always a danger that well-intended reforms will go awry. We have tried to be circumspect and cautious throughout. We do not believe, however, that our overall argument rests on unrealistic assumptions about citizen interest.

We vehemently *agree* with those who argue that political activity, including learning about political issues and candidates, is costly. We have *not* argued that citizens must be prepared to bear ever greater burdens and to make greater personal sacrifices on behalf of politics and civic activity. To the contrary, political institutions should always be constructed according to a certain economy of public participation. One way to get more citizens to vote, we argue, is to ask them to vote less frequently. The point can and should be generalized. One way to increase participation is to be reasonable in our expectations about the number and extent of the occasions on which we ask citizens to participate. Another is to invite participation when it matters most rather than for frivolous issues or in meaningless exercises.

Indeed, throughout this report we emphasize ways in which participation might be made less costly and more interesting. In our discussion of electoral institutions, we advocate making it easier to register to vote, easier to obtain information about polling places and voting procedures, and easier to get information about candidates' positions. We argue that presidential campaigns should be shorter so as to make it easier for potential voters to pay attention and learn about candidates and positions. We advocate ways of making elections more competitive (via nonpartisan redistricting in congressional districts, for example) because competitive elections are both more interesting and more worthy of interest. We argue for the importance of political parties—a topic that deserves far more attention than we give it here—in the form of local partisan elections, for example, so that citizens have the easy "cue" of the party label to make a rough and ready judgment about candidates' positions. All of these reforms and others—not to mention greater attention to civic education in schools—would improve the capacity of citizens to learn about candidates' positions and policy issues.

It is worth emphasizing that Fiorina, who may appear at first to be a decided skeptic with respect to our project, is not skeptical at all about the need for more participation. Acerbic as he is on the trials and burdens of participation, Fiorina calls for increased participation and recommends some of the sorts of measures we have advanced, including reform of partisan redistricting and other electoral reforms.[10] We agree with Fiorina and others that higher turnout is important partly because higher turnouts are liable to produce electorates that are less dominated by the ideological extremes and more reflective of the broad interests of the public as a whole.

Is there a danger that, in calling for additional deliberative opportunities and other new participatory opportunities, we could encourage the creation of institutions that will empower the zealous few at the expense of the many, further undermining government responsiveness to the good of all and public confidence in government? Our concern about such unintended consequences is part of the reason why we are especially cautious in recommending reforms at the metropolitan level and why we emphasize vexing trade-offs and call for experimentation with new institutions and new forms of governance. Details matter and consequences are difficult to predict. We offer no glib solutions, but we are not convinced that a warrant for general skepticism is proven.

We are not moral purists: we recognize and accept that a variety of motives lead people to get involved in civic affairs. We have, for example, called for realistic ways of making the experience of service more attractive and appealing to more citizens. We recognize that young adults may choose to serve for a mix of reasons that combine altruism with the desire to acquire useful skills, contacts, and credentials. If we have a guide here, after all, it is Alexis de Tocqueville, who argued for the centrality to civic engagement of "self-interest rightly understood."[11]

In the end, our project of seeking ways to promote greater participation, better informed participation, and better distributed participation has nothing to do with naive or unrealistic assumptions. Our argument is based on the best evidence available. We advance many reasons for thinking that participation matters deeply. Some of these might be considered "idealistic"—that politics calls forth the exercise and development of skills and capacities that are intrinsically valuable—but others are decidedly "realistic" by any standard: power, we insist, will be wielded by those who are active, engaged, and capable. We want government to be responsive to the interests of all, and we believe that more participation, more enlightened participation, and better distributed participation are crucial to that.

So far, we interpret the possible charge of utopianism, excessive hopefulness, or lack of realism as being based on the premise that citizens may not be up to the tasks of participation. There is an alternative basis for advancing this argument, namely, that institutional obstacles to more and better participation often serve the interests of elites, who will resist change. This is a large topic that we cannot address at length. We say only two things about it. One is that it seems clear that the general trajectory of American political history has been in the direction of greater inclusion and a progressive realization of some basic democratic ideals. "Government of, by, and for the people" has been incorporated into the Constitution to include more and more people in the political life of our country. We trust that this will continue.

We only add to this that "elites" are not a homogeneous group. Leadership also plays a role, and reformist leaders can, under the right circumstances, both discern underlying problems and make a big difference in addressing them. We have been told repeatedly, for example, that moving toward less partisan redistricting flies in the face of American political realities. But California Governor Arnold Schwarzenegger came out in early 2005 for nonpartisan districting commissions for congressional and state legislative seats, just as we were completing this conclusion.[12] "If we here in this chamber do not reform the government," Schwarzenegger warned state legislators, "the people will rise up and reform it themselves. And, you know something, I will join them. And I will fight with them." "Realism" should not blind us to possibilities for change.

IS THIS PROJECT MANIPULATIVE OR PATERNALISTIC?

It might seem not just arrogant but objectionably manipulative to reshape institutions and policy structures with the aim of altering other people's behavior and even their ideas and self-understandings. Does this smack of social engineering? Does it reflect a lack of respect for the freedom or autonomy of our fellow citizens, their capacity to reflectively and critically control their own lives? Are we being paternalistic in the sense that we are interfering with other people, sometimes without their consent, in the name of making them better off?

Obviously, our aim is to enhance our collective capacity to reform institutions and policies in order to promote improved civic life: a more active and capable citizenry and a more equitable distribution of civic activity. It is hard to see what is objectionable about this kind of "social engineering" or "manipulation." First and foremost, we openly submit these reflections to the court of public judgment and wish to contribute to a reflective public conversation about the formative role of institutions and policies; in this respect, our aim is the opposite of manipulation. Second, it is inevitable that we live within constructed and formative institutions: there is no alternative. There is no neutral or default baseline that would allow us as a political community to avoid making collective choices that will have far-reaching consequences. Third, we live within and are formed by these institutions as much as anyone else, and we are inviting others to join us in seeking to understand the civic stakes of the alternative political and social worlds that we construct. Living within institutions by which we are shaped does not preclude us from reflecting critically on these institutions (any more than being raised by our parents precludes critical reflection on their parenting practices). Therefore, the only question is which formative influences we should collectively promote. We want to call attention to, rather than to avoid, the questions of which consequences are desirable and how to promote them. Is there any greater ambition for social science than to improve citizens' capacities to answer these questions wisely?

Of course, we do not advocate restricting people's basic liberties for the sake of making them better or more virtuous citizens. We support rights of privacy, freedoms of speech and the press, protections for minorities, and the other essential guarantees of individual liberty and choice. Constitutional institutions including courts will continue to police the boundaries of democratic discretion.

The crux of charges of manipulation or paternalism is that people are being interfered with or are having power exercised over them without their consent. With respect to collective exercises of power that have the sort of far-reaching consequences that we have described, the only effective way of heading off worries about manipulation and paternalism is via more and more reflective participation that includes all groups in society. We have no way to avoid living in a collectively constructed world of institutions and policies, and no agency other than the people themselves can be trusted to make law for the people. Our entire project is, therefore, designed to respond to the worries that underlie charges of manipulation and paternalism: the sense that, via politics, some are unfairly exercising power over others. One premise of our project is, after all, the idea of democratic legitimacy discussed in chapter one: the notion that the law is legitimate only when it represents the reflective input of all, when it is genuinely an exercise in collective self-governance rather than an imposition of some on others.

IS OUR REPORT OBJECTIONABLY PARTISAN?

Some of the measures we propose might be charged with reflecting sympathy with the Democratic Party (our concern with lower levels of participation among the socioeconomically disadvantaged or our proposal that ex-felons should be reenfranchised). Others of our proposals, or failures to propose, could be portrayed as favoring Republicans (our failure to tackle campaign finance reform or our applause for the mobilizing work of churches). Because politics is ever-changing, it is typically difficult to determine the partisan implications of specific proposals.

In some respects at least, the 2004 election debunked the popular myth that higher participation always helps Democrats. Popular participation does not, by definition, favor any one party. Our discussion of concerted efforts to mobilize voters—whether by unions or through churches or by other means—are as likely to favor Republicans and Democrats and may even press both to change their appeals. A Republican Party committed to bringing more people into the electorate is, by the standards of our report, doing important civic work. We applaud the efforts of Republicans to reach out to Hispanics and other groups and their commitment to grassroots mobilization and get-out-the-vote drives, to mention only two prominent examples. We support similar mobilization efforts from the Democratic Party as well. Increased and more equal participation among all segments of the population is not the province of either party. (In recent decades, the Republicans have, for example, sometimes had an edge among younger voters, whose low levels of participation have been a special concern of ours).

We confess to being partisans of "small 'd' democracy." Favoring a party has never been our aim, nor have we self-consciously striven for partisan balance; instead, we recommend what we think is best for the nation. Readers must judge for themselves how well we have succeeded (remaining as self-conscious as they can of their own partisanship).

Conclusion

Some will say that our sights are too high, that what we have by way of democracy is good enough. But if Americans are satisfied with nothing short of ever-increasing wealth and health, ever-greater progress in science and medicine, and ever-better products of all sorts, if Americans deplore levels of academic achievement in schools that seem stagnant, and if with respect to every significant field of human endeavor Americans measure themselves against the rest of the world and strive to equal or surpass all others, why should we rest content with anything less than steady progress toward the realization of inclusive democratic ideals?

The Anti-Federalists were right to think that it would be difficult to realize rule by the people in a very large and diverse polity. We should not discount the intrinsic difficulties of our project nor be quick to lay the shortcomings of today's politics at the door of moral degeneration. We do some things well, and we can take pride in our achievements. We know enough, moreover, to promote a more vibrant and inclusive democratic life.

Social scientists have a role to play, we believe, both by bringing what they know (and the limits of what is known) to the attention of the public and by addressing more consistently the whole range of issues that we need to understand to improve democratic performance. They need to look beyond the characteristics of individuals and think more about the institutional contexts within which individuals are formed and act, and they need to study settings that are of enormous practical importance, including metropolitan areas, even if these settings present special difficulties to the application of scientific methods (and so seem less accessible to "science" than, say, elections).

Democracy will not be improved unless leaders in all fields play a role in bringing attention to democratic deficits and potential improvements. In the end, democracies' deficits will have to be addressed by democratic processes themselves: leaders can and will play an important role, but citizens themselves must be willing to support enlightened leaders. When it comes to improving democracy, there are at least two practical obstacles: Do we know enough, and do we care enough?

The fact is that our level of collective commitment to and concern about the overall legitimacy and quality of self-government may be undermined by the ways in which institutions have been designed. Too often, they foster polarization, challenge the inclusiveness of civic life, and discourage political learning and interest in politics. It remains to be seen whether, and under what conditions, Americans—leaders and citizens—are capable of mustering the will to improve democracy in America.

NOTES

Chapter One

1. See Arend Lijphart, "Unequal Participation: Democracy's Unresolved Dilemma," *American Political Science Review* 91 (1991): 1–14.

2. Robert D. Putnam, *Bowling Alone: The Collapse and Revival of American Community* (New York: Simon and Schuster, 2000).

3. Michael X. Delli Carpini and Scott Keeter, *What Americans Know about Politics and Why It Matters* (Yale University Press, 1996), p. 196.

4. Task Force on Inequality and American Democracy, "Inequalities of Political Voice" (American Political Science Association, 2004), available at www.apsanet.org/section_256.cfm [March 14, 2005].

5. Based on the authors' analysis of Monitoring the Future: A Continuing Study of American Youth (University of Michigan, Institute for Social Research, Survey Research Center, annual survey), available at www.monitoringthefuture.org/ [February 25, 2005].

6. Larry M. Bartels, "Partisanship and Voting Behavior, 1952–1996," *American Journal of Political Science* 44 (2000): 35–50.

7. Gregory B. Markus, "Civic Participation in American Cities" (University of Michigan, Institute for Social Research, February 2002), pp. 42–43.

8. Martin Gilens, "Public Opinion and Democratic Responsiveness: Who Gets What They Want from Government?" paper prepared for the annual meeting of the American Political Science Association, Chicago, September 2004; and Larry M. Bartels, "Economic Inequality and Political Representation," paper prepared for the annual meeting of the American Political Science Association, Boston, August 2002.

9. John Stuart Mill, "Representative Government," in *Three Essays* (Oxford University Press, 1960), p. 186.

10. John Stuart Mill, "The Subjection of Women," *Mill: Texts, Commentaries,* edited by Akin Ryan (New York: Norton, 1997), pp. 211–12.

11. See, for example, the evidence marshaled in Putnam, *Bowling Alone*.

12. "President: 'I Ask You to Be Citizens,'" *New York Times*, January 21, 2001, p. A15.

13. These include the Center for Information and Research on Civic Learning and Engagement (www.civicyouth.org), the National Alliance for Civic Education (www.cived.net), the Center for Civic Education (www.civiced.org), the Education Commission of the States (www.ecs.org), and the National Conference of State Legislatures (www.ncsl.org), among numerous others.

14. See Sidney Verba, Kay Lehman Schlozman, and Henry E. Brady, *Voice and Equality: Civic Voluntarism in American Politics* (Harvard University Press, 1995). See also Putnam, *Bowling Alone.*

15. Scott Keeter, Cliff Zukin, Molly Andolina, and Krista Jenkins, "The Civic and Political Health of the Nation: A Generational Portrait" (University of Maryland, Center for Information and Research on Civic Learning and Engagement, 2002).

16. John Dewey, *The Public and Its Problems* (Ohio University Press, 1954; reprint of New York: Henry Holt, 1927), pp. 206–09.

17. Michael X. Delli Carpini, Fay Lomax Cook, and Lawrence Jacobs, "Talking Together: Discursive Capital and Civic Deliberation in America," paper presented at the annual meeting of the American Political Science Association, Chicago, April 3–6, 2003; David M. Ryfe, "The Practice of Deliberative Democracy: A Study of Sixteen Deliberative Organizations," *Political Communication* 19 (2002): 359–77; James S. Fishkin, *The Voice of the People: Public Opinion and Democracy* (Yale University Press, 1995).

18. The foregoing three paragraphs are informed by Markus, "Civic Participation in American Cities," p. 10; and Keeter and others, "Civic and Political Health of the Nation."

19. Verba, Schlozman, and Brady, *Voice and Equality.*

20. See Adam Smith's discussion of the public responsibility for education in *The Wealth of Nations* (New York: Knopf, 1991), part III. Benjamin Constant's famous speech defending modern liberty—understood as "negative" liberty, or freedom from interference—closes with a call for public action to promote the capacities of citizens; Benjamin Constant, "The Liberty of the Ancients Compared with That of the Moderns," speech given at the Athenee Royal, in *Benjamin Constant: Political Writings,* edited by Biancamaria Fontana (Cambridge University Press, 1988). Alexis de Tocqueville's *Democracy in America* is a monumental account of the role of institutions and public policies of all sorts in promoting capable and active citizenship; Alexis de Tocqueville, *Democracy in America,* edited by J. P. Mayer (New York: Anchor Books, 1969).

21. E. E. Schattschneider, *The Semisovereign People: A Realist's View of Democracy in America* (New York: Holt, Rinehart and Winston, 1960).

22. Samuel P. Huntington, "The United States," in *The Crisis of Democracy: Report on the Governability of Democracies to the Trilateral Commission* (New York University Press, 1975), p. 115.

23. George Kateb, "The Moral Distinctiveness of Representative Democracy," *Ethics* 91 (April 1981): 357–74.

24. John R. Hibbing and Elizabeth Theiss-Morse, *Stealth Democracy: Americans' Beliefs about How Government Should Work* (Cambridge University Press, 2002).

25. Mancur Olson, *Logic of Collective Action: Public Goods and the Theory of Groups* (Harvard University Press, 1971). See also William H. Riker and Peter Ordeshook, "A Theory of the Calculus of Voting," *American Political Science Review* 61, no. 1 (March 1968): 25–42.

26. Albert O. Hirschman, *Exit, Voice, Loyalty: Responses to Decline in Firms, Organizations, and States* (Harvard University Press, 1970).

27. Hibbing and Theiss-Morse, *Stealth Democracy*; Tali Mendelberg, "The Deliberative Citizen: Theory and Evidence," in *Political Decision-Making, Deliberation, and Participation:*

Research in Micropolitics, vol. 6, edited by Michael X. Delli Carpini, Leonie Huddy, and Robert Y. Shapiro (Greenwich, Conn.: JAI Press, 2002); Jane J. Mansbridge, *Beyond Adversary Democracy* (University of Chicago Press, 1983).

28. Patrick Ellcessor and Jan E. Leighley, "Voters, Non-Voters, and Minority Representation," in *Representation of Minority Groups in the U.S.*, edited by C. E. Menifield (Lanham, Md.: Austin and Winfield, 2001). See also Raymond E. Wolfinger and Steven J. Rosenstone, *Who Votes?* (Yale University Press, 1980); Verba, Schlozman, and Brady, *Voice and Equality*. But see Kim Quaile Hill and Jan E. Leighley, "The Policy Consequences of Class Bias in State Electorates," *American Journal of Political Science* 36 (1992): 351–65; Zoltan Hajnal and Jessica Trounstine, "Where Turnout Matters: The Consequence of Uneven Turnout in City Politics," forthcoming in *Journal of Politics* 67, no. 2 (May 2005).

29. Josiah Ober, *Political Dissent in Democratic Athens: Intellectual Critics of Popular Rule* (Princeton University Press, 2001).

30. See, for example, Robert A. Dahl, *Who Governs? Democracy and Power in an American City* (Yale University Press, 1961). See also the classics from Samuel Stouffer, *Communism, Conformity, and Civil Liberties: A Cross-Section of the Nation Speaks Its Mind* (Garden City, N.Y.: Doubleday, 1955); Philip Converse, "The Nature of Belief Systems in Mass Publics," in *Ideology and Discontent*, edited by David E. Apter (New York: Free Press, 1964); Herbert McCloskey and John Zaller, *The American Ethos: Public Attitudes toward Capitalism and Democracy* (Harvard University Press, 1984).

31. Joseph Schumpeter, *Capitalism, Socialism, and Democracy*, 3rd ed. (New York: Harper and Row, 1950), p. 262.

32. Huntington, "The United States," p. 113. According to Huntington, surges in popular participation in the United States have "produced a substantial increase in governmental activity and a substantial decrease in governmental authority" (p. 64). As citizens mobilize to meet their needs, Huntington argues, government expenditures outrun revenues.

33. See Samuel P. Huntington, *American Politics: The Promise of Disharmony* (Harvard University Press, 1981).

34. See Madison's tenth federalist paper in Alexander Hamilton, John Jay, and James Madison, *The Federalist Papers*, edited by Clinton Rossiter (New York: New American Library, 1961).

35. See, especially, Jason Kaufman, *For the Common Good* (Oxford University Press, 2000). Also see the critiques of Putnam's version of social capital by Margaret Levi, "Social and Unsocial Capital: A Review Essay of Robert Putnam's *Making Democracy Work*," *Politics and Society* 24 (1996): 45–55; Sidney Tarrow, "Making Social Science Work across Space and Time: A Critical Reflection on Robert Putnam's *Making Democracy Work*," *American Political Science Review* 90 (1996): 389–97.

36. Hibbing and Theiss-Morse, *Stealth Democracy*, p. 216f.

37. Thomas Jefferson to William C. Jarvis, September 28, 1820, in *The Writings of Thomas Jefferson*, vol. 15, edited by Albert Ellery Bergh (Washington: Thomas Jefferson Memorial Association, 1907), p. 278.

38. See, for example, Scott Althaus, *Collective Preferences in Democratic Politics: Opinion Surveys and the Will of the People* (Cambridge University Press, 2003).

39. See, for example, Tom R. Tyler, *Why People Obey the Law* (Yale University Press, 1990).

40. See Hamilton, Madison, and Jay, *Federalist Papers*.

41. Dahl, *Who Governs*, p. 279. Dahl goes on to assert that, for political scientists, "instead of seeking to explain why citizens are not interested, concerned, and active, the task is to explain why a few citizens *are*."

42. Hibbing and Theiss-Morse, *Stealth Democracy*, p. 10.

43. Mansbridge, *Beyond Adversary Democracy*.

44. See John Stuart Mill, *On Liberty*, edited by David Bromwich and George Kateb (Yale University Press, 2003).

45. Hannah Fenichel Pitkin, "Justice: On Relating Public and Private," *Political Theory* 9, no. 3 (August 1981): 347; the reference to Tussman is from Joseph Tussman, *Obligation and the Body Politic* (Oxford University Press, 1968). And see the helpful discussion in Steven L. Elkin, *City and Regime in the American Republic* (University of Chicago, 1987), p. 149.

46. This discussion is indebted to Morris P. Fiorina with Samuel J. Abrams and Jeremy C. Pope, *Culture War? The Myth of a Polarized America* (New York: Longman Publishing, 2005); we discuss this further in chapter five.

47. Committee on Political Parties, "Toward a More Responsible Two-Party System: A Report of the Committee on Political Parties," supplement to the *American Political Science Review* 44, no. 3, pt. 2 (1950): 1–99.

Chapter Two

1. Robert D. Putnam, *Bowling Alone: The Collapse and Revival of American Community* (New York: Simon and Schuster, 2000).

2. Based on the authors' analysis of Monitoring the Future: A Continuing Study of American Youth (University of Michigan, Institute for Social Research, Survey Research Center, annual survey), available at www.monitoringthefuture.org/ [February 25, 2005].

3. Adam J. Berinsky, "The Perverse Consequences of Electoral Reform in the United States," *American Politics Research* 31, no. 10 (2004): 1–21.

4. This figure is as of November, 19, 2004. Taken from elections.gmu.edu/Voter_Turnout_2004.htm [February 25, 2005].

5. Richard A. Brody, "The Puzzle of Political Participation in America," in *The New American Political System*, edited by Anthony King (Washington: American Enterprise Institute, 1978), pp. 287–324; Richard W. Boyd, "Decline of U.S. Voter Turnout: Structural Explanations," *American Politics Quarterly* 9 (1981): 133–50; Stephen D. Shaffer, "A Multivariate Explanation of Decreasing Turnout in Presidential Elections, 1960–1976," *American Journal of Political Science* 25 (1981): 68–95; Paul R. Abramson and John H. Aldrich, "The Decline of Electoral Participation in America," *American Political Science Review* 76 (1982): 502–21; Paul Kleppner, *Who Voted? The Dynamics of Electoral Turnout, 1870–1980* (New York: Praeger, 1982); Ruy A. Teixeira, *Why Americans Don't Vote: Turnout Decline in the United States, 1960–1984* (New York: Greenwood Press, 1987); Carol A. Cassel and Robert C. Luskin, "Simple Explanations of Turnout Decline," *American Political Science Review* 82 (1988): 1321–30; Ruy A. Teixeira, *The Disappearing American Voter* (Brookings, 1992); Steven J. Rosenstone and John Mark Hansen, *Mobilization, Participation, and Democracy in America* (New York: Macmillan, 1993); Robert D. Putnam, "Bowling Alone: America's Declining Social Capital," *Journal of Democracy* 6 (1995): 65–78; Putnam, *Bowling Alone*; Martin P. Wattenberg, *Where Have All the Voters Gone?* (Harvard University Press, 2002).

6. Michael McDonald and Samuel Popkin, "Myth of the Vanishing Voter," *American Political Science Review* 95 (2001): 963–74.

7. McDonald and Popkin's estimates have met with criticism. See, for example, Richard B. Freeman, "What, Me Vote?" paper prepared for the Social Dimensions of Inequality Project (New York: Russell Sage Foundation, 2001). While further refinements of their estimates will undoubtedly be made, their basic point remains a valuable one: a proper accounting of changes in voter turnout rates requires careful attention to who can vote and who cannot.

8. Herbert B. Asher, *Presidential Elections and American Politics*, 5th ed. (Pacific Grove, Calif.: Brooks/Cole, 1992), p. 50.

9. See Michael J. Hanmer, "From Selection to Election and Beyond: Understanding the Causes and Consequences of Electoral Reform in America," Ph.D. dissertation, University of Michigan, 2004; Benjamin Highton and Raymond E. Wolfinger, "Estimating the Effects of the National Voter Registration Act of 1993," *Political Behavior* 20 (1998): 79–104; Stephen Knack, "Does 'Motor Voter' Work? Evidence from State-Level Data," *Journal of Politics* 57 (1995): 796–811; J. Eric Oliver, "Effects of Eligibility Restrictions and Party Activity on Absentee Voting and Overall Turnout," *American Journal of Political Science* 40 (1996): 498–513; Robert M. Stein, "Early Voting," *Public Opinion Quarterly* 62 (1998): 57–69; Michael D. Martínez and David Hill, "Did Motor Voter Work?" *American Politics Quarterly* 27 (1999): 296–315; Staci L. Rhine, "Registration Reform and Turnout Change in the American States," *American Politics Quarterly* 23 (1995): 409–26; Staci L. Rhine, "An Analysis of the Impact of Registration Factors on Turnout in 1992," *Political Behavior* 18 (1996): 171–85.

10. Putnam, *Bowling Alone*; Warren E. Miller and J. Merrill Shanks, *The New American Voter* (Harvard University Press, 1996).

11. Peter Levine and Mark Hugo López, "Youth Voter Turnout Has Declined, by Any Measure" (University of Maryland, Center for Information and Research on Civic Learning and Engagement, September 2002).

12. Circle Fact Sheet (www.civicyouth.org/research/products/fact_sheets_outside.htm) [June 17, 2005]. Figures 2-3 and 2-4 report voter turnout using the methodology developed by researchers at the Center for Information and Research on Civic Learning and Engagement (CIRCLE), drawing on data collected by the Census Bureau in the Current Population Survey. Only citizens are included in the calculations, while people who did not answer the voting question on the survey are excluded.

13. Data for 2004 data based on CIRCLE research.

14. Eric Plutzer, "Becoming a Habitual Voter: Inertia, Resources, and Growth in Young Adulthood," *American Political Science Review* 96 (2002): 41–57.

15. Task Force on Inequality and American Democracy, "Inequalities of Political Voice" (American Political Science Association, 2004), available at www.apsanet.org/section_256.cfm [March 29, 2005]. An earlier study found slightly greater levels of inequality, with the richest 20 percent of Americans engaging in various forms of participation at rates that are about four times those of Americans in the bottom 20 percent in terms of income. Sidney Verba, Kay Lehman Schlozman, and Henry E. Brady, *Voice and Equality: Civic Voluntarism in American Politics* (Harvard University Press, 1985), pp. 178–82.

16. Those interested in the relationship between inequality and participation should also read the report of the Task Force on Inequality and American Democracy, "Inequalities of Political Voice."

17. Henry E. Brady, Kay Lehman Schlozman, Sidney Verba, and Laurel Elms, "Who Bowls? The (Un)Changing Stratification of Participation," in *Understanding Public Opinion,* edited by Barbara Norrander and Cyde Wilcox (Washington: CQ Press, 2002), pp. 219–42.

18. Brady and others, "Who Bowls?"

19. Putnam, *Bowling Alone*.

20. National Election Studies, 1948–2000 Cumulative Data File.

21. Monitoring the Future.

22. Monitoring the Future.

23. Harold W. Stanley and Richard G. Niemi, *Vital Statistics on American Politics, 2003–2004* (Washington: CQ Press, 2004), pp. 174–75.

24. Pew Center for the People and the Press, "News Audiences Increasingly Politicized," available at people-press.org/reports/display.php3?ReportID=215 [July 26, 2004].

25. Scott Keeter, Cliff Zukin, Molly Andolina, and Krista Jenkins, "The Civic and Political Health of the Nation: A Generational Portrait" (University of Maryland, Center for Information and Research on Civic Learning and Engagement, 2002), available at www.civicyouth.org [February 25, 2005].

26. Michael X. Delli Carpini and Scott Keeter, *What Americans Know about Politics and Why It Matters* (Yale University Press, 1996), ch. 3.

27. G. Bingham Powell Jr., "American Voter Turnout in Comparative Perspective," *American Political Science Review* 80 (1986): 17–43.

28. We hasten to add that a link between current forms of campaign finance and low rates of civic engagement may exist; our point is only that researchers have yet to establish such a relationship.

29. Rosenstone and Hansen, *Mobilization, Participation, and Democracy.*

30. Jack Citrin, "Comment: The Political Relevance of Trust in Government," *American Political Science Review* 68 (1974): 973–88; Margaret Levi and Laura Stoker, "Political Trust and Trustworthiness," *Annual Review of Political Science* 3, no. 1 (2000): 475–507; and Rosenstone and Hansen, *Mobilization, Participation, and Democracy.*

31. Stephen D. Ansolabehere, Shanto Iyengar, Adam Simon, and Nicholas Valentino, "Does Attack Advertising Demobilize the Electorate?" *American Political Science Review* 88, no. 4 (1994): 829–38; Stephen D. Ansolabehere and Shanto Iyengar, *Going Negative: How Political Advertisements Shrink and Polarize the Electorate* (New York: Free Press, 1995); Larry M. Bartels, "Review of *Going Negative: How Political Advertisements Shrink and Polarize the Electorate,*" *Public Opinion Quarterly* 60, no. 3 (1996): 456–60; Steven Finkel and John Geer, "A Spot Check: Casting Doubt on the Demobilizing Effect of Attack Advertising," *American Journal of Political Science* 42, no. 2 (1998): 573–95; Richard R. Lau, Lee Sigelman, Caroline Heldman, and Paul Babbitt, "The Effects of Negative Political Advertisements: A Meta-Analytic Assessment," *American Political Science Review* 93, no. 4 (1999): 851–76; Kim Fridkin Kahn and Patrick J. Kenney, "Do Negative Campaigns Mobilize or Suppress Turnout? Clarifying the Relationship between Negativity and Perception," *American Political Science Review* 93, no. 4 (1999): 877–90; Martin P. Wattenberg and Craig Leonard Brians, "Negative Campaign Advertising: Demobilizer or Mobilizer?" *American Political Science Review* 93, no. 4 (1999): 891–900; Stephen D. Ansolabehere, Shanto Iyengar, and Adam Simon, "Replicating Experiments Using Aggregate and Survey Data: The Case of Negative Advertising and Turnout," *American Political Science Review* 93, no. 4 (1999): 901–10.

32. James Madison, "Second State of the Union Address," available at wikisource.org/wiki/James_Madison's_Second_State_of_the_Union_Address [March 19, 2005].

33. Delli Carpini and Keeter, *What Americans Know*; Samuel L. Popkin and Michael A. Dimock, "Political Knowledge and Citizen Competence," in *Citizen Competence and Democratic Institutions,* edited by Stephen L. Elkin and Karol Edward Soltan (Pennsylvania State University Press, 1999); Chris Chapman and Richard G. Niemi, "The Civic Development of Ninth- through Twelfth-Grade Students in the United States: 1996," NCES 1999-131 (Department of Education, Office of Educational Research and Improvement, 1999); Henry Milner, *Civic Literacy: How Informed Citizens Make Democracy Work* (Hanover, N.H.: University Press of New England, 2002).

34. Kim Fridkin Kahn and Patrick J. Kenney, *The Spectacle of U.S. Senate Elections* (Princeton University Press, 1999).

35. Larry M. Bartels, "Uninformed Votes: Information Effects in Presidential Elections," *American Journal of Political Science* 40 (1996): 194–230.

36. Delli Carpini and Keeter, *What Americans Know,* p. 196.

37. Judith Torney-Purta, Rainer Lehmann, Hans Oswald, and Wolfram Schulz, *Citizenship and Education in Twenty-eight Countries: Civic Knowledge and Engagement at Age Fourteen* (Amsterdam: International Association for the Evaluation of Educational Achievement, 2001).

38. Research concerning trends in civic education and the efficacy of various civic education strategies is summarized in John Patrick, "The Civic Mission of Schools: Key Ideas in a Research-Based Report on Civic Education in the United States" (University of Maryland, Center for Information and Research on Civic Learning and Engagement, May 2005). See also Richard G. Niemi and Julia Smith, "Enrollments in High School Government Classes: Are We Shortchanging Both Citizenship and Political Science Training?" *PS: Political Science and Politics* 34 (2001): 281–87. On the changing content of courses, see Nathaniel Leland Schwartz, "Civic Engagement: The Demise of the American High School Civics Class," unpublished honors thesis, Harvard University, 2002. Schwartz describes the older civics texts as "how-to" manuals.

39. James G. Gimpel, J. Celeste Lay, and Jason E. Schuknecht, *Cultivating Democracy: Civic Environments and Political Socialization in America* (Brookings, 2003).

40. Norman H. Nie, Jane Junn, and Kenneth Stehlik-Berry, *Education and Democratic Citizenship in America* (University of Chicago Press, 1996); John R. Zaller, *The Nature and Origins of Mass Opinion* (Cambridge University Press, 1992).

41. Wattenberg, *Where Have All the Voters Gone?*

42. National Center for Educational Statistics, *The NAEP 1998 Civics Report Card for the Nation,* NCES 2000-457, by A. D. Lutkus, A. R. Weiss, J. R. Campbell, J. Mazzeo, and S. Lazer (Department of Education, Office of Educational Research and Improvement, 1999), available at nces.ed.gov/pubsearch/pubsinfo.asp?pubid=2000457 [February 25, 2005].

43. Stéphane Baldi, Marianne Perie, Dan Skidmore, Elizabeth Greenberg, and Carole Hahn, "What Democracy Means to Ninth Graders: U.S. Results from the International IEA Civic Education Study," NCES 2001-096 (Department of Education, National Center for Education Statistics, 2001), available at nces.ed.gov/programs/quarterly/ vol_3/3_2/q5-1.asp [February 25, 2005].

44. Delli Carpini and Keeter, *What Americans Know,* p. 157 for both quotes.

45. Verba, Schlozman, and Brady, *Voice and Equality,* p. 353.

46. Joanne Miller and Wendy Rahn, "Identity-Based Feelings, Beliefs, and Actions: How Being Influences Doing," paper presented at the twenty-fifth annual scientific meeting of the International Society of Political Psychology, Berlin, July 2002.

47. Jan W. Van Deth, "Interest in Politics," in *Continuities in Political Action: A Longitudinal Study of Political Orientations in Three Western Democracies,* edited by M. Kent Jennings and others (New York: De Gruyter and Aldine 1990), p. 278.

48. On political knowledge, see, for example, Delli Carpini and Keeter, *What Americans Know*; on political mobilization, see, for example, Rosenstone and Hansen, *Mobilization, Participation, and Democracy.*

49. Important exceptions to this generalization include Ronald E. Inglehart, *Culture Shift* (Princeton University Press, 1990), and Jan W. Van Deth, "Interesting but Irrelevant:

Social Capital and the Saliency of Politics in Western Europe," *European Journal of Political Research* 37 (2000): 115–47. See also Miller and Rahn, "Identity-Based Feelings, Beliefs, and Actions."

50. Admittedly, political interest is the main focus of Charles E. Merriam and Harold F. Gosnell, *Non-Voting* (University of Chicago Press, 1924). On the conceptual distinction between activity and interest in activity, see Paul F. Lazarsfeld, Bernard Berelson, and Hazel Gaudet, *The People's Choice* (Columbia University Press, 1948). We thank Chris Achen for his acute comments on this section.

51. Robert C. Luskin, "Explaining Political Sophistication," *Political Behavior* 12 (1990): 331–61; Verba, Schlozman, and Brady, *Voice and Equality*.

52. Paul Allen Beck and M. Kent Jennings, "Family Traditions, Political Periods, and the Development of Partisan Orientations," *Journal of Politics* 53 (1991): 742–63.

53. Martin P. Wattenberg, *The Decline of American Political Parties: 1952–1994* (Harvard University Press, 1996); Norman H. Nie, Sidney Verba, and John R. Petrocik, *The Changing American Voter* (Harvard University Press, 1976).

54. Larry M. Bartels, "Partisanship and Voting Behavior, 1952–1996," *American Journal of Political Science* 44 (2000): 35–50.

55. Committee on Political Parties, "Toward a More Responsible Two-Party System," supplement to the *American Political Science Review* 44 (1950): 1–99.

56. Philip A. Klinkner, "Red and Blue Scare: The Continuing Diversity of the American Electoral Landscape," *The Forum* 2 (2004): 1–10; Morris P. Fiorina with Samuel J. Abrams and Jeremy C. Pope, *Culture War? The Myth of a Polarized America* (New York: Longman Publishing, 2005).

57. Bartels, "Partisanship and Voting Behavior."

58. Task Force on Inequality and American Democracy, "Inequalities of Political Voice."

59. Task Force on Inequality and American Democracy, "Inequalities of Political Voice," p. 22.

60. Larry M. Bartels, "Economic Inequality and Political Representation," paper prepared for the annual meeting of the American Political Science Association, Boston, August 2002.

61. Martin Gilens, "Public Opinion and Democratic Responsiveness: Who Gets What They Want from Government?" paper prepared for the annual meeting of the American Political Science Association, Chicago, September 2004, p. 27.

62. Rosenstone and Hansen, *Mobilization, Participation, and Democracy.*

63. Raymond E. Wolfinger, Benjamin Highton, and Megan Mullin, "How Post-Registration Laws Affect the Turnout of the Registered," *State Politics and Policy Quarterly* 5, no. 1 (Spring 2005).

64. Donald P. Gerber and Alan S. Green, *Get Out the Vote! How to Increase Voter Turnout* (Brookings, 2004).

65. Freeman, "What, Me Vote?"

66. Henry E. Brady, "An Analytical Perspective on Participatory Inequality and Income Inequality," paper prepared for the Social Dimensions of Inequality Project (New York: Russell Sage Foundation, 2003), p. 2.

67. Task Force on Inequality and American Democracy, "Inequalities of Political Voice"; Task Force on Inequality and American Democracy, "American Democracy in an Age of Rising Inequality," www.apsanet.org/section_256.cfm [March 29, 2005].

68. Sidney Verba, Norman Nie, and Jae-on Kim, *Participation and Political Equality: A Seven-Nation Comparison* (University of Chicago Press, 1978).

69. Verba, Schlozman, and Brady, *Voice and Equality*, p. 233.

70. Nancy Burns, Kay Lehman Schlozman, and Sidney Verba, *The Private Roots of Public Action: Gender, Equality, and Political Participation* (Harvard University Press, 2001); Sidney Verba, Nancy Burns, and Kay Lehman Schlozman, "Knowing and Caring about Politics: Gender and Political Engagement," *Journal of Politics* 59 (1997): 1051–72; Susan B. Hansen, "Talking about Politics: Gender and Contextual Effects on Political Proselytizing," *Journal of Politics* 59 (1997): 73–103; Kay Lehman Schlozman, Nancy Burns, Sidney Verba, and Jesse Donahue, "Gender and Citizen Participation: Is There a Different Voice?" *American Journal of Political Science* 39 (1995): 267–93.

71. Verba, Schlozman, and Brady, *Voice and Equality*, p. 1052; Delli Carpini and Keeter, *What Americans Know*, p. 157. Some reports of gender differences in political knowledge should be viewed cautiously, as a recent study estimates that approximately 50 percent of the knowledge gap between men and women can be explained by the fact that men are more likely to guess when asked survey questions about their political knowledge, artificially inflating gender disparities in knowledge. See Jeffery J. Mondak and Mary R. Anderson, "Gender-Based Differences in Political Knowledge," *Journal of Politics* 66, no. 2 (2004): 492–512.

72. Verba, Schlozman, and Brady, *Voice and Equality*, p. 1064; and Hansen, "Talking about Politics." Hansen finds this effect for 1992, but not for 1988, 1990, or 1994. In addition, one study finds that women who live in states with at least one statewide female politician are more likely to be politically knowledgeable and to feel that they can influence government. Burns, Schlozman, and Verba, *Private Roots of Public Action*, ch. 13. Similarly, adolescent girls are more politically engaged when viable female candidates run for major office. David E. Campbell and Christina Wolbrecht, "See Jane Run: Women Politicians as Political Role Models for Adolescents," paper presented at the annual meeting of the Midwest Political Science Association, Chicago, April 2004. This suggests that eliminating the gender imbalance in office holding and office seeking could help to cure enduring inequalities in civic engagement across men and women.

73. Jack Citrin and Benjamin Highton, "How Race, Ethnicity, and Immigration Shape the California Electorate" (San Francisco: Public Policy Institute of California, 2002), p. 16.

74. Verba, Scholzman, and Brady, *Voice and Equality*, p. 358.

75. Jan E. Leighley, *Strength in Numbers* (Princeton University Press, 2001).

76. Wendy K. Tam Cho, "Naturalization, Socialization, Participation: Immigrants and (Non-)Voting," *Journal of Politics* 61, no. 4 (November 1999): 1140–55. Her analysis reveals that the lack of English proficiency endures much longer in the Latino community than in the Asian American one. By the third generation, Asian Americans appear to be almost completely proficient, whereas one in five Latinos still is not (p. 1149). Louis DeSipio, "Immigrant Organizing, Civic Outcomes: Civic Engagement, Political Activity, National Attachment, and Identity in Latino Immigrant Communities," Paper 0208 (University of California, Irvine, Center for the Study of Democracy, 2002).

77. Citrin and Highton, "How Race, Ethnicity, and Immigration Shape the California Electorate"; Jan E. Leighley and Arnold Vedlitz, "Race, Ethnicity, and Political Participation: Competing Models and Contrasting Explanations," *Journal of Politics* 61 (1999): 1092–14; Pei-te Lien, "Ethnicity and Political Participation: A Comparison between Asian and Mexican Americans," *Political Behavior* 16 (1999): 237–64.

78. Citrin and Highton, "How Race, Ethnicity, and Immigration Shape the California Electorate," p. 78.

79. For an important account of the ways in which political choices have shaped the structure of the American media, see Paul Starr, *The Creation of the Media: The Political Origins of Modern Communications* (New York: Basic Books, 2004).

80. Jon Katz, quoted in Jane Mayer, "Bad News: What's Behind the Recent Gaffes at ABC?" *New Yorker*, August 14, 2000, pp. 30–36.

81. Matthew A. Baum and Samuel Kernell, "Has Cable Ended the Golden Age of Presidential Television?" *American Political Science Review* 93 (2000): 99–114.

82. Stephen Hess, "Dwindling TV Coverage Fell to New Low," November 7, 2000, available at www.brookings.org/GS/Projects/HessReport/week10.htm [November 15, 2004].

83. Larry M. Bartels and Wendy M. Rahn, "Political Attitudes in the Post-Network Era," paper presented at the annual meeting of the American Political Science Association, Washington, September 2000. See also Thomas E. Patterson, *The Vanishing Voter: Public Involvement in an Age of Uncertainty* (New York: Knopf, 2002); Lynn Vavreck, "The Reasoning Voter Meets the Strategic Candidate: Signals and Specificity in Campaign Advertising, 1998," *American Politics Quarterly* 29 (2001): 507–29.

84. Cass Sunstein, *Republic.com* (Princeton University Press, 2001); see also Elihu Katz, "And Deliver Us from Segmentation," *Annals of the American Academy of Political and Social Sciences* 546 (1996): 22–33.

85. Nielsen Media Research, "Trends in Media: Daily Newspapers per Household," available at www.tvb.org/nav/build_frameset.asp?url=/rcentral/index.asp [October 22, 2004].

86. Markus Prior, "News v. Entertainment: How Increasing Media Choice Widens Gaps in Political Knowledge and Turnout," unpublished ms., Princeton University.

87. Markus Prior, "Political Knowledge after September 11," *PS: Political Science and Politics* 35 (2002): 523–29.

88. Marty Cohen, Hans Noel, and John Zaller, "How Politicians Act When Voters Are Left in the Dark: The Effect of Local News on Quality of Political Representation," paper presented at the annual meeting of the American Political Science Association, Chicago, September 2–5, 2004. See also Richard G. Niemi, Lynda W. Powell, and Patricia L. Bicknell, "The Effect of Community-Congressional District Congruity on Knowledge of Congressional Candidates," *Legislative Studies Quarterly* 11 (1986): 187–201; and Douglas Arnold, *Congress, the Press, and Political Accountability* (Princeton University Press, 2004).

89. Patterson, *Vanishing Voter*, p. 99.

90. Norman Ornstein and Thomas E. Mann, *The Permanent Campaign and Its Future* (Washington: American Enterprise Institute, 2000); Sidney Blumenthal, *The Permanent Campaign: Inside the World of Elite Political Operatives* (Boston: Beacon Press, 1980).

91. Patterson, *Vanishing Voter*, pp. 111–13.

92. Ronald E. Weber, Harvey J. Tucker, and Paul Brace, "Vanishing Marginals in State Legislative Elections," *Legislative Studies Quarterly* 16 (1991): 29–47.

93. Kahn and Kenney, *The Spectacle of U.S. Senate Elections*.

94. Kahn and Kenney, *The Spectacle of U.S. Senate Elections*; Mark C. Westlye, *Senate Campaigns and Campaign Intensity* (Johns Hopkins University Press, 1991); Doris A. Graber, *Media Power in Politics* (Washington: CQ Press, 1990); Peter Clarke and Susan Evans, *Covering Campaigns: Journalism in Congressional Elections* (Stanford University Press, 1983).

95. Kahn and Kenney, *Spectacle of U.S. Senate Elections*; Paul Gronke, *The Electorate, the Campaign, and the Office: A Unified Approach to Senate and House Elections* (University of Michigan Press, 2001).

96. David R. Jones, "Party Polarization and Legislative Gridlock," *Political Research Quarterly* 54 (2001): 125–41. To the extent that we find a decrease in marginal seats in the Senate, it is for slightly different reasons: not a gerrymandering of districts, but an ideological sorting of populations by state, a possibility we discuss further in chapter three.

97. John R. Hibbing and Elizabeth Theiss-Morse, *Stealth Democracy: Americans' Beliefs about How Government Should Work* (Cambridge University Press, 2002).

98. Rosenstone and Hansen, *Mobilization, Participation, and Democracy*, ch. 5.

99. Michael G. Hagen, Richard Johnston, and Kathleen Hall Jamieson, "Effects of the 2000 Presidential Campaign," paper prepared for the annual meeting of the Midwest Political Science Association, Chicago, April 25–28, 2002. More technically, the campaigns purchased 35,000 gross rating points. A gross rating point is calculated by multiplying the percentage of a media market that is expected to see an ad by the number of times it is expected to see it. An advertiser who wants an entire media market to see an ad three times will purchase 300 gross rating points.

100. Keena Lipsitz, "The Significance of Rich Information Environments: Voter Knowledge in Battleground States during the 2000 Presidential Campaign," paper prepared for the annual meeting of the Midwest Political Science Association, Chicago, April 15–18, 2004.

101. Marc Hetherington, "Desire for Order and Political Choice: How Preferences for Child Rearing Polarize the Nation," paper presented at the Conference on the Polarization of American Politics: Myth or Reality? Princeton University, December 3–4, 2004.

102. Verba, Schlozman, and Brady, *Voice and Equality*; Rosenstone and Hansen, *Mobilization, Participation, and Democracy*; Green and Gerber, *Get Out the Vote!*

103. Theda Skocpol, *Diminished Democracy: From Membership to Management in American Civic Life* (University of Oklahoma Press, 2003).

104. Stanley and Niemi, *Vital Statistics*, p. 404.

105. Kenneth M. Goldstein and Travis N. Ridout, "The Politics of Participation: Mobilization and Turnout over Time," *Political Behavior* 24 (2002): 3–29.

106. Sometimes, mobilization can overcome simple obstacles: for example, by providing a way to get to the polls for those who might not otherwise make it. Indeed, evidence from the 1996 Current Population Survey shows that African Americans, women, the elderly, and those with less education (as compared to whites, males, the young, and the better educated) are more likely to claim that they do not go to the polls because of a lack of transportation. Lynn M. Capser and Loretta E. Bass, "Voting and Registration in the Election of 1996," Current Population Reports P20-504 (Census Bureau, July 1998).

107. Miller and Shanks, *New American Voter*; Donald P. Green and Roni Shachar, "Habit Formation and Political Behavior: Evidence of Consuetude in Voter Turnout," *British Journal of Political Science* 30 (2000): 561–73; Plutzer, "Becoming a Habitual Voter."

108. States can avoid motor-voter's provisions by instead adopting election-day voter registration (or, as in North Dakota, by not requiring registration at all). States that have election-day registration include Idaho, Maine, Minnesota, New Hampshire, Wisconsin, and Wyoming. Maine, however, is not exempt from motor-voter because some local officials require registration on election day to be done at a location other than the polling place. Minnesota has a state-level motor-voter program but did not implement the federal version.

109. Laws regarding the voting rights of ex-felons are in flux. As of June 2004, seven states have the most restrictive laws, which disenfranchise felons: Alabama, Florida, Iowa, Kentucky, Mississippi, Nebraska, and Virginia. Seven more states have laws that disenfranchise some ex-felons: Arizona, Delaware, Maryland, Nevada, Tennessee, Washington, and Wyoming.

110. Christopher Uggen and Jeff Manza, "Democratic Contraction? Political Consequences of Felon Disenfranchisement in the United States," *American Sociological Review* 67 (2002): 777–803.

111. Uggen and Manza, "Democratic Contraction?" If we count only African American ex-felons, the number is just over 500,000, or approximately 2 percent of the black voting-age population.

112. Numerous examples of problems faced by college students circulated on the Internet in the months prior to the election of 2004. Some problems were overcome simply by making the matter public or by giving street addresses to dormitories, among other strategies. Nonetheless, the difficulties probably discouraged many students from registering.

113. Putnam, *Bowling Alone*, p. 9.

114. Arthur H. Miller, Edie Goldenberg, and Lutz Erbring, "Type-Set Politics: The Impact of Newspapers on Public Confidence," *American Political Science Review* 73 (1979): 67–84.

115. For the first view, see Nancy Burns, Donald R. Kinder, and Wendy Rahn, "Social Trust and Democratic Politics," paper presented at the annual meeting of the Midwest Political Science Association, Chicago, April 3–6, 2003; for the second, see Eric M. Uslaner, *The Moral Foundations of Trust* (Cambridge University Press, 2002).

116. Eric M. Uslaner, "Civic Engagement in America: Why People Participate in Political and Social Life," available at www.bsos.umd.edu/gvpt/uslaner/democracycollaborative. pdf [March 19, 2005].

117. Putnam, *Bowling Alone*; Skocpol, *Diminished Democracy*.

118. Verba, Shlozman, and Brady, *Voice and Equality*, ch. 13–14 and pp. 518–21; Carol A. Cassel, "Voluntary Associations, Churches, and Social Participation: Theories of Turnout," *Social Science Quarterly* 80 (1999): 504–17; Oscar B. Martinson and E. A. Wilkening, "Religious Participation and Involvement in Local Politics throughout the Life Cycle," *Sociological Focus* 20 (1987): 309–18; Putnam, *Bowling Alone*; Rosenstone and Hansen, *Mobilization, Participation, and Democracy*.

119. Verba, Schlozman, and Brady, *Voice and Equality*.

120. Keeter and others, "Civic and Political Health of the Nation"; Krista Jenkins, Molly W. Andolina, Scott Keeter, and Cliff Zukin, "Is Civic Behavior Political? Exploring the Multidimensional Nature of Political Participation," paper presented at the annual meeting of the Midwest Political Science Association, Chicago, April 3–6, 2003.

121. Keeter and others, "Civic and Political Health of the Nation."

122. Verba, Schlozman, and Brady, *Voice and Equality*, ch. 4. See also Kay Lehman Schlozman, Sidney Verba, and Henry E. Brady, "Participation's Not a Paradox: The View from American Activists," *British Journal of Political Science* 25 (1995): 1–36.

123. Richard G. Niemi and Paul Herrnson, "Beyond the Butterfly: The Complexity of U.S. Ballots," *Perspectives on Politics* 1 (2003): 317–26; Raymond E. Wolfinger and Steven J. Rosenstone, *Who Votes?* (Yale University Press, 1980).

124. Mark N. Franklin, *Voter Turnout and the Dynamics of Electoral Competition* (Cambridge University Press, 2004).

125. Wolfinger, Highton, and Mullin, "How Post-Registration Laws."

126. Richard G. Niemi and Jane Junn, *Civic Education: What Makes Students Learn?* (Yale University Press, 1998).

127. National Association of Secretaries of State, *American Youth Attitudes on Politics, Citizenship, Government, and Voting* (Lexington, Ky., 1999), pp. 36–37.

128. This statement is based on unpublished research conducted by Elizabeth Addonizio of Yale University. See, for example, Elizabeth Addonizio, "Reducing Inequality in Political Participation: An Experiment to Measure the Effects of Voting Instruction on Youth Voter Turnout," paper presented at the annual meeting of the American Political Science Association, Chicago, September 2–5, 2004.

129. Torney-Purta and others, *Citizenship and Education in Twenty-Eight Countries.*

130. Clyde Wilcox, "Political Structures and Political Participation," Civic Engagement Working Paper 6 (College Park, Md.: The Democracy Collaborative/Knight Foundation Civic Engagement Project, 2003), p. 12.

131. It has also been noted that we might get more capable poll workers if election day were a national holiday, making the counting process easier.

132. Mary Fitzgerald, "Easier Voting Methods Boost Youth Turnout," Working Paper (University of Maryland, Center for Information and Research on Civic Learning and Engagement, 2003), available at www.civicyouth.org/PopUps/WP01%20Fitzgerald%20no%20cover.pdf [February 21, 2004].

133. Brian Pinaire and Milton Heumann, "Barred from the Vote: Public Attitudes toward the Disenfranchisement of Felons," paper presented at the National Symposium on Felon Disenfranchisement, September 30, 2002; Jeff Manza, Clem Brooks, and Christopher Uggen, "'Civil Death' or Civil Liberties: Public Attitudes towards Felon Disenfranchisement in the United States," unpublished ms. (Northwestern University, Department of Sociology, 2003).

134. Justification of ex-felon disfranchisement seems to rest on several arguments: (a) completing one's sentence, by itself, is not sufficient, and those who have committed felonies should continue to pay for their crimes unless they can further prove that they are rehabilitated; (b) permitting ex-felons to vote would endanger the public, perhaps allowing groups of them to vote against sheriffs and others involved in law enforcement; and (c) when raised as a matter for possible federal action, it is also argued that ex-felon enfranchisement is a matter of states' rights. All of these arguments were raised in the Senate debate on the issue in February 2002 (*Congressional Record*, pp. S798–809). The argument about groups voting against law enforcement officials was made in reference to "jailhouse blocs" (p. S802), but it is implicit in arguments about ex-felons.

135. A study of some sixty countries around the world finds only two countries outside the United States (Belgium and the Philippines) with any restrictions on voting by ex-felons. Belgium is the only one that imposes a lifetime ban, and that is restricted to felons who are imprisoned for five years or more. Louis Massicotte, André Blais, and Antoine Yoshinaka, *Establishing the Rules of the Game: Election Laws in Democracies* (University of Toronto Press, 2004), pp. 32–33.

136. Uggen and Manza, "Democratic Contraction?"

137. Bruce E. Cain, Karin MacDonald, and Michael P. McDonald, "From Equality to Fairness: The Path of Political Reform since Baker v. Carr," paper presented at the Conference on Competition, Partisanship, and Congressional Redistricting, Brookings Institution and Institute of Governmental Studies, Washington, April 16, 2004, p. 35. Cain and his colleagues argue that the Iowa redistricting process, which is so often lauded because the state

has a high proportion of competitive districts, is not an altogether reliable means of removing politics from redistricting (p. 37). For a survey of all the methods used in American legislative redistricting, see Michael P. McDonald, "A Comparative Analysis of Redistricting Institutions in the United States, 2001–02," *State Politics and Policy Quarterly* 4 (2004): 371–95.

138. Contrary to media coverage implying otherwise, the Texas legislature did not redistrict twice following the 2000 census. The legislature did not pass a plan following the census, leaving the task to the federal district court; the court, arguably, left intact a previous Democratic gerrymander. Yet the fact remains that two redistricting plans were implemented after the 2000 census.

139. *Davis* v. *Bandemer,* 478 U.S. 109 (1986).

140. *Vieth* v. *Jubelirer,* 541 U.S. 267 (2004).

141. Indeed, four of the dissenting justices offered their own definitions of excessive political gerrymandering.

142. Michael McDonald, "A Comparative Analysis of Redistricting Institutions," p. 380. For a discussion of bipartisan gerrymanders, see Bruce E. Cain, *The Reapportionment Puzzle* (University of California Press, 1984), pp. 160–66; and David Butler and Bruce E. Cain, *Congressional Redistricting: Comparative and Theoretical Perspectives* (New York: Macmillan Publishing, 1992), pp.152–53.

143. Cain, MacDonald, and McDonald, "From Equality to Fairness," pp. 26–27.

144. Cain, MacDonald, and McDonald, "From Equality to Fairness," pp. 29–30.

145. Schwarzenegger's proposal was inspired by the political boundaries drawn up in the 1990s by special masters appointed by the California Supreme Court after the legislature failed to adopt a redistricting plan. The special masters' plan produced a surprising number of congressional, state senate, and state assembly districts that changed parties—sometimes twice—over the next ten years. After the 2000 census, California reverted to a legislative districting process. Douglas Johnson, "Competitive Districts in California: A Case Study of California's Redistricting in the 1990s" (Claremont, Calif.: Rose Institute of State and Local Government, 2005), available at research.mckenna.edu/rose/publications/pdf/rose_ca_case_study.pdf [March 19, 2005].

146. Alan S. Gerber and Donald P. Green, "The Effects of Canvassing, Telephone Calls, and Direct Mail on Voter Turnout: A Field Experiment," *American Political Science Review* 94 (2000): 653–63.

147. Green and Gerber, *Get Out the Vote!*

148. Jim VandeHei and Mary Fitzgerald, "Kerry Stumps for N.M. Votes," *Washington Post,* August 9, 2004.

149. Franklin, *Voter Turnout.*

150. William D. Berry, Michael B. Berkman, and Stuart Schneiderman, "Legislative Professionalism and Incumbent Reelection: The Development of Institutional Boundaries," *American Political Science Review* 94 (2000): 859–74; John M. Carey, Richard G. Niemi, and Lynda W. Powell, "Incumbency and the Probability of Reelection in State Legislative Elections," *Journal of Politics* 62 (2000): 671–700; Gary W. Cox and Scott Morgenstern, "The Incumbency Advantage in Multimember Districts: Evidence from the States," *Legislative Studies Quarterly* 20 (1995): 329–49.

151. Wilcox, "Political Structures and Political Participation," p. 13.

152. Similarly, we encourage more attention to proposals that electoral college votes be awarded proportionally within a state, the subject of an unsuccessful ballot initiative in Col-

orado in 2004. The district plan, however, is often viewed as a less radical departure from the current system of electing the president. See Lawrence D. Longley, *The Politics of Electoral College Reform*, 2nd ed. (Yale University Press, 1975), ch. 3. For a revealing look at how difficult it has been historically to pass electoral reform at the state level, see Peter H. Argersinger, "Electoral Reform and Partisan Jugglery," *Political Science Quarterly* 119 (2004): 499–520.

153. See Stephen J. Wayne, *Is This Any Way to Run a Democratic Election?* 2nd ed. (Boston: Houghton Mifflin, 2003), p. 58.

154. Moreover, it is unclear that moving to a direct popular election would encourage presidential candidates to campaign in a more geographically dispersed fashion. Under such a scenario, they might simply focus on large urban areas with high concentrations of moderate and independent voters and ignore much of rural and small-town America altogether—just as smaller states at the Constitutional Convention feared might happen under a system of direct election. For reasons to adopt a system of direct election, despite the effects on campaigning, see George C. Edwards III, *Why the Electoral College Is Bad for America* (Yale University Press, 2004); Lawrence D. Longley and Neal R. Peirce, *The Electoral College Primer* (Yale University Press, 1996); Neal R. Peirce and Lawrence D. Longley, *The People's President: The Electoral College in American History and the Direct Vote Alternative* (Yale University Press, 1981).

155. They include efforts such as citizen juries, "citizen panels," deliberative polls, study circles, twenty-first-century town meetings, Americans Discuss Social Security, and the Oregon Health Decisions Project. For a discussion of these and related efforts, see John Gastil, *By Popular Demand: Revitalizing Representative Democracy through Deliberative Elections* (University of California Press, 2000); Ethan Lieb, *Deliberative Democracy in America: A Proposal for a Popular Branch of Government* (Yale University Press, 2004); Archon Fung, "Recipes for Public Sphere: Eight Institutional Design Choices and Their Consequences," *Journal of Political Philosophy* 11, no. 3 (September 2003): 338–67.

156. Bruce Ackerman and James Fishkin, *Deliberation Day* (Yale University Press, 2004).

157. Fishkin has conducted numerous polls around the world, often in conjunction with major media organizations, such as MacNeil/Lehrer Productions and Britain's Channel 4, and studies have demonstrated that deliberative polling does change the attitudes of participants. Robert C. Luskin, James S. Fishkin, and Roger Jowell, "Considered Opinions: Deliberative Polling in Britain," *British Journal of Political Science* 32 (2002): 455–87.

158. Simon Jackman, "Compulsory Voting," in *International Encyclopedia of the Social and Behavioral Sciences* (Oxford: Elesvier, 2001).

159. Mark N. Franklin, "Electoral Participation," in *Comparing Democracies: Elections and Voting in Comparative Perspective*, edited by Lawrence Le Duc, Richard G. Niemi, and Pippa Norris (Thousand Oaks, Calif.: Sage, 1996); Evan Schofer and Marion Fourcade-Gourinchas, "The Structural Contexts of Civic Engagement: Voluntary Association Membership in Comparative Perspective," *American Sociological Review* 66 (2001): 806–28. Costs of participation here refer to direct state subsidies for organizations: "In corporate countries, the state encourages all forms of collective organization as the main channel of political incorporation and usually provides generous support—provided that associations are large, nationwide, democratically run, and structured in a centralized way that authorizes negotiation and bargaining with administrative institutions" (p. 814). The authors refer to association memberships in corporate countries (that is, Scandinavia) as "automatic" rather than voluntary, and they find evidence that membership in associations in these countries is "dis-

sociated" from activity (that is, high levels of membership do not lead to high levels of activity), unlike in more voluntaristic and individualistic cultures, where membership and activity are highly related.

160. H. Wesley Perkins, *The Social Norms Approach to Preventing School- and College-Age Substance Abuse* (San Francisco: Jossey-Bass, 2003).

161. Verba, Schlozman, and Brady, *Voice and Equality*.

Chapter Three

1. Census Bureau, *1992 Census of Governments*, vol. 1, no. 1: *Government Organization;* vol. 1, no. 2: *Popularly Elected Officials* (Commerce Department, Economics and Statistics Administration, 1992).

2. David A. Bositis, *Black Elected Officials: A Statistical Summary, 2001* (Washington: Joint Center for Political and Economic Studies, 2003); National Association of Latino Elected and Appointed Officials (NALEO) Educational Fund, *2002 National Directory of Latino Elected Officials* (Los Angeles, 1993).

3. Survey sponsored by the Pew Internet and American Life Project.

4. Carmine Scavo, "Use of Participative Mechanisms by Large U.S. Cities," *Journal of Urban Affairs* 15 (1993): 93–109.

5. Data from the Community Associations Institute on U.S. Community Associations, available at www.caionline.org/about/facts.cfm [July 27, 2004].

6. Sidney Verba, Kay L. Schlozman, and Henry E. Brady, *Voice and Equality: Civic Volunteerism in American Politics* (Harvard University Press, 1995), p. 72.

7. Robert D. Putnam, *Bowling Alone: The Collapse and Revival of American Community* (New York: Simon and Schuster, 2000).

8. Michael Falcone, "What if They Held an Election and No One Ran?"*New York Times* (national edition), September 21, 2003, p. 30.

9. Putnam, *Bowling Alone*, p. 43. But Verba, Schlozman, and Brady, *Voice and Equality*, p. 72, report slight increases in some forms of community engagement.

10. Verba, Schlozman, and Brady, *Voice and Equality*, pp. 189–90.

11. According to the 2000 Social Capital Benchmark Survey, 79 percent of adults agree that "Living in [city name]" gives them "a sense of community or a feeling of belonging." See Cara Joy Wong, "Membership and Morality in American Politics: Obligation to Racial, National, and Geographic Communities," Ph.D. dissertation, University of California, Berkeley, 2002, p. 89.

12. Christine Kelleher and David Lowery, "Political Participation and Metropolitan Institutional Contexts," *Urban Affairs Review* 39 (2004): 728.

13. Robert A. Dahl, "The City in the Future of Democracy," *American Political Science Review* 61 (1967): 953–70. The quote is found on p. 964.

14. Census Bureau, *2002 Census of Governments*, vol. 1, no. 1: *Government Organization* (Government Printing Office, 2002).

15. Alexis de Tocqueville, *Democracy in America*, edited by J. P. Mayer (New York: Anchor Books, 1969), p. 63.

16. Robert L. Lineberry, *Equality and Urban Policy: The Distribution of Municipal Public Services* (Beverly Hills, Calif.: Sage, 1977), p. 10.

17. Stephen L. Elkin, *City and Regime in the American Republic* (University of Chicago Press, 1987), pp. 153–55.

18. Dahl, "City in the Future of Democracy," p. 954.

19. J. Eric Oliver, "City Size and Civic Involvement in Metropolitan America," *American Political Science Review* 94 (June 2000): 361–73; J. Eric Oliver, *Democracy in Suburbia* (Princeton University Press, 2001). See also Putnam, *Bowling Alone,* pp. 205–07, including references.

20. Frank Bryan, *Real Democracy: The New England Town Meeting and How It Works* (University of Chicago Press, 2004). See also Christian Albrekt Larsen, "Municipal Size and Democracy: A Critical Analysis of the Argument of Proximity Based on the Case of Denmark," *Scandinavian Political Studies* 25 (2002): 317–32.

21. However, a study of twelve metropolitan areas finds that municipal size does not matter for turnout in local legislative elections. Kelleher and Lowery, "Political Participation and Metropolitan Institutional Contexts."

22. This is an old claim; see, for example, Benjamin Constant, "The Liberty of the Ancients Compared with That of the Moderns," speech given at the Athenee Royal, in *Benjamin Constant: Political Writings,* edited by Biancamaria Fontana (Cambridge University Press, 1988), p. 314.

23. Bernard H. Ross and Myron A. Levine, *Urban Politics* (Itasca, Ill.: F. E. Peacock, 2001); Kelleher and Lowery, "Political Participation and Metropolitan Institutional Contexts."

24. Wendy M. Rahn and Thomas J. Rudolph, "A Tale of Political Trust in American Cities" (University of Illinois at Urbana-Champagne, Department of Political Science; University of Minnesota, Department of Political Science, 2005). Under review at *American Journal of Political Science.*

25. Putnam, *Bowling Alone,* pp. 119, 136–38.

26. Robert A. Dahl and Edward R. Tufte, *Size and Democracy* (Stanford University Press, 1973).

27. Herbert J. Storing, ed., *The Anti-Federalist: Writings by the Opponents of the Constitution* (University of Chicago Press, 1985), p. 245.

28. Grant McConnell, *Private Power and American Democracy* (New York: Alfred Knopf, 1966), pp. 366–67.

29. Paul E. Peterson, "Federalism, Economic Development, and Redistribution," in *Public Values and Private Power in American Politics,* edited by J. David Greenstone (University of Chicago Press, 1982), p. 257. See also Paul E. Peterson, *City Limits* (University of Chicago Press, 1981). Because local institutions are far more permeable, they are in a much weaker position than the national government when it comes to pursuing greater equality and other policies that generate "widespread repercussions" or broad and unconfined benefits. See McConnell, *Private Power,* ch. 10.

30. Iris Marion Young, *Justice and the Politics of Difference* (Princeton University Press, 1990); this idea is echoed by Putnam, *Bowling Alone,* pp. 208–10.

31. Douglas W. Rae, *City: Urbanism and Its End* (Yale University Press, 2003), pp. 30–31, quoting Richard Sennett. See also Gordon Allport, *The Nature of Prejudice* (Cambridge, Mass.: Addison-Wesley, 1954), on the importance of context and structure in shaping intergroup contact.

32. Social scientists find a negative relationship between community heterogeneity and the quantity of civic engagement. Rahn and Rudolph, "A Tale of Political Trust"; Alberto Alesina and Eliana La Ferrara, "Participation in Heterogeneous Communities," *Quarterly Journal of Economics* 115 (2000): 347–904; Dora L. Costa and Matthew E. Kahn, "Civic Engagement and Community Heterogeneity: An Economist's Perspective," *Perspectives on*

Politics 1 (2003): 103–11. See also John Hibbing and Elizabeth Theiss-Morse, *Stealth Democracy: Americans' Beliefs about How Government Should Work* (Cambridge University Press, 2002).

33. Alexander Hamilton, John Jay, and James Madison, *The Federalist Papers*, edited by Clinton Rossiter (New York: New American Library, 1961), p. 83.

34. Marc J. Perry and others, "Population Change and Distribution, 1990 to 2000" (Commerce Department, Economics and Statistics Administration, Census Bureau, April 2001), p. 5, available at www.census.gov/prod/2001pubs/c2kbr01-2.pdf [January 13, 2004].

35. William Fulton, Rolf Pendall, Mai Nguyen, and Alicia Harrison, "Who Sprawls the Most? How Growth Patterns Differ across the U.S." (Brookings, Center on Urban and Metropolitan Policy, July 2001).

36. Center on Urban and Metropolitan Policy, *Racial Change in the Nation's Largest Cities: Evidence from the 2000 Census* (Brookings, April 2001).

37. Yvette M. Alex-Assensoh, "Introduction: In Search of Black and Multiracial Politics in America," in *Black and Multiracial Politics in America,* edited by Yvette M. Alex-Assensoh and Lawrence J. Hanks (New York University Press, 2000).

38. William H. Frey, "Melting Pot Suburbs: A Study of Suburban Diversity," in *Redefining Urban and Suburban America: Evidence from Census 2000,* edited by Bruce Katz and Robert E. Lang (Brookings, 2003), p. 158.

39. John R. Logan, "Ethnic Diversity Grows, Neighborhood Integration Lags," in *Redefining Urban and Suburban America,* edited by Katz and Lang, p. 248. Among Latinos, 54 percent now reside in suburbs and 36 percent reside in central cities. Roberto Suro and Audrey Singer, *Latino Growth in Metropolitan America: Changing Patterns, New Locations* (Brookings, Center on Urban and Metropolitan Policy, and the PEW Hispanic Center, 2002), available at www.pewhispanic.org/site/docs/pdf/final_phc-brookings_paper-appendix-tables.pdf [February 17, 2005]. Nowadays, white flight is no longer the principal factor driving suburbanization. Increasing suburban diversity has been driven partly by the "new immigration": the dramatic movement of people from non-European countries to the United States since the repeal of racially discriminatory immigration laws in 1965. Alex-Assensoh and Hanks, eds., *Black and Multiracial Politics in America.* See also Audrey Singer, *The Rise of the New Immigrant Gateways* (Brookings, Center on Urban and Metropolitan Policy, February 2004); Ron Schmidt, Rodney Hero, Andy Aoki, and Yvette M. Alex-Assensoh, "Political Science, The New Immigration, and Racial Politics in the United States: What Do We Know? What Do We Need to Know?" paper presented at the annual meeting of the American Political Science Association, San Francisco, August 29–September 2, 2001.

40. William H. Frey, "Metro Magnets for Minorities and Whites: Melting Pots, the New Sunbelt, and the Heartland," Population Studies Center Research Report 02-496 (University of Michigan, Institute for Social Research, February 2002), available at www.psc.isr.umich.edu/pubs/papers/rr02-496.pdf [February 17, 2005]. Increases in diversity vary dramatically by region of the country, not to mention by metropolitan area. Frey finds only twenty-three melting-pot metropolitan areas, with significant regional differences in the trends, and concludes with the following: "It is important for commentators, political analysts, and those that monitor consumer behavior to take cognizance of these sharp regional divisions, rather than maintaining the illusion of a national melting pot." Nonetheless, while there are considerable regional differences, it is clear that the populations of Hispanics, blacks, and Asians in the nation's largest central cities are growing, while whites now represent less than half of the population in many of those places.

41. Figures on the number of governments are from the *Census of Governments* as reported in Census Bureau, *Statistical Abstract of the United States: 2002* (Government Printing Office, 2002), p. 260.

42. G. Ross Stephens and Nelson Wikstrom, *Metropolitan Government and Governance: Theoretical Perspectives, Empirical Analysis, and the Future* (Oxford University Press, 2000), p. 19.

43. Samuel Popkin, *The Reasoning Voter* (University of Chicago Press, 1991), p. 222. Popkin's focus is on the diffusion of power at the national level, but the same principles apply forcefully at the local level. See Curtis Wood, "Voter Turnout in City Elections," *Urban Affairs Review* 38 (2002): 214–15.

44. As Iris Marion Young states, "It is appropriate to ask whether the boundaries of a given polity correspond to the definition a polity ought to have in order properly to respond to moral requirements of justice." Iris Marion Young, *Inclusion and Democracy* (Oxford University Press, 2000), p. 222. See also Michael N. Danielson, *The Politics of Exclusion* (Columbia University Press, 1976).

45. Census Bureau, *2002 Census of Governments,* vol. 1, no. 1: *Government Organization.*

46. See Center on Urban and Metropolitan Policy, *Growth in the Heartland: Challenges and Opportunities for Missouri* (Brookings, 2002). See also David J. Barron, Gerald E. Frug, and Rick T. Su, *Dispelling the Myth of Home Rule: Local Power in Greater Boston* (Cambridge, Mass.: Rappaport Institute, 2004).

47. Edward L. Glaeser and Jacob L. Vigdor, "Racial Segregation: Promising News," in *Redefining Urban and Suburban America,* edited by Katz and Lang, pp. 211–34; David M. Cutler, Edward L. Glaeser, and Jacob L. Vigdor, "The Rise and Decline of the American Ghetto," *Journal of Political Economy* 3 (1999): 455–506.

48. Glaeser and Vigdor, "Racial Segregation."

49. Douglas S. Massey and Mary J. Fischer, "The Geography of Inequality in the United States, 1950–2000," in *Brookings-Wharton Papers on Urban Affairs 2003*, edited by William G. Gale and Janet Rothenberg Pack (Brookings, 2003), p. 11.

50. Paul A. Jargowsky, *Poverty and Place: Ghettos, Barrios, and the American City* (New York: Russell Sage Foundation, 1996).

51. Paul A. Jargowsky, *Stunning Progress, Hidden Problems: The Dramatic Decline of Concentrated Poverty in the 1990s* (Brookings, Center for Urban and Metropolitan Policy, May 2003).

52. Charles M. Tiebout, "A Pure Theory of Local Expenditures," *Journal of Political Economy* 66 (1956): 418.

53. Vicent Ostrom, Charles M. Tiebout, and Robert O. Warren, "The Organization of Government in Metropolitan Areas: A Theoretical Inquiry," *American Political Science Review* 44, no. 4 (1961): 831–42.

54. The most comprehensive treatment of local government using the public choice approach is Vincent Ostrom, Robert Bish, and Elinor Ostrom, *Local Government in the United States* (Oakland, Calif.: ICS Press, 1988).

55. The distinction between exit and voice as methods for holding organizations accountable is made by Albert O. Hirschman, *Exit, Voice, and Loyalty* (Harvard University Press, 1970).

56. One attempt to test these propositions, though, finds that government consolidation in Indianapolis in 1969 was followed by sharp declines in turnout in municipal elections. William Blomquist and Roger B. Parks, "Fiscal, Service, and Political Impacts of

Indianapolis-Marion County's Unigov," *Publius* 25 (1995): 37–54. This study is not a conclusive test because changes in other important variables, including size, coincided with consolidation. For a synthesis of the literature and an independent test of the effect of fragmented metropolitan government on civic engagement, see Christine Kelleher and David Lowery, "Central City Size, Metropolitan Institutions, and Political Participation: An Individual-Level Analysis of Twenty-five Urban Counties," paper presented at the annual meeting of the American Political Science Association, Chicago, September 2004.

57. Robert Stein, "Tiebout's Sorting Hypothesis," *Urban Affairs Quarterly* 23 (1987): 140–60.

58. Elkin, *City and Regime*, p. 149.

59. Michael Keating, *Comparative Urban Politics: Power and the City in the United States, Canada, Britain, and France* (Aldershot, U.K.: Edward Elgar, 1991), p. 115.

60. Myron Orfield captures this variety of suburbs with a typology focused on the fiscal condition of each municipality. Orfield's typology of suburbs includes at-risk segregated, at-risk older, at-risk low-density, bedroom-developing, affluent job centers, and very affluent job centers. Myron Orfield, *American Metropolitics: The New Suburban Reality* (Brookings, 2002).

61. Middle-class suburbs are defined as suburbs with per capita income between 75 and 125 percent of the regional per capita income. Todd Swanstrom, Colleen Casey, Robert Flack, and Peter Dreier, *Pulling Apart: Economic Segregation in the Top Fifty Metropolitan Areas, 1980–2000* (Brookings, Center on Urban and Metropolitan Policy, October 2004).

62. Orfield, *American Metropolitics*, p. 60.

63. Michael N. Danielson, *The Politics of Exclusion* (Columbia University Press, 1976).

64. Rae, *City*, pp. 30–31.

65. Oliver, *Democracy in Suburbia*.

66. McConnell, *Private Power*, p. 365.

67. Thomas Byrne Edsall and Mary Edsall, *Chain Reaction: The Impact of Race, Rights, and Taxes on American Politics* (New York: W. W. Norton, 1991).

68. Compounding the problem is the fact that local political institutions and groups in civil society are not doing all they could to incorporate and facilitate the civic engagement of new immigrants.

69. Rae, *City*, p. 421; Yvette Alex-Assensoh, *Neighborhoods, Family, and Political Participation in Urban America* (New York: Garland Publishing, 1998); John Bolland and Debra Moehle McCallum, "Neighboring and Community Mobilization in High-Poverty Inner-City Neighborhoods," *Urban Affairs Review* 38 (2002): 42–69. Jeffrey Berry, Kent Portney, and Ken Thomson, "The Political Behavior of Poor People," in *The Urban Underclass*, edited by Christopher Jencks and Paul Peterson (Brookings, 1991); Cathy Cohen and Michael Dawson, "Neighborhood Poverty and African American Politics," *American Political Science Review* 87 (1993): 286–302.

70. As reported by Bill Bishop, with the assistance of Robert Cushing, in a series of articles in the *Austin American-Statesman*, April 4, April 18, May 2, and May 30, 2004.

71. The research on contextual effects supports the conclusion that, as local political contexts become dominated by one political persuasion, minority political views tend to be stamped out or driven underground. Scholars have identified a number of causal pathways for this effect, including biased information, social learning, and reference groups. As Robert Huckfeldt and John Sprague observe, the probability that members of the political minority will have most of their interactions with members of the political majority "creates a

political bias favorable to political majorities and, thus, rather than being cohesive and resolute, political minorities suffer from the debilitating consequences of social bombardment by political messages that run counter to their own political inclinations. . . . In order to survive the loaded dice of social interaction within a bounded environment saturated with stochastically biased information—skewed partisan messages—political minorities may resort to withdrawal from the surrounding environment." Robert Huckfeldt and John Sprague, "Citizens, Contexts, and Politics," in *Political Science: The State of the Discipline II*, edited by Ada W. Finifter (Washington: American Political Science Association, 1993), p. 291. Huckfeldt and Sprague cite seven studies that support this generalization.

72. James G. Gimpel, J. Celeste Lay, and Jason E. Schuknecht, *Cultivating Democracy: Civic Environments and Political Socialization in America* (Brookings, 2003), p. 120.

73. Morris P. Fiorina, with Samuel J. Abrams and Jeremy C. Pope, *Culture War? The Myth of a Polarized America* (New York: Pearson Longman, 2005).

74. See Robert R. Rodgers, "This Land Is Your Land: The Politics of Open Space Preservation," Ph.D. dissertation, Princeton University, 2005.

75. For example, ethnographer M. P. Baumgartner describes a New Jersey suburb of the 1980s as having a culture of atomized, isolated individualism, a "moral minimalism" according to which suburbanites keep to themselves, ask little of their neighbors, and seek nothing in return. M. P. Baumgartner, *The Moral Order of a Suburb* (Oxford University Press, 1988). See also Margaret Kohn, *Brave New Neighborhoods: The Privatization of Public Space* (New York: Routledge, 2004).

76. For an introduction to new urbanist thinking, see Andres Duany, Elizabeth Plater-Zyberk, and Jeff Speck, *Suburban Nation: The Rise of Sprawl and the Decline of the American Dream* (New York: North Point Press, 2000), in particular appendix B, which reprints the official charter of the Congress for the New Urbanism, which was passed in 1996. See also Peter Calthorpe, *The Next American Metropolis: Ecology, Communities, and the American Dream* (New York: Princeton Architectural Press, 1993); Peter Katz, *The New Urbanism: Toward an Architecture of Community* (New York: McGraw-Hill, 1994).

77. Witold Rybczynski, *A Clearing in the Distance: Frederick Law Olmsted and America in the Nineteenth Century* (New York: Scribner, 1999).

78. Jane Jacobs, *The Death and Life of Great American Cities* (New York: Random House, 1961), p. 71.

79. Herbert J. Gans, *The Levittowners: Ways of Life and Politics in a New Suburban Community* (Columbia University Press, 1967). Gans does, however, acknowledge that the political commitments of Levittowners are parochial and do not address metropolitanwide issues.

80. Rae, *City*. Rae defines "urbanism" on pp. 18–19.

81. Oliver, *Democracy in Suburbia*, ch. 5.

82. Putnam, *Bowling Alone*, p. 213. Putnam estimates that sprawl accounts for approximately one-tenth of the decline in civic engagement that he documents in the book. Glaeser argues that commuting times in some cities—for example, New York City—are longer than for the average commuter in an auto, but that the experience of riding alone to work is different from rubbing elbows with diverse residents.

83. Stan Humphries, "Who's Afraid of the Big, Bad Firm: The Impact of Economic Scale on Political Participation," *American Journal of Political Science* 45 (July 2001): 678–99; Lance Freeman, "The Impact of Sprawl on Neighborhood Social Ties: An Exploratory Analysis," *Journal of the American Planning Association* 67 (Winter 2001): 69–78.

84. See Thad Williamson, "Sprawl, Politics, and Participation: A Preliminary Analysis," *National Civic Review* 9 (Fall 2002): 235–44, and "Does Sprawl Hinder Citizenship? The Impact of Local Socio-Spatial Characteristics on Nonelectoral Political Participation," paper prepared for the annual meeting of the Urban Affairs Association, Washington, April 1–3, 2004. See also his doctoral dissertation, "Sprawl, Justice, and Citizenship," Ph.D. dissertation, Harvard University, 2004.

85. In chapter four, we discuss some of the many nonpolitical civic groups that enhance personal connections and communications and facilitate the capacity of ordinary people for civic engagement.

86. Census Bureau, *1992 Census of Governments*, vol. 1, no. 2: *Popularly Elected Officials*.

87. Verba, Schlozman, and Brady, *Voice and Equality*, using 1990 Citizen Participation Study data, estimates calculated on weighted data.

88. Robert L. Morlan, "Municipal vs. National Election Voter Turnout: Europe and the United States," *Political Science Quarterly* 3 (1984): 461. See also Wood, "Voter Turnout in City Elections."

89. Wood, "Voter Turnout in City Elections."

90. Albert K. Karnig and B. Oliver Walter, "Decline in Municipal Voter Turnout: A Function of Changing Structure," *American Politics Quarterly* 11, no. 4 (1983): 491–505. See also Albert K. Karnig and B. Oliver Walter, "Municipal Voter Turnout during the 1980s: The Case of Continued Decline," in *State and Local Government and Politics: Essential Readings*, edited by H. A. Bailey and J. M. Shafritz (Itasca, Ill.: F. E. Peacock, 1993).

91. Zoltan L. Hajnal and Paul G. Lewis, "Municipal Institutions and Voter Turnout in Local Elections," *Urban Affairs Review* 38 (2003): 645–68.

92. Zoltan Hajnal and Jessica Trounstine, "Where Turnout Matters: The Consequences of Uneven Turnout in City Politics," forthcoming in *Journal of Politics* 67 (May 2005).

93. See, for example, Steven J. Rosenstone and John Mark Hansen, *Mobilization, Participation, and Democracy in America* (New York: Macmillan, 1993); Verba, Schlozman, and Brady, *Voice and Equality*.

94. Alan S. Gerber and Donald P. Green, "The Effects of Canvassing, Telephone Calls, and Direct Mail on Voter Turnout: A Field Experiment," *American Political Science Review* 94 (September 2000): 653–63.

95. Donald P. Green, Alan S. Gerber, and David W. Nickerson, "Getting Out the Vote in Local Elections: Results from Six Door-to-Door Canvassing Experiments," *Journal of Politics* 65 (November 2003): 1083–96. See also Verba, Schlozman, and Brady, *Voice and Equality*, pp. 134–39.

96. Putnam, *Bowling Alone*.

97. *New York Times* (national ed.), September 21, 2003, p. 30.

98. We do not mean to imply that the representation of African American and Latino communities as measured by the number of elected officials is in any sense proportional to their percentage of the population.

99. The Joint Center for Political and Economic Studies first gathered data on the number of African American elected officials in 1970. Of the 1,469 African Americans holding elective office in 1970, 42.4 percent (623) served at the municipal level and another 24.6 percent (362) served in education, with most of these persons serving on local school boards. In 1980, 72.7 percent ($N = 3,570$) of all African American elected officials served at the local level. In 1990, it was 72.3 percent ($N = 5,326$). David A. Bositis, *Black Elected Officials: A Statistical Summary, 2001* (Washington: Joint Center for Political and Economic Studies, 2003); NALEO, *2002 National Directory of Latino Elected Officials*.

100. See the discussion in Chandler Davidson and Bernard Grofman, *Quiet Revolution in the South: The Impact of the Voting Rights Act, 1965–1970* (Princeton University Press, 1994).

101. Paul Friesma, "Black Control of Central Cities: The Hollow Prize," *Journal of the American Institute of Planners* 35 (1969): 75–79; Albert K. Karnig and Susan Welch, *Black Representatives and Urban Policy* (University of Chicago Press, 1980); Adolph Reed, "The Black Urban Regime: Structural Origins and Constraints," in *Power, Community, and the City,* edited by Michael K. Smith, Comparative Urban and Community Research Series 1 (New Brunswick, N.J.: Transaction Books, 1988), pp. 138–89; Neil Kraus and Todd Swanstrom, "Minority Mayors and the Hollow Prize Problem," *PS: Political Science and Politics* 34 (March 2001): 99–105.

102. Douglas Yates, *The Ungovernable City: The Politics of Urban Problems and Policy Making* (MIT Press, 1977); Paul E. Peterson, *City Limits* (University of Chicago Press, 1981); Rufus Browning, Dale Marshall, and David Tabb, *Protest Is Not Enough: The Struggle of Blacks and Hispanics for Equality in Urban Politics* (University of California Press, 1984); Peter K. Eisenger, "Black Mayors and the Politics of Racial and Economic Advancement," *Urban Politics: Past, Present, and Future,* 2nd ed., edited by Harlan Hahn and Charles Levine (New York: Longman, 1984), pp. 249–58; William E. Nelson Jr., "Black Mayoral Leadership," *National Political Science Review* 2 (1990): 188–95; Michael Preston, "Symposium: Big City Black Mayors; Have They Made a Difference?" *National Political Science Review* 2 (1990): 129–95.

103. Russell D. Murphy, "Politics, Political Science, and Urban Governance: A Literature and a Legacy," *Annual Review of Political Science* 5 (2002): 63–85.

104. Amy Bridges, *Morning Glories: Municipal Reform in the Southwest* (Princeton University Press, 1997), p. 216. See also Michael Jones-Correa, "Immigrants, Blacks, and Cities," in *Black and Multiracial Politics in America,* edited by Alex-Assensoh and Hanks, p. 137. Jones-Correa emphasizes that the point of reforms was not to mobilize citizens but to perpetuate themselves.

105. Jessica L. Trounstine, "Urban Empires: Causes and Consequences of Biased Electoral Systems in American Cities," Ph.D. dissertation, University of California, San Diego, 2004. Trounstine asserts, "After machine and reform organizations secured election to office and were in a position to influence, if not control, policy, they sought to decrease competition and increase their probability of reelection" (p. 87). These efforts resulted in lower turnout in both machine and reform cities. See also Steven Erie's analysis of "entrenched machines": Steven Erie, *Rainbow's End: Irish-Americans and the Dilemmas of Urban Machine Politics, 1840–1985* (University of California Press, 1988).

106. Trounstine, "Urban Empires."

107. Robert R. Alford and Eugene C. Lee, "Voter Turnout in American Cities," *American Political Science Review* 62 (September 1968): 796–813; Karnig and Walter, "Decline in Municipal Voter Turnout"; Harvey Schuckman, "Political Participation in American Cities: Deconstructing the Role of Local Political Institutions," Ph.D. dissertation, University of Michigan, 2000.

108. Mayors do wield power unless, as in some cities, there is both a mayor and a manager, in which case the manager typically undermines the mayor's power.

109. Wood, "Voter Turnout in City Elections." See also Bridges, *Morning Glories*; Alford and Lee, "Voting Turnout in American Cities"; Karnig and Walter, "Decline in Municipal Voter Turnout."

110. See Schuckman, "Political Participation in American Cities," for African Americans and people of low socioeconomic status; see Luis Ricardo Fraga, "Domination through

Democratic Means: Nonpartisan Slating Groups in City Electoral Politics," *Urban Affairs Quarterly* 23 (June 1988): 528–55, for African Americans and Latinos. Fraga argues that, in the Southwestern cities he has studied, reform "governmental structures and their attendant party-type organizations . . . long serve[ed] to minimize the effective representation of minority community interests in city government [by preventing] the election of their first-choice candidates." See also Rahn and Rudolph, "A Tale of Political Trust," with respect to a negative relationship between political trust and at-large elections among African Americans.

111. Karnig and Welch, *Black Representatives and Urban Policy*.

112. Lawrence Bobo and Franklin D. Gilliam Jr., "Race, Sociopolitical Participation, and Black Empowerment," *American Political Science Review* 84 (1990): 377–93. There is also recent preliminary evidence that the presence of a black mayor is related to trust in local government among African Americans. Melissa Marschall, "The Attitudinal Effects of Minority Incorporation: Examining the Racial Dimensions of Trust in Urban America," paper presented to the annual meetings of the International Society for Political Psychology, Lund, Sweden, July 15–18, 2004. However, some scholars are less certain about the relationship between reform institutions and minority participation; see, for example, Fraga, "Domination through Democratic Means," p. 551.

113. John P. Pelissero, "The Political Environment of Cities in the Twenty-first Century," in *Cities, Politics, and Policy: A Comparative Analysis,* edited by John P. Pelissero (Washington: CQ Press, 2003), p. 18.

114. Wood, "Voter Turnout in City Elections."

115. Hajnal and Lewis, "Municipal Institutions and Voter Turnout in Local Elections." Local elections held at the same time as midterm congressional elections and presidential primaries increase voter turnout by 26 and 25 percent, respectively.

116. Hajnal and Lewis mention several important objections and concerns about concurrent elections, including lack of voter attentiveness to and knowledge of local issues; longer, more complex, and confusing ballots; the swamping of local concerns by state and national issues; and the prospect of increased partisanship.

117. See Fiorina, *Culture War,* ch. 8. We are grateful to Jessica L. Trounstine for her expert assistance on this section.

118. Schuckman, "Political Participation in American Cities."

119. Rahn and Rudolph, "A Tale of Political Trust." However, low levels of trust may also spur participation, especially when combined with high levels of efficacy or political interest. Margaret Levi and Laura Stoker, "Political Trust and Trustworthiness," *Annual Review of Political Science* 3 (2000): 475–508; see especially pp. 486–88.

120. Michael Jones-Correa, *Between Two Nations: The Political Predicament of Latinos in New York City* (Cornell University Press, 1998); Rodolfo O. de la Garza and Louis DeSipio, "Between Symbolism and Influence: Latinos and the 2000 Elections," in *Muted Voices: Latinos and the 2000 Election,* edited by Rodolfo O. de la Garza and Louis DeSipio (New York: Rowman and Littlefield Publishers, 2005), pp. 13–65; Adrian D. Pantoja, Ricardo Ramírez, and Gary M. Segura, "Citizens by Choice, Voters by Necessity: Patterns in Political Mobilization by Naturalized Latinos," *Political Research Quarterly* 54 (2001): 729–50; Wendy K. Tam Cho, "Naturalization, Socialization, Participation: Immigrants and (Non-)Voting," *Journal of Politics* 61 (1999): 1140–55; Pei-te Lien, M. Margaret Conway, and Janelle Wong, *The Politics of Asian Americans* (New York: Routledge, 2004).

121. Jones-Correa, "Immigrants, Blacks, and Cities"; Gary Gerstle and John Mollenkopf, "The Political Incorporation of Immigrants Then and Now," in *E Pluribus Unum? Contem-*

porary and Historical Perspectives on Immigrant Political Incorporation (New York: Russell Sage Foundation, 2001).

122. For argument and evidence that local party politics can generate increased civic engagement, see Trounstine, "Urban Empires," ch. 4; Bridges, *Morning Glories.*

123. Census Bureau, *Statistical Abstract of the United States 2000* (Government Printing Office, 2000), p. 299; Census Bureau, *2002 Census of Governments,* vol. 1, no. 1: *Government Organization.*

124. For a review of the scholarship on special districts, see Kathryn Foster, *The Political Economy of Special-Purpose Government* (Georgetown University Press, 1997), especially ch. 2.

125. Nancy Burns, *The Formation of American Local Governments: Private Values in Public Institutions* (Oxford University Press, 1994), p. 25.

126. Foster, *Political Economy of Special-Purpose Government,* shows that special districts tend to drive up the cost of government and "bias" spending toward development and routine services to residents and businesses over social services. Some argue that the overlapping jurisdictions created by the proliferation of special districts tend to result in higher taxes, not greater efficiency in service provision; see Christopher Berry, "Piling On: The Fiscal Effects of Jurisdictional Overlap" (Harvard University, Department of Government, n.d.).

127. Burns, *Formation of American Local Governments,* p. 116.

128. A good example is when citizens force highway engineers to consider the effects of their projects on the community or the environment. For a profound reflection on the problems of leaving highway building to experts and engineers, see Robert A. Caro, *The Power Broker: Robert Moses and the Fall of New York* (New York: Vintage Books, 1974).

129. See Cheryl Simrell King, Camilla Stivers, and others, *Government Is Us: Public Administration in an Anti-Government Era* (Thousand Oaks, Calif.: Sage Publications, 1998), and John Forester, *The Deliberative Practitioner: Encouraging Participatory Planning Processes* (MIT Press, 1999).

130. Verba, Schlozman, and Brady, *Voice and Equality,* pp. 51, 72.

131. For example, of all of the census-designated central cities with populations between 50,000 and 250,000 in eighteen states chosen randomly from across the United States, 90 percent had citizen seats on local boards and commissions. Katherine Cramer Walsh, "Local Governance and Intergroup Dialogue Programs," unpublished ms. (University of Wisconsin, n.d.).

132. Verba, Schlozman, and Brady, *Voice and Equality,* p. 51.

133. Putnam, *Bowling Alone,* p. 43. But Verba, Schlozman, and Brady, *Voice and Equality,* p. 72, report slight increases in some forms of community engagement, including contacting public officials.

134. Putnam, *Bowling Alone,* p. 43.

135. Christopher F. Karpowitz, "Having a Say: Public Hearings, Deliberation, and American Democracy," Ph.D. dissertation, Princeton University, 2005.

136. David J. Greenstone and Paul E. Peterson, *Race and Authority in Urban Politics: Community Participation and the War on Poverty* (New York: Russell Sage Foundation, 1973), pp. 2–6.

137. U.S. Congress, *An Act to Mobilize the Human and Financial Resources of the Nation to Combat Poverty in the United States,* Public Law 88-452, 88 Cong. 2nd sess. (Government

Printing Office, 1964), p. 9, quoted in Greenstone and Peterson, *Race and Authority*, pp. 4–5.

138. Carmen Sirianni and Lewis Friedland, *Civic Innovation in America: Community Empowerment, Public Policy, and the Movement for Civic Renewal* (University of California Press, 2001), pp. 35–43; Dennis R. Judd and Todd Swanstrom, *City Politics: Private Power and Public Policy*, 4th ed. (New York: HarperCollins College Publishers, 2004), pp. 378–79; see also Richard Cole, *Citizen Participation and the Urban Policy Process* (Lexington, Mass.: Lexington Books, 1974).

139. Daniel Patrick Moynihan, *Maximum Feasible Misunderstanding: Community Action and the War on Poverty* (New York: Macmillan, 1970).

140. Scott Allard, "Intergovernmental Relationships and the American City: The Impact of Federal Policies on Local Policy-Making Processes," Ph.D. dissertation, University of Michigan, 1999. The effects were, some argue, especially pronounced among low-income residents and across racial boundaries. John Clayton Thomas, *Between Citizen and City: Neighborhood Organizations and Urban Politics in Cincinnati* (University Press of Kansas, 1986), pp. 38, 41. Since many Model Cities grants went to African American residents, the legislation helped to break down racial barriers in local politics. Allard, "Intergovernmental Relationships and the American City," p. 180. The program served as a political training ground for residents, as the experience helped to launch various attempts to gain elected office at the local and state levels. Peter Eisinger, "The Community Action Program and the Development of Black Political Leadership," in *Urban Policy Making*, edited by Dale R. Marshall (Beverly Hills, Calif.: Sage, 1979), pp. 127–44; Sallie Marston, "Citizen Action Programs and Participatory Politics in Tucson," in *Public Policy for Democracy*, edited by Helen Ingram and Steven Rathgeb Smith (Brookings, 1993), pp. 119–35.

141. Scavo's survey excludes Chicago, Los Angeles, and New York. All three of these cities have systems of neighborhood councils. See also William M. Rohe and Lauren Gates, *Planning with Neighborhoods* (University of North Carolina Press, 1985), p. 8.

142. Carmine Scavo, "Use of Participative Mechanisms by Large U.S. Cities," *Journal of Urban Affairs* 15 (1993): 93–109.

143. Jeffrey M. Berry, Kent Portney, and Ken Thomson, *Rebirth of Urban Democracy* (Brookings, 1993).

144. See, for example, Judith Martin and Paula Pentel, "What the Neighborhoods Want: The Neighborhood Revitalization Program's First Decade," *American Planning Association Journal* 68, no. 4 (2002): 435–49; Susan Fainstein, "An Evaluation of the Minneapolis NRP," CUPR Policy Report 13 (Center for Urban Policy Research, January 9, 1995); Susan S. Fainstein, and Clifford Hirst, "Neighborhood Organizations and Community Planning: The Minneapolis Neighborhood Revitalization Program," in *Revitalizing Urban Neighborhoods*, edited by W. Dennis Keating, Norman Krumholz, and Philip Star (University Press of Kansas, 1996), pp. 96–111; Edward G. Goetz and Mara S. Sidney, "Revenge of the Property Owners: Community Development and the Politics of Property," *Journal of Urban Affairs* 16 (1994): 319–34.

145. See Juliet Musso, Alicia Kitsuse, Evan Lincove, Michael Sithole, and Terry Cooper, "Planning Neighborhood Councils in Los Angeles: Self-Determination on a Shoestring," Neighborhood Participation Project Report (University of Southern California, School of Planning, Policy, and Development, April 30, 2002).

146. See Rohe and Gates, *Planning with Neighborhoods*, pp. 75–84. About a third of neighborhood councils elect representatives by committee, another third have elections in

which neighborhood residents vote, and a quarter have volunteer memberships. Very few neighborhood councils have representatives that are appointed by the mayor or city council. Three-quarters of these councils are administered by cities' planning or development agencies. On the dimension of government support, almost all of the councils receive information and data from the city, 80 percent receive staff assistance, and 55 percent receive public money. In response to surveys, these councils claim to do far more than communicate preferences to city councilors or agencies: 80 percent say they develop neighborhood plans, and 67 percent monitor the activities and projects of agencies. Such organizational surveys, however, reveal little about the character of neighborhood politics and engagement. It appears that many neighborhood council systems are moribund or powerless.

147. Fainstein and Hirst, "Neighborhood Organizations and Community Planning."

148. See Saul Alinsky, "The War on Poverty: Political Pornography," *Journal of Social Issues* 21 (January 1965): 42.

149. Berry, Portney, and Thomson, *Rebirth of Urban Democracy*, p. 81.

150. See Bryan, *Real Democracy*; Joseph F. Zimmerman, *The New England Town Meeting: Democracy in Action* (Westport, Conn.: Praeger, 1999); Jane Mansbridge, *Beyond Adversary Democracy* (University of Chicago Press, 1983).

151. See Amy Gutmann and Dennis Thomson, *Democracy and Disagreement* (Harvard University Press, 1996); James Bohman, *Public Deliberation: Pluralism, Complexity, and Democracy* (MIT Press, 1996); James S. Fishkin, *Democracy and Deliberation: New Directions for Democratic Reform* (Yale University Press, 1992).

152. See Archon Fung, *Empowered Participation: Reinventing Urban Democracy* (Princeton University Press, 2004).

153. See David M. Ryfe, "The Practice of Deliberative Democracy: A Study of Sixteen Deliberative Organizations," *Political Communication* 19 (2002): 359–77; Mark Button and Kevin Mattson, "Deliberative Democracy in Practice," *Polity* 31 (1999): 609–37; Katherine Cramer Walsh, *Talking about Politics: Informal Groups and Social Identity in American Life* (University of Chicago Press, 2004), pp. 191–94. For historical antecedents, see Kevin Mattson, *Creating a Democratic Public: The Struggle for Urban Participatory Democracy during the Progressive Era* (Pennsylvania State University Press, 1997).

154. Patricia Reichler and Polly B. Dredge, *Governing Diverse Communities: A Focus on Race and Ethnic Relations* (Washington: National League of Cities, 1997).

155. Beyond the direct participants, the event catalyzed a much wider discussion in the pages of city newspapers and in New York generally. See Kennedy School of Government, "Listening to the City: Rebuilding at New York's World Trade Center Site," Case 1687.0 and 1687.1 (Harvard University, April 2003).

156. Michael Delli Carpini, Lawrence R. Jacobs, and Fay Lomax Cook, "Does Political Deliberation Matter? The Impact of Discursive Participation on Civic and Political Behavior," paper presented at the annual meeting of the American Political Science Association, Chicago, September 2–6, 2004.

157. See Hibbing and Theiss-Morse, *Stealth Democracy*; Tali Mendelberg, "The Deliberative Citizen: Theory and Evidence," in *Political Decision-Making, Deliberation, and Participation, Research in Micropolitics*, vol. 6, edited by Michael X. Delli Carpini, Leonie Huddy, and Robert Y. Shapiro (Greenwich, Conn.: JAI Press, 2002); Mansbridge, *Beyond Adversary Democracy*; Karpowitz, *Having a Say*.

158. Scavo, "Use of Participative Mechanisms," p. 102.

159. Jacobs, *Death and Life of Great American Cities*.

160. See Robert J. Sampson, Stephen W. Raudenbush, and Felton Earls, "Neighborhoods and Violent Crime: A Multilevel Study of Collective Efficacy," *Science* 277 (August 1997): 918–24.

161. Putnam, *Bowling Alone*, pp. 130–31, 465 (note 38).

162. Susan Crawford and Peggy Levitt, "Social Change and Civic Engagement: The Case of the PTA," in *Civic Engagement in American Democracy*, edited by Theda Skocpol and Morris P. Fiorina (Brookings, 1999), pp. 249–96.

163. Crawford and Levitt, "Social Change and Civic Engagement," report that membership statistics in parent-teacher organizations are not recorded.

164. Crawford and Levitt, "Social Change and Civic Engagement," especially pp. 283–84.

165. Scholars working at Indiana University's Workshop in Political Theory and Policy Analysis have produced important work in this arena. See also Lawrence Susskind and Michael Elliott, *Paternalism, Conflict, and Coproduction: Learning from Citizen Action and Citizen Participation in Western Europe* (New York: Plenum Press, 1983).

166. See Gordon P. Whitaker, "Coproduction: Citizen Participation in Service Delivery," *Public Administration Review* 40 (May-June 1980): 240–46; Stephen L. Percy, "Citizen Participation in the Coproduction of Urban Services," *Urban Affairs Quarterly* 19 (June 1984): 431–46; R. K. Wilson, "Citizen Coproduction as a Mode of Participation: Conjectures and Models," *Journal of Urban Affairs* 3 (1981): 37–49.

167. For example, while many neighborhood associations simply provide input or advice to city agencies, the Minneapolis Revitalization Project allocates $400 million over twenty years to individual neighborhood associations to implement projects around housing, services, and amenities. The very different levels of influence and power associated with different forms of community participation are described in Sherry Arnstein's classic article, "A Ladder of Citizen Participation," *American Institute of Planning Journal* (July 1969): 216–24.

168. Fiorina, *Culture War*.

169. Fung, *Empowered Participation*.

170. Fung, *Empowered Participation*.

171. See Saul Alinksy, *Rules for Radicals* (New York: Random House, 1971); Saul Alinksy, *Reveille for Radicals* (University of Chicago Press, 1946); Sanford D. Horwitt, *Let Them Call Me Rebel: Saul Alinsky, His Life and Legacy* (New York: Alfred A. Knopf, 1990); Robert Fisher, *Let the People Decide: Neighborhood Organizing in America* (New York: Twayne Publishers, 1994).

172. Fisher correctly observes that neighborhood organizing "is not inherently reactionary, conservative, liberal, or radical, nor is it inherently democratic and inclusive or authoritarian and parochial. It is above all a political method." Fisher, *Let the People Decide*, p. 221.

173. Rohe and Gates, *Planning with Neighborhoods*, p. 21; Richard L. McCormick, "Public Life in Industrial America, 1877–1917," in *The New American History*, edited by Eric Foner (Temple University Press, 1990), pp. 93–117, as cited in Putnam, *Bowling Alone*.

174. Of the major community organizing enterprises, the Industrial Areas Foundation—specifically the Texas Industrial Areas Foundation—has received by far the greatest attention from scholars and journalists. See, for example, Mark R. Warren, *Dry Bones Rattling: Community Building to Revitalize American Democracy* (Princeton University Press, 2001); Mary Beth Rogers, *Cold Anger: A Story of Faith and Power in Politics* (University of North Texas Press, 1990); Paul Osterman, *Gathering Power: The Future of Progressive Politics in America* (Boston: Beacon Press, 2003); Dennis Shirley, *Valley Interfaith and School Reform: Organiz-*

ing for Power in South Texas (University of Texas Press, 2002); Michael Gecan, *Going Public: An Inside Story of Disrupting Politics as Usual* (Boston: Beacon Press, 2002); Benjamín Márquez, *Constructing Identities in Mexican-American Political Organizations: Choosing Issues, Taking Sides* (University of Texas Press, 2003). On PICO, see Richard Wood, *Faith in Action: Religion, Race, and Democratic Organizing in America* (University of Chicago Press, 2002).

175. Harry Chatten Boyte, *The Backyard Revolution: Understanding the New Citizens' Movement* (Temple University Press, 1980). A weakness of the community organizing literature is that it focuses mostly on groups on the political left.

176. ACORN claims 150,000 member families and 700 neighborhood chapters in fifty-one cities. Mark Warren and Richard Wood estimate that the faith-based community organizational field "includes about 4,000 member institutions, of which 87 percent are religious congregations and 13 percent are non-congregational institutions (NCIs) like unions, public schools, and a diverse array of other community organizations. The religious congregations involved represent between 1 and 1.5 percent of all congregations in the country." Mark R. Warren and Richard Wood, *Faith-Based Community Organizing: The State of the Field* (Jericho, N.Y.: Interfaith Funders, 2001).

177. Fisher, *Let the People Decide*, p. 60. But see Osterman, *Gathering Power*, p. 64.

178. Urban scholars have focused detailed attention on the role of accessible political institutions and coalition building in facilitating empowerment and mobilization in minority communities. Rufus P. Browning, Dale Roger Marshall, and David H. Tabb, *Protest Is Not Enough: The Struggle of Blacks and Hispanics for Equality in Urban Politics* (University of California Press, 1984); Rufus P. Browning, Dale Rogers Marshall, and David H. Tabb, *Racial Politics in American Cities*, 3rd ed. (New York: Longman, 2003); Wilbur Rich, ed., *The Politics of Minority Coalitions: Race, Ethnicity, and Shared Uncertainties* (Westport, Conn.: Praeger, 1996). African Americans and Latinos have become politically empowered in cities with accessible political institutions, which allowed members of previously disenfranchised groups to become part of the governing coalition that determines public policy, coordinates institutional arrangements, and influences the distribution of scarce municipal resources. William Nelson, "Black Mayoral Leadership," *National Political Science Review* 2 (1990): 188–95; Preston, "Symposium: Big-City Black Mayors."

179. Noah Pickus, *Immigration and Citizenship in the Twenty-first Century* (Lanham, Md.: Rowman and Littlefield, 1998); Louis DeSipio, *Counting on the Latino Vote: Latinos as a New Electorate* (University of Virginia Press, 1996); Pei-te Lein, *The Making of Asian America through Political Participation* (Temple University Press, 2001); Jones-Correa, *Between Two Nations*; Ronald Schmidt Sr., *Language Policy and Identity Politics in the United States* (Temple University Press, 2000). One study by Segura, García, and Pachón finds that Latinos who are citizens (especially the native born), more educated, and English dominant are more likely to participate in traditional civic affairs. Gary M. Segura, F. Chris García, and Harry Pachón, "Estimating and Understanding Social Capital and Its Political Effects among Latinos in the United States," paper delivered at the annual meeting of the Western Political Science Association, Long Beach, Calif., March 22–24, 2002.

180. More than 20 percent of Americans are immigrants or the children of immigrants, and nearly a third of all Americans are of nonwhite and non-European descent. By a slim margin, African Americans are no longer the largest minority group in the United States, having been eclipsed in 2000 by a rapidly growing population of Latinos. In the past decade, Asians doubled the size of their population to more than 4 percent of Americans.

181. Jones-Correa, *Between Two Nations*; Wong, *Membership and Morality in American Politics*.

182. Kristi Andersen and Jessica Wintringham, "Political Parties, NGOs, and Immigrant Incorporation: A Case Study," workshop on immigrant incorporation, Syracuse University, March 21, 2003; Rodolfo O. de la Garza and Briant Lindsay Lowell, *Sending Money Home: Hispanic Remittances and Community Development* (Lanham, Md.: Rowman and Littlefield Publishers, 2002).

183. Karthick Ramakrishnan, *Immigrant America: Changing Demographics and Political Participation* (Stanford University Press, 2005).

184. Ricardo Ramírez, Alan Gerber, and Donald Green, "Report on NALEO *La Voz del Pueblo*, 2002" (2002).

185. Roger Waldinger, *Still the Promised City? African Americans and New Immigrants in Postindustrial New York* (Harvard University Press, 1996).

186. See Kim Geron, Enríque de la Cruz, Leland T. Saito, and Jaideep Sing, "Asian Pacific Americans' Social Movements and Interests Groups," *PS: Political Science and Politics* 34 (2001): 619–24; Carol Hardy-Fanta, *Latina Politics, Latino Politics: Gender, Culture, and Political Participation in Boston* (Temple University Press, 1992); Benjamín Márquez and James Jennings, "Representation by Other Means: Mexican American and Puerto Rican Social Movement Organizations," *PS: Political Science and Politics* 33 (2000): 541–46.

187. Hometown associations within Latino immigrant communities have become major centers of civic activity. The primary identity of these groups is to villages and towns in home countries. Hometown associations have been directly responsible for raising funds and in-kind contributions to promote a variety of urban development projects, including the building of churches, schools, roads, and water wells, all in countries of origin. Although there is no systematic survey of their presence in U.S. communities, such information would indicate the full scope of civic engagement of some immigrant communities. Our traditional categories of civic engagement may need to be expanded to comprehend this growing segment of urban populations.

188. See Steven Rathgeb Smith, "The New Politics of Contracting: Citizenship and the Nonprofit Role," in *Public Policy for Democracy*, edited by Ingram and Smith, pp. 198–221.

189. John P. Kretzmann, John L. McKnight, and Nicole Turner, *Voluntary Associations in Low-Income Neighborhoods: An Unexplored Community Resource* (Northwestern University, Institute for Policy Research, 1996).

190. For more on the role of black churches, see Fred Harris, *Something Within: Religion in African American Political Activism* (Oxford University Press, 1999); Yvette M. Alex-Assensoh, "Taking the Sanctuary to the Streets: Religion, Race, and Community Development in Columbus, Ohio," *Annals of the American Academy of Political Science* 594 (July 2004): 79–92; Alison Calhoun-Brown, "African-American Churches and Political Mobilization: The Psychological Impact of Organizational Resources," *Journal of Politics* 63 (3): 886–901; Omar McRoberts, *Streets of Glory: Church and Community in a Black, Urban Neighborhood* (University of Chicago Press, 2003).

191. Mildred Warner, "Innovative Economic Development Strategies" (Cornell University, June 2001), available at www.cce.cornell.edu/restructuring/doc/reports/econdev/ieds. htm [February 27, 2004].

192. See Randy Stoecker, "The CDC Model of Urban Redevelopment: A Critique and an Alternative," *Journal of Urban Affairs* 19 (1997): 1–22.

193. See Julia Koschinsky and Todd Swanstrom, "Theories of Nonprofit-Government Collaboration: The Case of Community Development," in *Non-Profits in Urban America*,

edited by Richard C. Hula and Cynthia Jackson-Almeria (Westport, Conn.: Greenwood Press, 2000), pp. 65–92; and Bishwapriya Sanyal, "Beyond the Theory of Comparative Advantage: Political Imperatives of the Government-Nonprofit Relationship," in *Shelter and Society: Theory, Research, and Policy for Nonprofit Housing,* edited by Theodore C. Koebel (State University of New York Press, 1998). The Koebel volume has a number of articles that address the obstacles keeping housing nonprofits from realizing their potential.

194. Barbara Ferman, *Challenging the Growth Machine: Neighborhood Politics in Chicago and Pittsburgh* (University Press of Kansas, 1996).

195. For the general argument that nonprofits can become dominated by governments as they succumb to the contract regime, see Steven Rathgeb Smith and Michael Lipsky, *Non-profits for Hire: The Welfare State in the Age of Contracting* (Harvard University Press, 1993). For evidence on the specific case of CDCs, see Jordan Yin, "The Community Development Industry System," *Journal of Urban Affairs* 20, no. 2 (1998): 137–57; and Benjamín Márquez, "Mexican American Community Development Corporations and the Limits of Directed Capitalism," *Economic Development Quarterly* 7 (1993): 287–95. For a more optimistic take on the democratic potential of CDCs, see Herbert J. Rubin, *Renewing Hope within Neighborhoods of Despair: The Community-Based Development Model* (State University of New York Press, 2000).

196. See Social Capital Community Benchmark Survey, available at www.cfsv.org/community survey/ [February 28, 2005].

197. Richard C. Rich, "A Political Economy Approach to the Study of Neighborhood Organizations," *American Journal of Political Science* 24 (November 1980): 559–92.

198. Oliver, *Democracy in Suburbia,* p. 79.

199. See Matthew Crenson, *Neighborhood Politics* (Harvard University Press, 1983). Rich and Oliver differ, however, about the explanation for this pattern. Rich hypothesizes that formation of, and participation in, neighborhood associations corresponds to the ratio of resources in the neighborhood to the demand for public goods. Poor neighborhoods have many needs, but few resources to address those needs, whereas wealthy neighborhoods have few needs, but many resources. These mismatches between needs and resources result in low participation and collective action. In middle-income neighborhoods, Rich argues, local participation can mobilize moderate resources to address manageable needs. In contrast, Oliver argues that communities in the middle-income range are more likely to be economically diverse and that diversity begets conflict, which, in turn, generates participation. Oliver, *Democracy in Suburbia,* pp. 86–93. Oliver argues that both poor and wealthy communities are more homogeneous and less conflictual, with individuals in such communities less likely to be drawn into the political process.

200. Figures are from the Community Associations Institute, which is the trade association for homeowners associations, as cited in Evan McKenzie, *Privatopia: Homeowner Associations and the Rise of Residential Private Government* (Yale University Press, 1994), p. 11, and on the Community Associations Institute website: www.caionline.org [February 28, 2005].

201. A 1989 report by the Advisory Commission on Intergovernmental Relations (ACIR) asserts that homeowners associations "account for the most significant privatization of local government responsibilities in recent times." ACIR, *Residential Community Associations: Private Governments in the Intergovernmental System?* (Washington, 1989), p. 18.

202. According to the 2001 Annual Housing Survey, 7 million Americans live in gated communities: these almost always involve a community association and further accentuate

their exclusionary character by controlling public access. Edward J. Blakely and Mary Gail Snyder, *Fortress America: Gated Communities in the United States* (Brookings, 1999).

203. Nelson argues that the benefits of homeowners associations should be spread to existing poor and inner-city neighborhoods. At least two obstacles present themselves immediately to this scheme: (1) most inner-city poor are renters, not homeowners; (2) almost all homeowners associations are founded by real estate developers when they build the subdivision, and it would be difficult to impose the legal structure of a homeowners association on existing neighborhoods. See Robert H. Nelson, "Privatizing the Neighborhood: A Proposal to Replace Zoning with Private Collective Property Rights to Existing Neighborhoods," in *The Voluntary City*, edited by David T. Beito, Peter Gordon, and Alexander Tabarrok (University of Michigan Press, 2002), pp. 307–70.

204. McKenzie, *Privatopia*, p. 22.

205. McKenzie, *Privatopia*, p. 18.

206. The covenants, conditions, and restrictions prohibit behaviors that are perceived as harming property values. These rules cover an incredibly broad range of activities, from determining acceptable paint colors to banning clotheslines or basketball hoops and imposing rules about pets, cars, and guests. Everyone who purchases property in the development becomes a member of the homeowners association and is subject to the rules.

207. Cited in Robert Jay Dilger, *Neighborhood Politics: Residential Community Associations in American Governance* (New York University Press, 1992), p. 140.

208. Analysis of court records in the Houston metropolitan area identifies more than 15,500 filings between 1985 and 2001 that could have resulted in foreclosure against owners in homeowners associations. See www.HOAdata.org, as reported in Motoko Rich, "Homeowner Boards Blur Line of Just Who Rules the Roost," *New York Times,* July 27, 2003.

209. Dilger, *Neighborhood Politics*, p. 7.

210. Rodgers, *This Land Is Your Land.*

211. E. E. Schattschneider, *The Semisovereign People: A Realist's View of Democracy in America* (New York: Holt, Rinehart and Winston, 1960), ch. 1.

212. Douglass S. Massey and Nancy L. Denton, *American Apartheid: Segregation and the Making of the Underclass* (Harvard University Press, 1993).

213. Charles M. Haar, *Suburbs under Seige: Race, Space, and Audacious Judges* (Princeton University Press, 1996).

214. Because privileged suburban enclaves derive direct public and private benefits from their exclusivity and fiscal autonomy (better public services, including schools, and the higher home values associated with the superiority of schools and public services), important constituencies will be opposed to residential integration. But fair housing laws are supported in principle by the majority of Americans. Martin D. Abravanel, "Public Knowledge of Fair Housing Law: Does It Protect against Housing Discrimination?" *Housing Policy Debate* 3 (2002): 469–504.

215. Additional normative concerns, in particular whether and when members of immigrant groups have fulfilled the responsibilities concomitant with the privileges of the franchise, should regulate these proposed extensions. Allowing noncitizens to vote could also result in a noticeable backlash from native citizens. Any community considering extending voting to noncitizens must take into account the risks of such a backlash. Because schools are often the first place immigrants interact with local government, we believe that public school officials should reach out to the parents of immigrant children, in their native language, and lessen the barriers that fan alienation, although this recommendation takes us

too far from the matters we have investigated in this report. See, for example, Alejandro Portes and Ruben G. Rumbaut, *Legacies: The Story of the Immigrant Second Generation* (University of California Press, 2001); Ruben G. Rumbaut and Alejandro Portes, eds., *Ethnicities: Children of Immigrants in America* (University of California Press, 2001).

216. Many reforms, such as state court litigation aimed at curbing local exclusionary powers, state legislative impositions of consolidated regional governments, or special-purpose regional authorities, may well depress political and civic participation.

217. David Barron refers to this as the "baseline problem." David J. Barron, "A Localist Critique of the New Federalism," *Duke Law Journal* 51 (2001): 377–433.

218. Orfield, *Metropolitics*.

219. Gerald E. Frug, "Beyond Regional Government," *Harvard Law Review* 115, no. 7 (2002): 1763–836; David J. Barron, "Reclaiming Home Rule," *Harvard Law Review* 116, no. 8 (2003): 2255–386; David J. Barron, Gerald E. Frug, and Rick T. Su, *Dispelling the Myth of Home Rule: Local Power in Greater Boston* (Cambridge, Mass.: Rappaport Institute for Greater Boston, 2004). See also Gerald Frug, *City Making: Building Communities without Building Walls* (Princeton University Press, 1999) and Richard Briffault, "Localism and Regionalism," *Buffalo Law Review* 48 (2000): 1–30.

220. Generally, Frug and Barron argue that local home-rule powers are much weaker than generally believed and that states often restrict the powers of local governments to collaborate regionally. Barron argues, for example, that certain common local powers should be reduced: powers to engage in exclusionary zoning, maintain municipal boundaries, and refuse to share property tax revenues, while localities should exercise greater powers in other domains such as the enactment of inclusionary zoning and antidiscrimination ordinances. Such changes, he contends, would create incentives for citizens and officials in current localities to address, rather than exacerbate, sprawl and spatial stratification. Barron, "Reclaiming Home Rule."

221. Frug, "Beyond Regional Government."

222. See Frug, "Beyond Regional Government," especially the discussion of the General Assembly of the Puget Sound Regional Council (covering the four-county region of greater Seattle), which he calls "the only large-scale regional planning organization in the nation," p. 1803.

223. Robert D. Putnam, Lewis M. Feldstein, and Don Cohen, *Better Together: Restoring the American Community* (New York: Simon and Schuster, 2003). However, the challenge of diversity is not as great in Portland as it is in many other metropolitan areas.

224. Blomquist and Parks, "Fiscal, Service, and Political Impacts."

225. It took the availability of cheap cars, advances in housing construction, the development and extension of the AC electric grid, and other factors to unleash the great decentering of the metropolis. Economists Edward L. Glaeser and Mathew E. Kahn are unequivocal about the causes: sprawl is ubiquitous, expanding, and irresistible, and it has a single root cause—the technological superiority of the automobile. Edward L. Glaeser and Mathew E. Kahn, "Sprawl and Urban Growth," forthcoming in *Handbook of Urban and Regional Economics*, vol. 4, pt. 2, edited by Vernon Henderson and Jacques Thisse (North Holland: Elsevier). And see Rae, *City*.

226. For syntheses of the scholarly literature on the role of public policies in suburbanization, see Kenneth T. Jackson, *Crabgrass Frontier: The Suburbanization of the United States* (Oxford University Press, 1985); Peter Dreier, John Mollenkopf, and Todd Swanstrom, *Place Matters: Metro Politics for the Twenty-Frst Century* (University Press of Kansas, 2001), esp. ch. 4.

227. Barron, "A Localist Critique of the New Federalism."

Chapter Four

1. Paul Arnsberger, "Charities and Other Tax-Exempt Organizations, 2000," *Statistics of Income* 23 (Fall 2003): 122–36. See also Lester Salamon, ed., *The State of Nonprofit America* (Brookings, 2002).

2. Alexis de Tocqueville, *Democracy in America*, edited by J. P. Mayer (New York: Anchor Books, 1969), p. 189.

3. Tocqueville, *Democracy in America*, p. 189.

4. Tocqueville, *Democracy in America*, pp. 62–84; 270–76; 286–87, 301–08; also, the laws of property and inheritance, pp. 51–54.

5. Robert D. Putnam, *Bowling Alone: The Collapse and Revival of American Community* (New York: Simon and Schuster, 2000), p. 19.

6. Putnam, *Bowling Alone*, p. 121.

7. Sidney Verba, Kay Lehman Schlozman, and Henry E. Brady, *Voice and Equality: Civic Volunteerism in American Politics* (Harvard University Press, 1995), p. 309.

8. Putnam, *Bowling Alone*, p. 66.

9. Jeffrey M. Berry, Kent E. Portney, and Ken Thomson, *The Rebirth of Urban Democracy* (Brookings, 1993), p. 279.

10. Miriam Galston, "Civic Renewal and the Regulation of Nonprofits," *Cornell Journal of Law and Public Policy* 13, no. 289 (2004): 401.

11. See, for instance, Carol Cassel, "Voluntary Associations, Churches, and Social Participation Theories of Turnout," *Social Science Quarterly* 80 (1999): 504.

12. Nancy Rosenblum argues, however, that even these exclusionary and racist groups, so long as they are law-abiding, may serve an important social function in moderating the effects or tendencies of the most extreme members. See Nancy Rosenblum, *Membership and Morals* (Princeton University Press, 2000).

13. Theda Skocpol, *Diminished Democracy: From Membership to Management in American Civic Life* (University of Oklahoma Press, 2003).

14. Independent Sector, "Giving and Volunteering in the United States, 2001" (Washington, 2001).

15. The most recent census estimates put the number of volunteers in 2004 at 64.5 million. See Bureau of Labor Statistics, "Volunteering in the United States, 2004" (Washington, 2004).

16. Independent Sector, "Giving and Volunteering in the United States, 2001."

17. Virginia Hodgkinson with Kathryn Nelson and Edward Sivak Jr., "Individual Giving and Volunteering," in *The State of Nonprofit America*, edited by Salamon, p. 404.

18. Linda J. Sax, Alexander Astin, and others, *The American Freshman: National Norms for Fall 2003* (University of California, Los Angeles, Higher Education Research Institute, 2004).

19. Putnam, *Bowling Alone*, p. 129.

20. Jeffrey L. Brudney, "The Perils of Practice: Reaching the Summit," *Nonprofit Management and Leadership* 9 (1999): 385–98.

21. E. J. Dionne, *The Vitality of Society Rests on the Independent Sector*, Conversations with Leaders Series (Washington: Independent Sector, 2000).

22. It is worth noting, however, that the long period of decline of youth interest in politics reversed itself in 2003. The UCLA study showed an uptick in the number of youth who

said that "keeping up to date with political affairs" is a very important life goal and in the number of students who said that they discuss politics frequently; Sax and others, *The American Freshman*. Equally significant is the fact that the number of eighteen- to twenty-four-year-olds who voted in the 2004 election rose significantly from previous elections, both as a total number (10.5 million versus 8.7 million in 2000) and as a percentage (42.3 percent as against 36.5 percent in 2000); Center for Information and Research on Civic Learning and Engagement, "Youth Voting in the 2004 Election" (University of Maryland, 2004).

23. Although we are optimistic about the connection between volunteering and increased political engagement, we are mindful of the deep tension in the short-term and long-run data. How is it possible to reconcile a positive correlation between volunteering and political activity in cross-sectional data (data at a particular moment in time across different groups of people) and a steady decrease in political activity in the time-series data (data of particular cohorts tracked over time) while volunteering is on the rise? It seems impossible for both to be true over an extended period of time. One possible resolution to this tension can be seen in the recent upturn in political interest and activity of younger Americans across a wide variety of indicators. Perhaps increased volunteerism is beginning to have payoffs in political engagement. For a longitudinal analysis across generations, see M. Kent Jennings and Laura Stoker, "Social Trust and Civic Engagement across Time and Generations," *Acta Politica* 39 (2004): 342–79.

24. Diana Owen, "Service Learning and Political Socialization," *PS: Political Science and Politics* 33 (September 2000): 638–40.

25. John Patrick, "The Civic Mission of Schools: Key Ideas in a Research-Based Report on Civic Education in the United States" (University of Maryland, Center for Information and Research on Civic Learning and Engagement, May 2005), p. 27.

26. Lester M. Salamon, "The Resilient Sector," in *The State of Nonprofit America,* edited by Salamon, pp. 3–4.

27. Murray Weitzman, Nadine Jalandoni, Linda Lampkin, and Thomas Pollack, *The New Nonprofit Almanac and Desk Reference* (San Francisco: Jossey-Bass, 2002), pp. 13–21.

28. Weitzman and others, *The New Nonprofit Almanac,* p. 73.

29. See, generally, Steven Rathgeb Smith and Michael Lipsky, *Nonprofits for Hire* (Harvard University Press, 1993); Lester M. Salamon, *Partners in Public Service* (Johns Hopkins University Press, 1995).

30. The nonprofit sector includes a great variety of organizations and groups, but the term "nonprofit" is a misnomer. Ironically, nonprofits are not prohibited from making a profit. Should they make one, nonprofits are simply forbidden from distributing it to owners or shareholders.

31. Peter Frumkin, *On Being Nonprofit* (Harvard University Press, 2002), p. 2.

32. Paul C. Light, *The True Size of Government* (Brookings, 1999), p. 1.

33. Steven Rathgeb Smith, "Social Services," in *The State of Nonprofit America,* edited by Salamon, p. 165.

34. S. Wojciech Sokolowski and Lester M. Salamon, "The United States," in *Global Civil Society,* edited by Lester M. Salamon and others (Johns Hopkins Center for Civil Society Studies, 1999), p. 276.

35. Confusion often arises because 501(c)(3)s are only one type of nonprofit and tax-exempt organization. Twenty-six other types of organizations are exempt from federal income taxation under section 501 of the Internal Revenue Code. For instance, 501(c)(5)s

are labor unions, 501(c)(6)s are business associations, and 521s are farmer cooperatives. Lester M. Salamon, *America's Nonprofit Sector*, 2nd ed. (New York: Foundation Center, 1999), p. 8. Although all twenty-seven categories of nonprofits are exempt from income tax, only the 501(c)(3)s can offer tax deductibility to donors.

36. U.S. Code, Title 26, sec. 501.

37. Stephanie Strom, "New Equation for Charities: More Money, Less Oversight," *New York Times*, November 17, 2003, p. E1. In 2000 the IRS recognized 676,783 of these 501(c)(3)s as "active." See Arnsberger, "Charities and Other Tax-Exempt Organizations."

38. Jeffrey M. Berry with David F. Arons, *A Voice for Nonprofits* (Brookings, 2003), p. 9.

39. Alan Altshuler and David Luberoff, *Mega-Projects* (Brookings, 2003).

40. Barbara Ferman, *Challenging the Growth Machine* (University Press of Kansas, 1996).

41. Clarence N. Stone, Jeffrey R. Henig, Bryan D. Jones, and Carol Pierannunzi, *Building Civic Capacity* (University Press of Kansas, 2001).

42. American Association of Fundraising Counsel, *Giving USA 2003* (Washington: Trust for Philanthropy, 2004).

43. Independent Sector, "Giving and Volunteering in the United States, 2001."

44. Hodgkinson with Nelson and Sivak Jr., "Individual Giving and Volunteering," p. 394. Lowering tax rates reduces the financial incentives to donate to charitable causes. People donate for reasons other than the tax deductibility of their contributions, but the tax benefit is no small matter and economists believe that the tax rate affects contribution patterns. Thus declining tax rates, from President Reagan's 1981 tax cuts through President George W. Bush's 2001 tax cuts, may help to explain why individuals, especially wealthy individuals, have been giving less as a percentage of their income. Evelyn Brody and Joseph J. Cordes, "Tax Treatment of Nonprofit Organizations: A Two-Edged Sword?" in *Nonprofits and Government*, edited by Elizabeth T. Boris and C. Eugene Steuerle (Washington: Urban Institute, 1998), pp. 141–75.

45. Congressional Budget Office, "The Estate Tax and Charitable Giving" (Washington, July 2004).

46. Berry with Arons, *A Voice for Nonprofits*, pp. 57–65.

47. The amount of money that an H elector can spend on lobbying is tied to a sliding scale based on the budget of the nonprofit. The 20 percent figure is for the smallest nonprofits (up to an annual budget of $500,000). An additional one-quarter of the direct lobbying limit can be spent on grassroots efforts. Advocacy before administrative agencies is not limited in any way. See Bob Smucker, *The Nonprofit Lobbying Guide*, 2nd ed. (Washington: Independent Sector, 1999), p. 55.

48. Berry with Arons, *A Voice for Nonprofits*, pp. 60–74. Using a random sample of IRS Form 990 filers and a comparison sample of H-electing organizations that are otherwise similar, they measured the impact of 501(c)(3)s on advocacy.

49. Jeffrey M. Berry, "Nonprofit Groups Shouldn't Be Afraid to Lobby," *Chronicle of Philanthropy*, November 27, 2003, pp. 33–35.

50. Steven Rathgeb Smith, "The New Politics of Contracting: Citizenship and the Nonprofit Role," in *Public Policy for Democracy*, edited by Helen Ingram and Steven Rathgeb Smith (Brookings, 1993), pp. 213–18.

51. Joe Soss, "Lessons of Welfare: Policy Design, Political Learning, and Political Action," *American Political Science Review* 93 (1999): 363–80.

52. Leslie Lenkowsky, "Foundations and Corporate Philanthropy," in *The State of Nonprofit America*, edited by Salamon, pp. 355–86.

53. Paul C. Light, *Pathways to Nonprofit Excellence* (Brookings, 2002), pp. 5–12.

54. At the Berger Foundation, for example, seven directors awarded themselves bonuses totaling $4.2 million as a reward for successful investments. Beth Healy, "Foundations Veer into Business," *Boston Globe*, December 3, 2003, p. 1.

55. Albert B. Crenshaw, "Charities' Tax Breaks Scrutinized," *Washington Post*, June 21, 2004, p. A1.

56. Brad Wolverton, "Rethinking Charity Rules," *Chronicle of Philanthropy*, July 22, 2004, p. 33.

57. Grant Williams, "Accountability Law Spurs Charities to Make Changes," *Chronicle of Philanthropy*, November 25, 2004, p. 29.

58. Michael Brintnall, "Developing Management and Leadership Capacity: Strategic Goals for the Independent Sector," paper prepared for delivery at the annual conference of the Association for Research on Nonprofit Organizations and Voluntary Action, New Orleans, November 2000.

59. Carol F. Stoel, "Improving Postsecondary Education through the Nonprofit Sector," in *New Partnerships: Higher Education and the Nonprofit Sector,* edited by Elinor Miller Greenberg (San Francisco: Jossey-Bass, 1982).

60. Judith R. Saidel, "Expanding the Governance Construct: Functions and Contributions of Nonprofit Advisory Groups," *Nonprofit and Voluntary Sector Quarterly* 27 (1998): 421–36.

61. Debra Blum, "Three Pittsburgh Foundations Halt Grants to Schools," *Chronicle of Philanthropy*, July 25, 2002, p. 18.

62. National Association of Schools of Public Affairs and Administration, "Guidelines for Graduate Professional Education in Nonprofit Organizations: Management and Leadership" (Washington, 1998), available at www.naspaa.org/accreditation/seeking/reference/guidelines.asp#graduate [February 25, 2005].

63. Throughout this chapter, the term "church" is meant to include all places of worship, including synagogues, mosques, and temples.

64. Verba, Schlozman, and Brady, *Voice and Equality*.

65. David E. Campbell, "Acts of Faith: Churches and Political Engagement," *Political Behavior* 26, no. 2 (2004): 155–80.

66. Fredrick Harris, *Something Within: Religion in African-American Political Activism* (Oxford University Press, 1999).

67. Omar McRoberts, *Streets of Glory: Church and Community in a Black Urban Neighborhood* (University of Chicago Press, 2003); Arthur E. Paris, *Black Pentecostalism* (University of Massachusetts Press, 1982); Frances Kostaleros, *Feeling the Spirit: Faith and Hope in an Evangelical Black Storefront Church* (University of South Carolina Press, 1995); and Yvette M. Alex-Assensoh, "Taking the Sanctuary to the Streets," *Annals of the American Academy of Political and Social Science* 594 (July 2004): 79–91.

68. Michael Jones-Correa, "Political Participation: Does Religion Matter?" *Political Research Quarterly* 54 (2001): 751–70.

69. Mark R. Warren, *Dry Bones Rattling: Community Building to Revitalize American Democracy* (Princeton University Press, 2001).

70. Mark Chaves and William Tsitsos, "Congregations and Social Services: What They Do, How They Do It, and With Whom," *Nonprofit and Voluntary Sector Quarterly* 30 (December 2001): 669.

71. Chaves and Tsitsos, "Congregations and Social Services," p. 671.

72. Mark Chaves, "Religious Congregations," in *The State of Nonprofit America*, edited by Salamon, p. 284.

73. For helpful discussions of charitable choice and the faith-based initiative, see E. J. Dionne and Ming Hsu Chen, eds., *Sacred Places, Civic Purposes: Should Government Help Faith-Based Charity?* (Brookings, 2001); Jo Renee Formicola, Mary C. Segers, and Paul Weber, *Faith-Based Initiatives and the Bush Administration: The Good, the Bad, and the Ugly* (Lanham, Md.: Rowman and Littlefield, 2003); and Charles L. Glenn, *The Ambiguous Embrace: Government and Faith-Based Schools and Social Agencies* (Princeton University Press, 2000).

74. In terms of legal status, labor unions are nonprofits under section 501(c)(5) of the tax code. Thus they do not qualify for tax-deductible donations under section 501(c)(3).

75. Benjamin Radcliff, "Organized Labor and Electoral Participation in American National Elections," *Journal of Labor Research* 22 (2000): 408. Also see Peter Francia, *The Future of Organized Labor in Congressional Politics* (New York: Columbia University Press, forthcoming).

76. According to a Peter Hart Research Associates survey done on election night, updated November 3, 2004, available at www.aflcio.org/issuespolitics/ns11032004.cfm [February 25, 2005]: "More than 90 percent of union members say they received information from their unions on issues in the presidential campaign crucial to working families. The survey among 1,135 active and retired union members included 400 additional members in Ohio and had a 3.5 percent margin of error." Consider also the following two quotes from the AFL-CIO website (www.aflcio.org/issuespolitics/politics/ppp_movement.cfm [February 25, 2005]): "The heart and soul of that strategy is growth of the nation's strongest grassroots network of political activists. In the 1996, 1998, 2000, and 2002 election cycles, the AFL-CIO committed voluntary contributions by affiliates to increase voter registration, education, and mobilization. None of the money went to political candidates. The difference was noticeable. More than 4.8 percent of members of union households added their names to the voter rolls between 1992 and 2000. Those new voters meant that union households represented 26 percent of the vote in 2000, up from 19 percent in 1992." Finally, as posted on November 15, 2004, available at www.aflcio. org/aboutaflcio/wip/wip11152004.cfm [February 25, 2005], "More than 5,500 full-time staff and union members worked in battleground states—up from 1,500 in 2000. More than 225,000 volunteers participated in the Labor 2004 program. Union members knocked on more than 6 million doors in neighborhood walks that ran daily in many states since Labor Day. Volunteers called millions of union members and passed out more than 32 million leaflets at workplaces and in neighborhoods—including more than 6 million in Ohio alone. Union members reached out at 257 phone banks with 2,322 lines running in sixteen states. The AFL-CIO's program sent out more than 30 million pieces of mail to union households."

77. Henry S. Farber and Bruce Western, "Accounting for the Decline of Unions in the Private Sector, 1973–1998," *Journal of Labor Research* 22 (2001): 459–85.

78. See www.bls.gov/news.release/union2.nr0.htm [December 3, 2004].

79. Bureau of Labor Statistics, *Current Population Survey. Table 3. Union Affiliation of Employed Wage and Salary Workers by Occupation and Industry* (Department of Labor, 2003).

80. Task Force on Inequality, "American Democracy in an Age of Rising Inequality" (American Political Science Association, 2004), available at www.apsanet.org/section_256.cfm [March 27, 2005], p. 10.

81. Margaret Levi, "Organizing Power: Prospects for the American Labor Movement," *Perspectives on Politics* 1 (2003): 45–68. Also see Bernhard Ebbinghaus and Jelle Visser, "When Institutions Matter: Union Growth and Decline in Western Europe, 1950–1995," *European Sociological Review* 15, no. 2 (1999): 1–24.

82. Immanual Ness and Stuart Eimer, eds., *Central Labor Councils and the Revival of American Unionism: Organizing for Justice in Our Communities* (Armonk, N.Y.: M. E. Sharpe, 2001).

83. J. David Greenstone, *Labor in American Politics* (New York: Vintage Books, 1969). Also see Taylor Dark, *The Unions and the Democrats: An Enduring Alliance,* 2nd ed. (Cornell University Press, 2001); and Francia, *The Future of Organized Labor.*

84 Francia, *The Future of Organized Labor,* compares the Sweeney years with those of his predecessor and documents considerable improvement in the influence of organized labor on electoral outcomes.

85. See Levi, "Organizing Power," pp. 57–58, for an elaboration of some of these actions. Also see Margaret Levi, "Capitalizing on Labor's Capital," in *Social Capital and Poor Communities,* edited by Mark E. Warren, Susan Saegert, and Phil Thompson (New York: Russell Sage Foundation, 2001); and Margaret Levi, David J. Olson, and Erich Steinman, "Living Wage Campaigns and Laws," in *The Encyclopedia of American Social Movements,* edited by Immanual Ness (New York: M. E. Sharpe, 2004), pp. 1471–81.

86. Harris Wofford, "The Politics of Service," in *United We Serve: National Service and the Future of Citizenship,* edited by E. J. Dionne, Kayla Meltzer Drogosz, and Robert Litan (Brookings, 2003), p. 46.

87. Harris Wofford and Steven Waldman, "AmeriCorps the Beautiful?" *Policy Review* (September-October 1996): 28–33.

88. Stephen Bates, *National Service: Getting Things Done?* Cantigny Conference Series Special Report (Chicago: Robert R. McCormick Tribune Foundation, 1996), p. 33.

89. Doug Bandow, "National Service or Government Service?" *Policy Review* (September-October 1996); and see Bates, *National Service,* pp. 44–46.

90. Martin Anderson, remarks at Cantigny Conference on National and Community Service, sponsored by the Robert R. McCormick Tribune Foundation, July 15–16, 1997.

91. Wofford, "Politics of Service," p. 51.

92. Charles Moskos quoting Bush in "Patriotism Lite Meets the Citizen Soldier," in *United We Serve,* edited by Dionne, Drogosz, and Litan, p. 40.

93. For evidence that the National Labor Relations Board has been more pro-business under Republican presidents and more pro-labor under Democrats, see Terry Moe, "Control and Feedback in Economic Regulation: The Case of the NLRB," *American Political Science Review* 79 (1985): 1094–116; also Robert J. Flanagan, "Compliance and Enforcement Decisions under the National Labor Relations Act," *Journal of Labor Economics* 7 (1989): 257–80; Margaret Levi, Matt Moe, and Theresa Buckley, "Institutionalizing Trustworthiness through the NLRB?" in *Distrust,* edited by Russell Hardin (New York: Russell Sage Foundation, 2004), pp. 106–35.

94. See, for example, Torben Iversen, *Contested Economic Institutions: The Politics of Macroeconomics and Wage Bargaining in Advanced Democracies* (Cambridge University Press, 1999).

95. Suzanne Mettler, *Soldiers to Citizens: The G.I. Bill and the Making of the Greatest Generation* (Oxford University Press, 2005). Mettler's research also finds that government pol-

icy can profoundly shape gender, racial, and ethnic inequalities in patterns of participation and conceptions of citizenship. See also *Dividing Citizens: Gender and Federalism in New Deal Public Policy* (Cornell University Press, 1998).

96. Andrea Campbell, *How Policies Make Citizens: Senior Citizen Activism and the American Welfare State* (Princeton University Press, 2003).

Chapter Five

1. Herbert J. Storing and Murray Dry, eds., *The Anti-Federalist: Writings of the Opponents of the Constitution* (University of Chicago Press, 1981), Brutus I, 2.9.16, pp. 114–15.

2. Storing and Dry, eds., *The Anti-Federalist*. The second federalist paper also emphasizes that Americans in 1787 shared common ancestry, language, and religion; contrast the argument of the tenth federalist paper, with its emphasis on the advantages of governance in an "extended republic"; Alexander Hamilton, James Madison, and John Jay, *The Federalist Papers*, edited by Clinton Rossiter (New American Library, 1961).

3. See the discussion of these issues in chapter three.

4. See the discussion of Morris Fiorina, below.

5. For an innovative account of the possibilities of bringing democratic values to the workplace, see Brooke Manville and Josiah Ober, *A Company of Citizens* (Harvard Business School Press, 2003).

6. Jean-Jacques Rousseau, *The Social Contract*, translated by Maurice Cranston (Penguin Books, 1968), line 1.

7. Kenneth T. Jackson, *Crabgrass Frontier: The Suburbanization of the United States* (Oxford University Press, 1985), p. 11.

8. Jackson, *Crabgrass Frontier*, p. 3.

9. Morris P. Fiorina, with Samuel J. Abrams and Jeremy C. Pope, *Culture War? The Myth of a Polarized America* (New York: Pearson Longman, 2005), p. 96.

10. See Fiorina, *Culture War*, pp. 104–13.

11. Alexis de Tocqueville, *Democracy in America*, edited by J. P. Mayer (New York: Anchor Books, 1969).

12. John M. Broder, "Schwarzenegger Proposes Overhaul of Redistricting," *New York Times*, January 6, 2005, p. A16.

THE AUTHORS

Yvette Alex-Assensoh
Indiana University

Jeffrey M. Berry
Tufts University

Michael Brintnall
American Political Science
    Association

David E. Campbell
University of Notre Dame

Luis Ricardo Fraga
Stanford University

Archon Fung
Harvard University

William A. Galston
University of Maryland

Christopher F. Karpowitz
Princeton University

Margaret Levi
University of Washington

Meira Levinson
Boston Public Schools

Keena Lipsitz
Queens College–City University
    of New York

Stephen Macedo
Princeton University

Richard G. Niemi
University of Rochester

Robert D. Putnam
Harvard University

Wendy M. Rahn
University of Minnesota

Rob Reich
Stanford University

Robert R. Rodgers
Princeton University

Todd Swanstrom
Saint Louis University

Katherine Cramer Walsh
University of Wisconsin–
    Madison

INDEX

Absentee voting, 55
Accountability, 12; of nonprofit organizations, 136–40
Ackerman, Bruce, 61
Advertising, political campaign, 31, 46
Altshuler, Alan, 130
Alinsky, Saul, 97
American Federation of Labor-Congress of Industrial Organizations, 143, 144–45
American Political Science Association, 16–17
AmeriCorps, 95, 123, 146, 147
Anderson, Martin, 147
Arizona, 56, 58
Arons, David, 134
Associational affiliation: American tradition and culture, 119; benefits of civic engagement, 5; business associations, 130; coproduction of public services, 95; future prospects, 122; nongovernment organizations in local politics, 97–104, 113; patterns and trends, 19, 27, 50, 66, 121, 122, 153; political significance, 120–21; possible negative aspects, 121; scope of, 117–18; significance of, for civic engagement, 117, 119–22, 148, 152–53; strategies for enhancing civic life through, 118–19, 122, 131, 148–52, 163–64; structural factors, 119; types of associations

and organizations, 118. *See also* Charitable organizations; Labor union; Nonprofit organizations; Religious organizations

Barron, David, 109
Bartels, Larry, 36, 42
Baucus, Max, 137
Berinsky, Adam, 21
Berry, Jeffrey, 93, 120, 134
Bishop, Bill, 79
Boards and committees, 91
Boston, 92
Brady, Henry, 34–35, 38, 52, 120
British Colombia, 61
Brudney, Jeffrey, 124
Bryan, Frank, 70
Burns, Nancy, 90
Bush, George W., 5

California, 88
Campaign finance, 3, 37; voter turnout and, 30–31
Campus Compact, 123
Charitable giving, 116, 131–33
Charitable organizations, 118; accountability, 137; concerns about government support, 146–47; political and advocacy activities, 133–35; strategies for strengthening civic engagement through, 149; trends, 118. *See also*

Philanthropic foundations; Volunteer
and charity work
Chaves, Mark, 142
Chicago, 94, 96–97, 98, 100, 101
Churches. *See* Religious organizations
Citizen Corps, 123
City Year, 123
Civic engagement: benefits of, 4–5, 12–13;
causes of declines in, 2–4, 14; challenges
for disadvantaged communities, 78–79;
citizen qualities as determinants of,
170–72; coproduction of public services,
95, 162; costs of, 13; critical dimensions,
8; current state, 16, 17, 156–59; definition and scope, 6–8; elite resistance to
expansion of, 174–75; equality issues,
9–10, 166–67; indicators of, 1, 4, 7; low
levels of, as positive, 10–12; motivation,
6; national service participation and,
148; neighborhood governance and, 93;
partisanship in strategies to promote,
176–77; progressive-era reforms and,
86–89; quality of, 8–9, 164–66; quantity
of, 8, 156–57, 161–64; rationale for promoting, 10, 14–15, 16, 174, 175–76,
177–78; research goals, 19; research
methodology, 17; significance of associational life for, 117, 119–22, 148, 152–53;
size and diversity of community and,
155–56; sociodemographic patterns, 2;
socioeconomic homogeneity of communities and, 78; strategies for promoting, 5–6, 159–61, 167–70; trends, 1–2,
20, 21, 175; urban design and, 80–82. *See
also* Education to promote civic engagement; Political participation
Civilian Conservation Corps, 146
Civil rights, 176
Cohen, Marty, 43
Colorado, 57
Community Action Program, 91–92
Community development corporations,
101, 113, 130
Community involvement, 5, 7; commuting
time and, 81; homeowners associations,
102–04; neighborhood councils, 91–93;
neighborhood organizations, 100–02;

political significance, 120; public safety
programs, 96. *See also* Political partici-
pation; Volunteer and charity work
Community organizing, 97–99
Commuting, 81
Congressional elections: competitiveness,
45–47; incumbent advantage, 3, 45;
polarization trends, 79–80
Coproduction of public services, 95, 162
Corporation for National and Community
Service, 146
Corporation for National Service, 123
Crenson, Matthew, 102
Cultural factors, 49–52, 62–64, 171–72

Dahl, Robert, 68, 69
Davis v. Bandemer, 57
Delli Carpini, Michael, 34
Democratic governance: accountability of
nonprofit organizations, 136–38; constitutional principles, 13–14; homeowners association rules, 103; importance of
associational life, 119; importance of
local politics, 68–69, 158; local jurisdiction, 71; negative effects of encouraging
citizen involvement, 11–12, 172–75;
population diversity and, 71–72,
155–56; role of civic engagement, 4, 12,
13, 14–15, 178; special district rules and,
89–90
Dewey, John, 7
Dionne, E. J., 124
Disadvantaged population: civic engagement trends, 2, 9; community organizing
among, 97–99; democratic governance
and, 13; in metropolitan political life, 18;
nongovernmental groups acting on
behalf of, 19, 100–01; nonprofit organization activities on behalf of, 134–35,
157, 167; obstacles to civic engagement,
78–79, 167; political effects of
progressive-era reforms, 87; political
knowledge, 34; political mobilization of,
48; political participation, 27, 37–39, 38,
52, 85, 96, 97, 166–67; social stratification of communities, 77–79, 158, 165
Discrimination, 9–10

Economic status: challenges for cities, 85–86; civic engagement trends, 9–10; community involvement and, 102; nonprofit sector, 116, 126; political access and, 38; political knowledge and, 34; political participation and, 37–39, 66, 96, 157; segregation in metropolitan areas, 75, 77–79, 106, 158, 165; strategies for encouraging community diversity, 107–08, 165–66; voting behavior and, 25, 27

Edsall, Mary, 78

Edsall, Thomas Byrne, 78

Educational attainment: civic engagement and, 101; current affairs knowledge and, 28; political knowledge and, 32–34; political participation and, 23; voting behavior and, 54

Education to promote civic engagement, 6; public school trends, 1; settings for, 6, 7–8, 160, 171; understanding of political process, 14–15; voter education, 53–54

Elections, generally: campaign advertising, 31, 46; campaign financing, 30–31, 37; campaign length, 44, 161–62; competitiveness of, 3, 20, 45–47, 58, 64, 161, 163, 173; congressional, 45–47, 79–80; election day as holiday, 55; election-day registration, 55; frequency, 32, 87–88, 163; hours of voting, 55; local politics, 83–86, 87–88; mail-in balloting, 55; media coverage, 41–42, 43–44; negative public perceptions, 3; nonpartisan, 87; quality of, 9; supply of candidates, 84–85. *See also* Elections, specific; Presidential elections; Voter turnout

Elections, specific: *1952* presidential, 28; *1956* presidential, 2; *1960* presidential, 22, 46; *1992* presidential, 35; *1996* presidential, 35; *2000* presidential, 22, 28, 42, 46; *2002* congressional, 20; *2004* congressional, 3, 20; *2004* presidential, 2, 20, 22, 25, 36

Electoral college, 60, 161

Equality and justice issues, 9–10, 18, 157; political participation, 38–39, 52, 53, 96–97; social stratification of communities, 78–79, 158; strategies to encourage

community diversity, 165–66; strategies to enhance civic engagement, 166–67

Estate tax, 132–33

Families, 63–64

Federal Advisory Committee Act, 129

Felons, 22–23, 48–49, 56, 64, 166

Ferman, Barbara, 101, 131

Fiorina, Morris P., 79, 172–74

Fishkin, James, 61

Florida, 55

Flournoy, Melissa, 138

Freedom Corps, 123, 147

Freeman, Richard, 38

Frey, William, 74

Frug, Gerald, 109

Frumkin, Peter, 127

Fung, Archon, 96

Galston, Miriam, 121

Gans, Herbert, 81

Gender differences: political knowledge and interest, 34, 39; political participation, 27, 39; voting behavior, 27

Gerber, Alan, 59, 84

Gilens, Martin, 38

Gimpel, James G., 33, 79

Grassley, Charles, 137

Green, Donald, 59, 84

Greenstone, David, 144

Hajnal, Zoltan, 84

H-election regulations, 133–34, 135, 149

Hibbing, John, 10, 11

Higher Education Act (*1998*), 55

Homeowners associations, 102–04, 121

Housing policies, 107–08, 165–66

Huntington, Samuel, 11

Immigrant population, 22–23, 40, 71, 166; determinants of political behavior, 88; political mobilization of, 48, 98, 99–100, 107, 108

Incumbency, 3, 9, 20, 45; proportional representation and, 59–60; redistricting and, 57–58

Internet, 41

Jackson, Kenneth T., 172
Jacobs, Jane, 80
Jefferson, Thomas, 12
Job training programs, 127–28
Jones-Correa, Michael, 88

Keeter, Scott, 7, 34, 51

Labor unions, 47, 118, 130; collective bargaining arrangements, 151; obstacles to organizing, 144, 151–52; outreach activities, 143, 144; political significance, 143, 144–45; strategies for strengthening civic engagement through, 151–52, 167; trends, 118, 143–44
Landrum-Griffin Act, 144
Levittown, N.J., 81
Light, Paul, 127
Local politics: boards and committees, 91; community diversity and, 71–72, 107–08; community size and, 69–71, 82, 104; determinants of participation, 66, 69–70, 82, 88, 96; election schedule, 87–88; electoral, 83–86; government structure, 68; importance of, in democratic governance, 68–69, 158; influence of homeowners associations, 104; jurisdiction, 71, 80, 108–11, 114–15; neighborhood councils, 91–93; nongovernmental organizations in, 97–104, 113; obstacles to civic engagement, 156–57; opportunities for participation, 68, 69, 72, 82–83, 90–91, 96–97; polarization trends, 79–80; strategies to revitalize political life, 111–12, 162–63; trends, 66, 67–68; voter turnout, 83–84. *See also* Metropolitan areas
Luberoff, David, 130

Madison, James, 11–12, 32, 72
Madison, Wis., 107
Mail-in balloting, 48, 55
Markus, Gregory B., 4
Mayors, 87
McConnell, Grant, 71, 78
McDonald, Michael, 22, 23
Media, 41–44; campaign advertising, 31,

46; newspapers, 28, 42; strategies for increasing political participation, 63
Metropolitan areas, 18; coproduction of public services, 95, 162; determinants of civic engagement, 73; economic challenges, 85–86; fragmentation of political structure and power, 74–77, 80, 104–05, 106, 165; growth patterns, 73; management structures, 87, 88; need for new political institutions, 106, 108–11; neighborhood councils, 92; obstacles to political participation, 68, 104–05; physical design, political effects of, 80–82; political participation, 66; population diversity, 73–74, 75, 107–08, 165–66; social stratification in, 77–79, 106; special districts, 89–90, 112, 157; strategies for improving political participation, 68, 104–14, 162. *See also* Local politics
Meyerson, Adam, 138
Military service, 145–46, 152
Miller, Joanne, 35
Minnesota, 61, 92, 113
Moderate voters, 2, 3, 46

National Labor Relations Act, 144, 151
Negotiated Rulemaking Act, 129
Neighborhood councils, 91–93, 113–14
Neighborhood organizations, 100–02
New Haven, Conn., 81, 84
Newspaper industry, 28, 42
New York City, 92, 94
Nickelson, David, 84
Noel, Hans, 43
Nonprofit organizations, 116; accountability, 136–38, 139–40, 149–50; activities, 127; boards and advisory groups, 139, 149–50; economic significance, 126; employment, 126; in enhancement of civic engagement, 121, 157; financial management, 136, 137; government relations, 130–31; government support, 127–28, 129–30; international comparisons, 128; leadership development, 138–39, 140; political significance, 124–25; regulation, 129–30, 138; restric-

tions on political activity, 118, 130, 133–35, 149, 167; social service delivery, 127–28, 130; strategies for strengthening civic engagement through, 149–50, 153, 167; tax policies, 128–29, 131–33; types of, 118, 127; volunteerism in, 126–27. *See also* Associational affiliation; Charitable organizations; Philanthropic foundations; Religious organizations; Volunteer and charity work

Oliver, Eric, 70, 81, 102
Olson, Mancur, 10–11
O'Neill, Thomas P. ("Tip"), 68
Oregon, 55
Orfield, Myron, 77, 109
Owen, Diana, 125–26

Paternalism, 175–76
Peace Corps, 146
Pennsylvania, 57
Peterson, Paul, 115
Philanthropic foundations, 116; accountability, 137, 138, 140; economic significance, 116; regulatory environment, 118; strategies for strengthening civic engagement through, 149. *See also* Associational affiliation; Nonprofit organizations
Pitkin, Hannah, 15
Pittsburgh, 101, 139
Points of Light Foundation, 123
Polarization, political: among elites, 36–37, 45–46, 47, 157–58; causes of, 164, 165; within communities, 79–80, 157, 158, 165; strategies for reducing, 164, 165; voter participation and, 174
Political institutions and practices: accountability in, 12; benefits of civic engagement, 14–15; campaign advertising, 31, 46; campaign financing, 3, 30–31, 37; campaign length, 44; as cause of civic decline, 2–4, 14, 160; conflict resolution, 14–15; educative role, 6, 8, 14–15, 160; fragmentation of, in metropolitan areas, 74–77, 80, 104–05, 106, 165; local structure, 68, 69–70, 91;

machine politics, 86; mobilizing institutions, 47–48; need for new metropolitan governance institutions, 106, 108–11; negative public perceptions, 3, 31, 50; neighborhood councils, 91–93, 113–14; nongovernmental organizations and groups, 19, 97–104, 113–14; nonpartisan elections, 87; progressive-era reforms, 86–89, 106, 156–57, 162; in promoting civic engagement, 14; proportional representation, 59–60; public understanding, 32–34; significance of nonprofit association activity, 124–25; special districts, 89–90, 162–63; strategies for improving participation, 38, 55–62; term limits, 31; voter registration procedures, 30, 48–49, 55; voter turnout and, 23, 30. *See also* Elections, generally; Polarization, political; Political participation
Political participation: burden of, for citizens, 13, 173–74; campaign contributions, 37; campaign factors discouraging, 44–45; campaign involvement, 27–28; childhood development as factor in, 35; as civic duty, 51–52, 62; community size and, 69–71, 82; cultural factors, 49–52, 62–64, 171–72; current affairs knowledge, 27, 28–30, 42; current state, 16; determinants of, 3–4, 52; educational attainment and, 23, 54; family role in determining, 63–64; forms of, 7; goals, 15; as indicator of civic engagement and, 6–7; local factors, 66, 67, 114–15; local opportunities, 82–90; low levels of, as positive, 10–11; mandatory, 62–63; media factors, 41–44; mobilization efforts, 47–48, 58–59, 84; moving to new jurisdiction versus, 11, 12–13, 76–77; negative outcomes of, 11, 172–74; obstacles to, 18, 41–49, 52–53, 160; partisanship and, 35–37, 164; personal factors, 32–40, 53–54, 159–60; political interest and, 34–35; political scandal and, 31; quality of, 8–9, 60; rationale for improving, 53; restrictions on nonprofit organizations, 118, 130,

133–35, 149, 167; role of labor unions, 143, 144–45; role of religious organizations, 50–51, 124, 141–42; settings and opportunities for deliberative engagement, 60–62, 94, 159; significance of nonpolitical associations, 120–21; social capital factors, 49–51; sociodemographic differences, 39–41, 52, 157, 166; socioeconomic differences, 18, 27, 37–39; strategies for improving, 18, 21, 40, 53–64, 85, 104–14, 160–62, 166–67; structural factors, 30, 41–49, 52–53, 55–62, 108–11, 160; supply of political candidates, 84–85; trends, 1–2, 18, 27–30, 66; for unjust or oppressive goals, 11–12; urban design and, 80, 81–82; volunteerism as substitute for, 125; zealotry, 172–73. *See also* Elections, generally; Political institutions and practices; Voter turnout

Popkin, Samuel, 22, 23, 74
Portland, Ore., 113
Portney, Kent, 93, 120
Presidential elections, 173; competitiveness, 45, 46, 161; electoral college reform, 60, 161; length of campaign, 44–45, 161–62; polarization trends, 79; primary process, 3, 44, 161–62; voter turnout, 83. *See also* Elections, specific
Primary process, 3, 44
Prior, Markus, 42
Progressive-era political reforms, 86–89, 106, 156–57, 162
Proportional representation, 59–60
Protesting and demonstrating, 7
Public opinion: current affairs knowledge, 27, 28–30, 42; news sources, 42–43; of partisan politics, 3; trust in political institutions, 31, 50
Public policy: benefits of citizen participation, 12–13; educative role, 6; incentives for charitable giving, 131–33; negative effects of citizen involvement, 11; role of citizen groups in formation and implementation, 130–31; strategies to increase citizen involvement, 113; to support associational life, 118–19, 122,

131; support for social service delivery by nonprofit organizations, 127–28
Public safety, 95, 96
Puerto Rico, 55
Putnam, Robert, 50, 70, 81, 102, 120, 124

Race and ethnicity: civic engagement trends, 2, 9–10; community diversity and democratic functioning, 71–72; local political participation, 83–84, 85, 87; metropolitan growth patterns, 73–74, 75; neighborhood organizations, 100–01; political coalitions, 85; political knowledge patterns, 34; political participation and, 39–40, 52, 157; role of church in civic life, 141–412; segregation in metropolitan areas, 106, 158, 165; social stratification of communities, 77–79, 158; strategies for encouraging community diversity, 107–08, 165–66; trends among elected officials, 66, 85–86; voter turnout patterns, 25–27, 49; voting assistance for minority communities, 55
Rae, Douglas, 78, 81, 115
Rahn, Wendy, 35, 42, 70
Red Cross, 137
Redistricting, 3, 173, 175; depoliticizing, 56–58; frequency of, 57, 161; to improve political participation, 18, 56–58, 161, 164; media markets and, 43; polarizing effects of, 164
Religious organizations, 100–01, 116, 118; civic role, 141; government support for, 142–43; influence on political participation, 50–51; political significance, 124, 141–42; in social service delivery, 142–43; strategies for strengthening civic engagement through, 150
Resistance to change, 174–75
Rich, Richard C., 102
Rousseau, Jean-Jacques, 171

Salamon, Lester, 126
Scavo, Carmine, 92, 95
Schlozman, Kay, 34–35, 52, 120
Schools, 6; civic education in, 171; civics and government courses, 32; interven-

tions to increase voter turnout, 54, 63; parent-teacher associations, 95; sorting model, 32–33

Schumpeter, Joseph, 11, 12

Schwarzenegger, Arnold, 175

September *11* terrorist attacks, 28, 43, 147

Service learning programs, 125–26, 157, 164

Settlement house movement, 98

Skocpol, Theda, 50, 121

Smith, Al, 14

Social capital, 49–51, 80, 120

Social engineering, 175–76

Social services, 19, 127–28, 130, 142–43

Social studies, 33

Space Shuttle Challenger, 43

Special districts, 74, 89–90, 112, 157, 162–63

St. Louis, 75

Starr, Paul, 41

Stone, Clarence, 131

Sunstein, Cass, 42

Sweeney, John, 145

Taft-Hartley Act, 144

Takoma Park, Md., 108

Tax policies, 128–29, 131–33, 149, 163, 167

Teach for America, 95, 123

Technology, 114, 172; communications, 41

Term limits, 31

Texas, 57

Theiss-Morse, Elizabeth, 10, 11

Thomson, Ken, 93, 120

Tiebout, Charles, 76

Tocqueville, Alexis de, 68–69, 119

Trounstine, Jessica, 84

Trust in political institutions, 31, 50

Tsitsos, William, 142

United Way, 137

Verba, Sidney, 34–35, 47, 52, 120

Vermont, 70

Vieth v. *Jubelirer,* 57

Virtue, civic, 170–72

Volunteer and charity work, 7, 116, 118; coproduction of public services, 95; economic value, 116, 123; involvement in political campaigns, 27–28, 47–48; local boards and committees, 91; motivation, 125; national service, 19, 145–48, 152, 163; organizational types, 118, 123, 125, 127; patterns among young people, 51, 123; patterns and trends, 19, 51, 66, 116, 122–24; political involvement and, 125–26; political significance, 124–25; quality of, 124; recommendations for public funding, 19; regulatory environment, 118; service learning programs, 125–26, 164; strategies for enhancing civic life through, 118, 163–64; youth involvement, 51, 123. *See also* Associational affiliation; Charitable organizations; Nonprofit organizations

Volunteers in Service to America, 146

Voter turnout, 1; among young people, 25; associational affiliation and, 121; competitiveness of political races and, 3, 22, 57, 58, 64, 161; determinants of, 30–32; duty motivation, 51–52, 62; economic status of voters and, 25, 27; educational attainment of potential voters, 23; eligible population, 22–23; as indicator of civic engagement, 7; influence of labor unions, 143; interest in politics and, 34–35; international comparison, 23; local elections, 66, 83–84, 87–88; mandatory, 62–63; negative campaign advertising and, 31; partisanship and, 36–37, 165, 174, 177; perception of political efficacy and, 31; proportional representation and, 59–60; significance of low levels of, 11; sociodemographic differences, 25–27, 39; special district elections, 90; strategies for improving, 21, 38, 53–54, 55–56, 59, 63, 173; structural factors, 23, 30, 52–53; trends, 2, 20, 22–27, 66, 83–84, 156; trust in government and, 31, 50; voter registration and, 23–25, 30, 48–49, 55. *See also* Political participation

Voting Rights Act (*1965*), 39, 55, 85

Watergate, 31
Welfare, 127, 142
White, Kevin, 92
Wilcox, Clyde, 55
Williamson, Thad, 81–82
Wood, Curtis, 87

Young people: civic engagement trends, 2, 9; college students, 49, 55; current affairs knowledge, 28; involvement in political campaigns, 27–28; motivation for volunteering, 125; perceptions of civic duty and responsibility, 51; political knowledge and interest, 34, 35; political mobilization of, 48; political participation trends, 18, 20, 51, 166; strategies to increase voter turnout, 54, 55, 63, 64, 166; volunteer work, 51, 123, 124; voting behaviors, 25; voting registration, 49, 55

Zaller, John, 43
Zealotry, 172–73
Zoning laws, 107, 165–66